FRAUDS OF AMERICA

OR

BEWARE OF SHAMS

HOW THEY ARE WORKED AND HOW TO FOIL THEM

The Tricks and Methods of All Kinds of Frauds and Swindlers, from the Petty Sneak-Thief to the Cleverest Schemes of the Expert Bank Robber, Fully Exposed

FOR THE PROTECTION OF THE AMERICAN PUBLIC

BY

E. G. REDMOND

ASSISTED BY EMINENT EXPERTS

Appropriately Illustrated with Full-Page Half-Tone Engravings Made Expressly for this Book

J. L. NICHOLS & CO.

Manufacturing Publishers of Popular Subscription Books on the Exclusive Territory Plan

TORONTO, ONT. NAPERVILLE, ILL. ATLANTA, GA.

THE
FRAUDS
OF
AMERICA
REDMOND
THE
FRAUDS
OF
AMERICA

PREFACE.

For the protection of the community in general from all classes of depredators this book is intended. The methods of catching victims by fraudulent and swindling practices has never before been given in full to the public. We have now for the first time, in this book, given a truthful and reliable exposé of the multifarious schemes, swindles and dodges practiced on the American public. Scarcely a day passes but the press reports depredations of one kind or another from all parts of the country. The burglar, safe-breaker, sneak-thief, swindler, confidence man, forger, check-raiser and counterfeiter are ever on the alert, and the reason these rascals are usually successful is owing to the fact that the public is unacquainted with the way they work.

This book exposes all manner of thievery, swindling, robbery, etc.—the *modus operandi*—in a plain and practical way. For the protection of the people of America from all classes of thieves and rascals this work is written. It is the result of years of careful application and untiring work by experts, and will be found of inestimable value to the public. It is not a detective story, or work of fiction, but a book of facts, instructive, interesting and educational.

The country is filled with adventurers, rascals great and small, with men so industrious in uncanny lines as to cause one to admire the persistent pluck with which they energetically go ahead to their own ruin, employing faculties for their own destruction which rightfully utilized might make them not only solid and respectable citizens, but brilliant and impressive.

In writing this volume and exposing the ways of frauds and swindlers who ply their vocation upon the public, the aim has been to educate, instruct and put the public on their guard against the schemes and wiles of designing men of all kinds by exposing in detail their methods. Barnum once said, "The American people want to be humbugged." This is not absolutely correct. It is true that many people want to get something for nothing, and hence fall an easy victim to the suave confidence man. But we take the position that "*An ounce of prevention is worth a pound of cure*," and fully believe that no person who reads this book will ever be "taken in" by a swindler. It exposes the entire business from the petty sneak-thief to the cleverest schemes of the expert bank robber.

In conclusion, the author desires to express his thanks to the many gentlemen who have materially assisted in the preparation of this book, and also for the fidelity and perseverance with which writers on special subjects have discharged their duties. To them every reader will owe a debt of grateful appreciation.

With the sincere hope that our efforts may aid in foiling every scheme of the great army of Frauds, we confidently send this volume forth.

E. G. REDMOND.

CHICAGO, ILL., March 27, 1902.

CONTENTS.

LIST OF ILLUSTRATIONS.

CHAPTER I.

AMERICA'S EDUCATED CRIMINAL CLASS.

POPULAR ERROR IN REGARD TO INTELLIGENCE OF CRIMINALS—REQUIREMENTS TO BE AN ACCOMPLISHED RASCAL—WHAT CRIMINAL HISTORY SHOWS—CARE AND DETAIL USED BY SWINDLERS—EDUCATED CRIMINALS TO BE FEARED—MYSTERY AND FASCINATION IN CRIME—DOES THE PUBLIC ENJOY BEING HUMBUGGED, SWINDLED AND DECEIVED?—LIVING BY ONE'S WITS A FINE ART—PRIDE OF PROFESSIONAL CRIMINALS—CAUSE OF INCREASE IN CRIME—OUR CROWDED CITIES—MODE OF PUNISHMENT FOR EVIL DOERS—PROTECTION TO SOCIETY—CURIOUS FACTS ABOUT FACES OF DISHONEST MEN—CONDITION OF THE INSTINCTIVE CRIMINAL—CRIMINAL PHYSIOGNOMY AND SCIENCE—RISE OF CRIME'S TIDE.

The great mass of the American people, aside from those who have had experience in hunting and shadowing criminals, labor under the popular delusion that the most daring criminals of to-day are a lot of tough, ignorant men, with little or no education at all, who would do almost anything else than work honestly for a living. If people would but stop to consider the subject a moment they would readily discover their error. There are, it is true, a large number of swindlers, thieves, pickpockets, thugs and criminals of a like class who have but a scant knowledge of books, literature or other educational propensities, but they are only to be found among the lower class of criminals. The most notorious criminals the world has ever produced have been men and women of high culture and refinement, well educated and thoroughly posted on all that is transpiring. It is this class of people who make the most successful and at the same time most dangerous criminals. It requires men of education to swindle, crack a safe, rob a bank, jewelry store or forge a paper. To be a successful confidence operator requires the man to be well educated in matters of all natures, to be a fluent talker, a person of refinement and polite address and a good judge of character.

Criminal history shows that the most successful jobs are always planned and executed by men of education; the details of some of the great forgeries that have taken place, of the numerous bank robberies and burglar's exploits, all go to show the direction of a brain of no ordinary person, being proof positive that the persons planning the work possessed both education and talent. First class criminals are exceedingly hard to cope with and are the most dangerous to handle by the officers. They do not generally do things in a rush or by halves. Great care is given to all the minor details of their work, and it often takes weeks and months before they are ready to put their plans into operation. They study all the possibilities of the job; the chances of success and the way of escape in case of failure; how they can cover all traces of the work and throw the guilt or suspicion upon the more unfortunate of their class who have bad reputations and who are likely to be brought up and possibly convicted on suspicion of being the guilty parties. Educated crooks are always to be feared, not only by the public against whom they are constantly devising ways and means to relieve of their valuables, but by detectives of a lesser grade. This latter class they do not hesitate to sacrifice if their desired ends can be successfully accomplished, while the detective finds it a task of no little moment to gain even the faintest clue to their operations.

There is, after all, a good deal of satisfaction in being superstitious. To be able to charge all puzzling or inexplicable occurrences to invisible, supernatural agency is a convenient method of getting rid of troublesome doubts or wearisome inquiry into hidden causes. A poor solution of a difficulty may not, to a profound thinker, be better than none, but it is infinitely more comforting to ordinary human beings. Men feel, moreover, that in acknowledging that there may be truth in astrology, charlatanism and all the rest, they have been in a manner brought into a mystic brotherhood; and most people have a certain secret notion that the very confession of faith is in some way a sort of propitiatory offering to unseen powers. Mystery has always a fascination for man, and almost any scheme of deception can succeed if it can but veil itself in a semi-obscurity and pique the awestruck curiosity of the ignorant. A very small basis of truth serves as a sufficient basis upon which to erect a very substantial structure of delusion, as the history of innumerable quacks and impostors has testified through all the centuries since civilization began. It is not so much that men like to be deceived as that they enjoy deceiving themselves under the pretense that they stand in the presence of some inscrutable mystery, before which, since human reason is sure to prove unavailing, it is foolish to attempt to be reasonable or logical at all. To be freed from thinking, is, after all, the delight which ensnares more of mankind than any other temptation.

Living by one's wits has become a fine art, and it is a profession that is more liberally patronized than any other by the present generation. One of America's leading detectives remarked that there were about seventy-five thousand people in a city the size of Chicago that would bear watching. There isn't a bank, insurance office, dry goods store, restaurant or hotel, that does not employ men to watch their customers, and there is hardly a business house in the country that has not some system of watching its employes. Everybody at this day seems to be afraid of everybody else.

Professional criminals pride themselves quite as much upon their ability as men engaged in legitimate occupations. A thief, for instance is as vain of his superiority over other thieves as a lawyer, politician, or clergyman might be whose talents had elevated him to a commanding position in the eyes of the people. And the talented thief is as much courted and sought after as the successful man in the honest walks of life. The other thieves will say: "He is a good man to know; I must make his acquaintance." But the thief who has earned a reputation is particular about the company he keeps and is scornful in his demeanor toward another thief whom he does not consider his professional equal. Caste exists among criminals as well as among other classes.

Men and women who are not living merely for to-day must be deeply interested in the efforts which practical philanthropists are making to discover the causes of crime and to remedy the mischievous conditions which now prevail to such an alarming extent. Hidden away to a considerable degree in the great mass of figures which came into being through the operations of the census bureau are facts that should shock every good citizen. With all the warmth of eulogy the story of wonderful progress has been told again and again, but only a few references have been made to the abnormal growth of what may be termed the criminal class. Forty years ago there was but one criminal to 3,500 good or reasonably good citizens. According to the last census the proportion was one in 786.5; an increase of 445 per cent. in a period during which the population increased but 170 per cent. Never in the nation's history has educative work of all descriptions been nearly so active as at present, yet the increase in the number of those who were confined in penitentiaries and jails and reformatory institutions is almost twice as rapid as the speed of populative growth.

The true explanation of this unsatisfactory state of things is not far to seek. It is almost entirely to be attributed to the growing tendency of the community to become concentrated in large cities. A highly concentrated population fosters lawless and immoral instincts in such a multitude of ways that it is only an expression of literal exactitude to call the great cities of to-day the nurseries of modern crime. Statistics of all kinds show this, but it can easily be ascertained without the aid of any figures. The aggregation of large multitudes within a very limited area must increase the chances of conflict, and consequently multiply the occasions for crime.

A population in this crowded condition has also to be restrained and regulated at every turn by a huge network of laws, and as every new law forbids something which was permitted before a multiplication of laws is inevitably followed by an increase of crime.

The prevention of crime should be the great object with the philanthropist. The obvious remedy is, if possible, to aid the individual in overcoming the temptation to evil or to crime. The remedy must be general, gradual, and constant. It consists in religious, moral, intellectual, and industrial education of the children, especially of the poor and unfortunate and the weakling classes. The most certain preventive is the early incarnation of good habits in children, which becoming part and parcel of their nervous organization are an unconscious force when passion, perplexity, or temptation tend to make them lose self-control. Little can be expected from palliative remedies for social diseases so long as this educational remedy is not thoroughly carried out.

Locking a man up for committing a crime does not always cure him. It is now proven that affixed penalties to certain crimes accomplishes practically nothing, for it is based on a wrong principle. The length of confinement ought confessedly to be adjusted to the needs of the prisoner. He should not be discharged from his moral hospital until there is reasonable assurance that he is cured. He certainly should not be turned loose on society, on the mere expiration of a formal sentence, when it is known he will begin anew on his old life. Protection to society, as well as the reformation of the criminal, call for the retention of the latter until he can be trusted with his liberty, and affords proof that he is fitted to take his place in the world as a useful, law-abiding citizen. This system alone permits the fullest scope to reformatory methods, and leaves the court the right of sentencing indefinitely, and to the tribunal which has to do with the prisoner's release, to say when there is reasonable ground for faith that if discharged he will not prove either a burden or menace to society. Where conduct and character afford no such grounds he should be incarcerated for life, just as we would retain in asylums hopeless lunatics.

This form of sentence was first put into operation in a modified form by Maconochie at Norfolk Island in 1836 with a success in the way of reformatory results from the start which was unequalled. Now the best authorities in penology in all countries not only commend it, but the opinion is fast becoming general that it is a necessary feature in every reformatory system of prison discipline. Of course it implies in prison management the highest wisdom and integrity, and especially the banishment of partisan politics therefrom. It makes the dominant idea of prison administration manhood-making, and not money-making.

Every one knows that men's passions, propensities, and peculiarities, as well as their callings, are reflected in their faces, but it is only the few who have made the study of physiognomy an especial pursuit who are gifted with the power of reading those faces. Some police officials and judges, who have served long terms on the bench, lawyers in large practice, and doctors of eminence possess the power of interpreting physiognomies more largely than other people. But any one can acquire the rudiments of the art by dint of study.

It is as impossible to disguise a face as a handwriting. When the expert comes the disguise is torn off and the face tells the true story of the spirit inside the body. One only needs to visit the penitentiary to realize how undeniably vice writes its sign manual on the features. It is not the drunkard only whose red nose, flabby cheeks and rheumy eyes betray him; it is the sensualist whose vice is read in his lips, the knave whose propensity is revealed in the shape of his mouth, the man of violence is surrendered by his eyes. An experienced detective, policeman, or a trained jailer seldom needs to ask the crime of which the prisoner was guilty. He can tell it by his face.

It is quite evident that in the future the study of physiognomy is going to be pursued more vigorously than it has been. As a means of preventing crime it may prove invaluable. How constantly do we hear of men "falling from grace," as the phrase goes. Yet these men must have carried their crime in their faces for a long time. If any one had been able to read their features the mischief might have been averted. It is well known that every man's face is more or less stamped by the pursuit he follows. An experienced observer can generally detect a lawyer, or a doctor, or a merchant, or a clerk, or a mechanic, or a clergyman, by merely studying his face.

The instinctive criminal is a social parasite. The conclusion is irresistible that he is is organically morbid. He will proceed to any extreme, and life and property, separating him from the accomplishment of his wishes, are but barriers to be overcome. The occasional criminal is largely a negative creature, who yields himself when temptation and the stimulus of opportunity exceed his resistive power. The habitual and professional criminal represents degree rather than kind. Criminality is to him a profession, a fine art, and susceptible of division into specialties.

The average heads of criminals and those of ordinary people probably do not vary much in size. A large brain does not necessarily indicate great intelligence any more than a small one mental deficiencies. This being true, as little importance can be attached to the weight of brains of criminals. The weight of Oliver Cromwell's brain was 82.29 ounces; Lord Byron's, 79 ounces; Cuvier's, 64 ounces; Ruloff's, a thief and murderer, 59 ounces; adult idiot's, 54.95 ounces; Daniel Webster's, 53.50 ounces, and Gambetta's that of the size of a microcephalic idiot.

A face may either attract or repel; its lines indicate firmness and decision or weakness and sensuousness. In physiognomy may be traced fineness or brutality, surfeit or privation, gentleness or irascibility; yet from a consideration of the face it is assuming too much to predicate the form of criminal tendencies, if any, on the subject. Criminal physiognomy is not yet an exact science. The practical criminalogist regards criminality as bred in the bone and born in the flesh, and the etiology of crime to be looked for chiefly in heredity and environment, using the word environment in its most liberal sense, ante and post natal, and whatever cause, in whatever way, that exerts a deleterious influence upon nutrition and the functions of organic life, voluntary and involuntary.

Little is being done in this country in criminal anthropology that can compare with the studies and researches that are being carried on in Italy, France, and Germany. The student unacquainted with the languages of these countries pursues his studies at a disadvantage, owing to the paucity of literature in English upon the subject.

The tide of crime is steadily rising. The level of criminality, it is well known, is rising, and has been rising during the whole of the present century, throughout the civilized world. Its prevention and cure is a perplexing study and is engaging the thoughts and energies of our best men.

CHAPTER II.

FORGERY AS A PROFESSION.

FORGERS, CHECK AND DRAFT RAISERS—HOW PROFESSIONAL FORGERS AND CHECK RAISERS WORK—VALUABLE POINTS FOR BANKERS AND BUSINESS MEN—PERSONNEL OF A PROFESSSIONAL FORGERY GANG—THE SCRATCHER, LAYERDOWN, PRESENTER AND MIDDLEMAN—HOW BANKS ARE DEFRAUDED BY RAISED AND FORGED PAPER—DETAILED METHOD OF THE WORK—DIVIDING THE SPOILS—ACTION IN CASE OF ARREST—EMPLOYING ATTORNEYS—WHAT "FALL" MONEY IS—DUTIES OF A SHADOW—PREVENTING A CONFESSION—FIXING A JURY—POLITICIANS WITH A PULL—PROTECTING CRIMINALS—FULL DESCRIPTION OF HOW CHECKS AND DRAFTS ARE ALTERED—ALTERATIONS, ERASURES AND CHEMICALS—FAVORITE TRICK OF FORGERS—GAINING THE CONFIDENCE OF A BANK—LATEST MODE OF IMITATING A PRIVATE CHECK—PHOTOGRAPHING A SIGNATURE—HOW CHECKS ARE SECURED OUT OF CHECK BOOKS—HOW STOLEN UNSIGNED BANK NOTES AND BONDS ARE PLACED IN CIRCULATION—THE DETECTION OF FORGERS—HOW TO EXAMINE SIGNATURES—SCHEME ADOPTED BY EUROPEAN BANKERS—ALTERING A CHECK—THE VALUE OF SAFETY PAPER—SUCCESSFULLY RAISING CHECKS WITH A NEW SCHEME—BANKS SWINDLED BY RAISED PAPER—LIABILITY OF THE MAKER OF A CHECK—COURT DECISIONS—POINTS ABOUT RAISING CHECKS AND DRAFTS—CHEMICALS USED TO OBLITERATE WRITTEN FIGURES—RAISING ANY PAPER—ALERT CASHIERS AND TELLERS—DIFFERENT METHODS OF PROTECTION.

Professional forgers usually make their homes in large cities. They are constantly studying schemes and organizing gangs of men to defraud banks, trust companies and money lenders by means of forged checks, notes, drafts, bills of exchange, letters of credit, and in some instances altering registered government and other bonds, and counterfeiting the bonds of corporations. These bonds they dispose of or hypothecate to obtain loans on.

A professional forgery gang consists of: First, a capitalist or backer; second, the actual forger, who is known among his associates as the "scratcher;" third, the man who acts as confidential agent for the forger, who is known as the "middleman" or the "go-between;" fourth, the man who presents the forged paper at the bank for payment, who is known as the "layer-down" or "presenter."

When it is necessary to have a capitalist or backer connected with a gang, he furnishes the funds for the organization, frequently lays out the plans of work and obtains the genuine paper from which the forgeries are made. He will, when necessary, find the engraver, the lithographer, and, most important of all, the "professional" forger, who will do the actual forgery work.

The professional forger has, as a rule, considerable knowledge of chemicals, which enables him to alter checks, drafts, bills of exchange, letters of credit, or to change the names on registered bonds. He is something of an artist, too, for with a fine camel's hair brush he can restore the most delicate tints in bank safety paper, where the tints have been destroyed by the use of acids; in fact, no bank safety paper is a protection against him. When the amount of the genuine draft or check is perforated in the paper, certain professional forgers have reached that point in their work where they fill up the perforations with paper pulp, then with a hot iron press it out so that it is a very difficult matter to detect the alterations even with the use of the finest microscope. This done and the writing cleaned off the face of the draft, check, letter of credit or bill of exchange, with only the genuine signature left and the tints on the paper restored, the forger is prepared to fill up the paper for any amount decided upon.

The backer or capitalist is rarely known to any member of the gang outside of the "go-between," whom he makes use of to find the forger. He very rarely allows himself to become known to the men who "present" the forged paper at the banks. If the forgery scheme is successful, the backer receives back the money paid out for the preparation of the work, as well as any amount he may have loaned the "band" to enable them to open accounts at banks where they propose placing the forged paper. He is also allowed a certain percentage on all successful forgeries. This percentage will run from 20 to 30 per cent., but where the backer and forger are working together, their joint percentage is never less than 50 per cent.

The duties of the "middleman" or "go-between" are to receive from the forger or his confidential agent the altered or forged paper. He finds the man to "present" the same, accompanies his confederates on their forgery trips throughout the country, acts as the agent of the backer in dealing out money for expenses, sees that their plan of operations is carried out, and, in fact, becomes the general manager of the band. He is in full control of the men who act as "presenters" of the forged paper. If there be more than one man to "present" the paper, the middleman, as a rule, will not allow them to become known to each other. He meets them in secluded places, generally in little out-of-the-way saloons. In summer time a favorite meeting place is some secluded spot in the public parks. At one meeting he makes an appointment for the next meeting. He uses great care in making these appointments, so that the different "presenters" do not come together and thereby become known to each other. The middleman is usually selected for his firmness of character. He must be a man known among criminals as a "staunch" man, one who cannot be easily frightened by detectives when arrested, no matter what pressure may be brought to bear upon him. He must have such an acquaintanceship among criminals as will enable him to select other men who are "staunch" and who are not apt to talk and tell their business, whether sober or under the influence of liquor. It is from among this class of acquaintances that he selects the men to "present" the forged paper. It is an invariable rule followed by the backer and forger that in selecting a middleman they select one who not only has the reputation of being a "staunch" man, but he must also be a man who has at least one record of conviction standing against him. This is for the additional protection of the backer and forger, as they know that in law the testimony of an accomplice who is also an ex-convict, should he conclude to become a state's witness, would have to be strongly corroborated before a court or jury in order to be believed.

As the capitalist and forger, for self-protection, use great care in selecting a "middleman," the middleman to protect himself also uses the same care in the selection of men to "present" the forged paper. He endeavors, like the backer and forger, to throw as much protection around himself as possible, and for the same reasons he also uses ex-convicts as the men to "present" the forged paper at the banks. The "presenters" are of all ages and appearances, from the party who will pass as an errand boy, messenger, porter or clerk, to the prosperous business man, horse trader, stock buyer, or farmer. When a presenter enters a bank to "lay down" a forged paper, the "go between" will sometimes enter the bank with him and stand outside the counter, noting carefully if there is any suspicious action on the part of the paying teller when the forged paper is presented to him, and whether the "presenter" carries himself properly and does his part well. But usually the middleman prefers waiting outside the bank for the "presenter," possibly watching him through a window from the street. If the "presenter" is successful and gets the money on the forged paper, the middleman will follow him when he leaves the bank to some convenient spot where, without attracting attention, he receives the money. He then gives the presenter another piece of forged paper, drawn on some neighboring bank. They go from bank to bank, usually victimizing from three to five banks in each city, their work being completed generally in less than an hour's time. All money obtained from the various banks on the forged paper is immediately turned over to the middleman, who furnishes all the money for current expenses. After the work is completed the presenters leave the city by different routes, first having agreed on a meeting point in some neighboring city. The "presenters" frequently walk out of the city to some outlying station on the line of the road they propose to take to their next destination. This precaution is taken to avoid arrest at the depot in case the forgery is discovered before they can leave the city. At the next meeting-point the middleman, having deducted the expenses advanced, pays the "presenters" their percentage of the money obtained on the forged paper.

A band of professional forgers before starting out always agree on a basis of division of all moneys obtained on their forged paper. This division might be about as follows: For a presenter where the amount to be drawn does not exceed $2,000, 15 to 25 per cent.; but where the amount to be drawn is from $3,000 to $5,000 and upwards, the "presenter" receives from 35 to 45 per cent. The price is raised as the risk increases, and it is generally considered a greater risk to attempt to pass a check or draft of a large denomination than a smaller one. The middleman gets from 15 to 25 per cent. His work is more, and his responsibility is greater, but the risk is less. There are plenty of middlemen to be had, but the "presenters" are scarce. The "shadow," when one accompanies the band, is sometimes paid a salary by the middleman and his expenses, but at other times he is allowed a small percentage, not to exceed 5 per cent. and his expenses, as with ordinary care his risk is very slight. The backer and forger get the balance, which usually amounts to from 50 to 60 per cent. The expenses that have been advanced the men who go out on the road are usually deducted at the final division.

In case of the arrest of one of the "presenters" in the act of "laying down" forged paper, the middleman or shadow immediately notifies other members of the band who may be in the city. All attempts to get money from the other banks are stopped, and the other members of the band leave the city as best they can to meet at some designated point in a near-by city. Out of their first successful forgeries a certain sum from each man's share is held by the "middleman" to be used in the defense of any member of the band who may be arrested on the trip. This money is called "fall money," and is used to employ counsel for the men under arrest, or to do anything for them that may be for their interest. Any part of this money not used is paid back in proportion to the amount advanced to the various members of the band from whose share it has been retained. Sometimes, however, in in forming a band of forgers there is an understanding or agreement entered into at the outset that each man "stand on his own bottom"—that is, if arrested, take care of himself. When this is agreed to, the men arrested must get out as best they can. Under these circumstances there is no assessment for "fall money," but usually the men who present the paper insist on "fall money" being put up, as it assures them the aid of some one of the band working earnestly in their behalf and watching their interests, outside of the attorney retained.

When a "middleman" is exceedingly cautious and not entirely satisfied with the "presenters," he will sometimes have an assistant. This is where the "shadow" comes in. This shadow will, under the directions of the "middleman," follow the presenter into the bank and report fully on his actions. He sometimes catches the "presenter" in an attempt to swindle his companions by claiming that he did not get the money, but had to get out of the bank in a hurry and leave the check or draft, as the paying teller was suspicious. A "presenter" caught at this trick is sometimes sent into a bank to present a forged check where the bank has been previously warned of his coming by an anonymous letter, written by or at the instigation of one of the leaders. This is done as a punishment for his dishonesty, and as a warning to the other "presenters," not to attempt this treachery. Usually, however, a dishonest member is quietly dropped. The "shadow" will follow the "presenters" from the time they get the forged paper from the middleman until they hand the money over to him. A good "shadow" is always useful to tho middleman, who does not allow him to become known to his confederates.

When one of the party is arrested, an attorney is at once sent to him. As a rule, in selecting an attorney, one is employed who is known as a good criminal lawyer. It is also preferred that he should be a lawyer who has some political weight. The middleman employs the attorney, and pays him out of the "fall money." The arrested man is strictly instructed by the attorney to do no talking, and is usually encouraged by the promise that they will have him out in a short time. In order to keep him quiet, this promise is frequently renewed by the attorney acting for the "middleman." This is done to prevent a confession being made in case the arrested man should show signs of weakening. Finally, when he is forced to stand trial, if the case is one certain of conviction, the attorney will get him to plead guilty, with the promise of a short sentence, and will then bargain to this end with the court or prosecutor. Thus guided by the attorney selected and acting for the "middleman" and his associates, the prisoner pleads guilty, and frequently discovers, when it is too late, that he has been tricked into keeping his mouth shut in the interests of his associates. It is but fair to state, however, that if money can save an arrested party, and if his associates have it, they will use it freely among attorneys or "jury fixers," where the latter can be made use of, and frequently it is paid to politicians who make a pretense of having a "pull" with the prosecuting officers of the court.

In most instances when checks are sent out they are not seen again by the maker for a period of days. As business houses of any considerable magnitude always have a comfortable balance with their bankers, ample time and an abundance of cash are thus placed at the disposal of the check-raisers.

As to the best methods of raising checks so that the fraud will not be readily detected, much depends upon the way in which they are written. The style of handwriting, the texture and quality of the paper, and the chemical properties of the inks, are points which are necessary to be considered.

Many checks may be altered to a larger amount by the mere addition of a stroke of the pen here or the erasure of a line, by means of chemicals, in some other place. For instance, take a check of $100, no matter how it may be written, there are five or six different ways in which it may be altered to a much larger amount, and in such a manner as to defy the scrutiny of the most careful bank teller. It may be made into six hundred by merely adding the "S" loop to the "O," dotting the first part of the "n" to make of it an "i," and crossing the connecting stroke between the "n" and the

" e " to form the " x." To complete the change it will be found necessary to erase with chemicals part of the " e."

A check for one hundred dollars may also be easily altered to eight hundred dollars, especially when sufficient space has been left between the " one " and the " hundred," as follows: Add to the " O " the top part of an " E," dot part of the " n " to form an " i," connect the remaining part of the " n " with the " e," forming the loop of a " g," and then add " ht." The figure " 1 " is very easily changed to " 8."

Sometimes a small capital it used for an " o." In this case an alteration into " Four " hundred is easily accomplished by simply prefixing a capital " F " and transforming the " e " into an " r," the " n " being made to serve as a " u."

Another change frequently made is to " Ten " hundred. It is done simply by adding the stem and top part of the " T " to the " O " and changing the first part of the " u " to an " e."

Of course, any of the foregoing changes may be made with equal facility whether the amount be " hundred " or " thousand."

Two hundred, if anything, is a much easier amount to alter than one hundred. It is done in the following manner: Make an " F " by simply crossing the " T;" dot the first part of the " w " to make an " i," and change the " o " into an " e." The figure " 2 " can be made into a perfect " 5 " by simple adding the top part of the " 5 " to it."

Three hundred is not so easily altered; still it may be done by changing the word " hundred " into " thousand "—an alteration which is by no means rare, and which is quite simple, especially when the word is begun with a small " h." The modus operandi is as follows: Place a capital " T " before the " h;" change the first part of the " u " into an " o," connecting it with the second part, which, with the first part of the "u," will form a "u;" change the second part of the "u" to an "s;" erase the top part of the "d," making of it an "a," and complete the alteration by making an "n" of the "r" and "e." This alteration may appear to be somewhat complicated, but a trial of it according to direction will show how nicely it may be done.

"Four" is another easy amount to alter. It is done by extending the second part of the "u" into a "t," and adding the "y" loop to the "r." "Five" is changed into "Fifty" and "Fifteen." "Six," "Seven," "Eight," and "Nine" are changed into "Sixty," "Seventy," "Eighty," and "Ninety" by simply affixing the syllable "ty." "Twenty" is another easily changed amount; all that is necessary to make "Seventy" of it is to make an "S" of the "T," and change the first part of the "w" into an "e." To make the alteration perfect, the top part of the "T" must be erased with chemicals.

In regard to the chemicals used to erase ink, much depends upon the ink. For most writing fluids and copying inks, which are in daily use, a saturated solution of chloride of lime is the best eraser known, and when properly made is very quick and effective in its work. It may be applied with a glass pointed pen, to avoid corrosion, or with a clean bit of sponge. It acts as a powerful bleach, and with it the face of a check may be washed as white as before it was written upon. When inks have become dry and hard, sometimes carbolic or acetic acid is used effectively with the chlorine. The application of any alkali or acid to the clean polished surface of a check will, of course, destroy the finish and leave a perceptible stain, but the work of covering up these traces is quite as simple as removing the ink in the first place.

A favorite trick of forgers, and check and draft raisers, who operate on an an extensive scale, is for one of them to open an office in a city and represent himself as a cattle dealer, lumber merchant, or one looking about for favorable real estate investments. His first move is to open a bank account, and then work to get on friendly terms with the cashier. He always keeps a good balance—sometimes way up in the thousands—and deports himself in such a manner as to lead to the belief that he is a highly honorable gentleman, and the bank officials are led to the belief that he will eventually become a very profitable customer.

Occasionally he has a note, for a small amount to begin with, always first-class two-name paper, and he never objects—usually insists—in paying a trifle more than the regular discount. At first the bank officials closely examine the paper offered, and of course find that the endorsers are men of high standing, and then their confidence in the "cattle king" is unbounded. Gradually the notes increase in amount, from a thousand to fifteen hundred dollars, and from fifteen hundred to two or three thousand. The notes are promptly paid at maturity. After the confidence of the bank people has been completely gained, the swindler makes a strike for his greatest effort. He comes in the bank in a hurry, presents a sixty-day note, endorsed by first-class men, for a larger amount than he has ever before requested, and it generally happens that he gets the money without the slightest difficulty. Then he has a sudden call to attend to important business elsewhere. When the note or notes mature, it is discovered to be a very clever forgery. This has been done time and again, and it is rare that the forger has been apprehended.

The latest mode is for the forger to imitate a private check by the photo-lithographic method, after having obtained a signed check. The signature, after being photographed, is carefully traced over with ink, and the body of the check is filled up for whatever amount is desired. The maker of the check is requested to identify the person who holds it, and as a general thing he does not wait to see the money paid. The moment his back is turned, the layer-down palms the small check and presents the large one. This way of obtaining money is without the assistance of a middleman.

Private marks on a check are no safeguards at all, although a great many merchants believe they can prevent forgery by making certain dots, or seeming slips of the pen, which are known only to the paying-teller and themselves. This precaution becomes useless when the forger uses the camera. Safe-breakers are often called upon by forgers and asked to secure a sheet of checks out of a check book. When this is accomplished a few canceled checks are taken at the same time. These are given to the forger and he fills them up for large amounts, after tracing or copying the signature. The safe burglars receive a percentage on the amount realized. If your safe, vault or desk is broken open where your check-book is kept, carefully count the leaves in your check-book, also your canceled checks. If any are missing notify the banks and begin using a different style of check immediately. The sneak-thief, while plying his trade, often secures unsigned bonds of some corporation which has put the signed bonds in circulation, leaving the rest unsigned until the next meeting of the directors.

Frequently unsigned bonds are left in the bank vault for safe keeping. These are stolen and sent to the penman or "scratcher." Then a genuine signed bond is purchased, from which the signatures are copied and then forged. The same trick has been played on unsigned bank notes, but on the bank notes almost any name will do, as no person looks at the signature as long as the note appears genuine.

The ingenuity of a countless army of sharpers is constantly at work in this country, devising plans to obtain funds dishonestly, without work, but, in fact, they often expend more time, skill and labor in carrying out their nefarious schemes, than would serve to earn the sum they finally secure, by honest labor. Every banker must, therefore, be on his guard, and should acquaint himself with the most approved means of detecting and avoiding the most common swindlers. This is just as necessary as it is to lock his books and cash in his safe before going home.

Next to the counterfeiter, the forger in the most dangererous criminal in business life. Transactions involving the largest sums of money are completed on the faith in the genuineness of a signature. Hence every effort should be made to acquire the art of detecting an imitation at a glance. This can only be done by considerable practice. It is asserted that every signature has character about it which can not be perfectly copied, and which can always be detected by an experienced eye. This is problematical, but certainly a skillful bank-teller can hardly be deceived by the forgery of a name of a well-known depositor.

A banker and business man should accustom himself to scrutinize closely the signatures of those with whom he deals. He should cut off their names from the backs of checks and notes, and paste them in alphabetical order in an autograph book devoted to that purpose, and compare any suspicious signature with the genuine one.

In consequence of the numerous frauds committed by forged checks, some of the European bankers have adopted the custom of sending with their letter of advice a photograph of the person in whose favor the credit has been issued, and to stop the payment when the person who presents himself at the bank does not resemble the picture. If this practice were to become universal, the object of preventing frauds could be well attained.

Many banks have been swindled in the following manner:

A check, say for ten dollars, is obtained from a depositor of a bank, and a blank check exactly like the filled-in check is secured. The two checks are laid one upon the other, so that the edges are exactly even. Both checks are then torn irregularly across, and in such a way that the signature on the filled check appears on one piece and the amount and name of the payee on the other. The checks having been held together while being torn, of course one piece of the blank check will exactly fit the other piece of the filled check. The swindler then fills in one piece of the blank check with the name of the payee and an amount to suit himself, takes it with the piece of the genuine check containing the signature to the bank, and explains that the check was accidently torn. The teller can put the pieces together, and as they will fit exactly, the chances are that he will think that the pieces are parts of the same check, and becomes a victim of the swindle. The trick, of course, suggests its own remedy.

It is a well known fact that there are banks in the country that have paid thousands of dollars on raised checks, and decided that it was cheaper for them to pocket the loss than to have the facts become known. The New York Court of Appeals holds that the maker of a check is obliged to use all due diligence in protecting it, and the omission to use the most effectual protection against alterations is regarded as an evidence of neglect.

Here are a few points about raising checks and drafts that should be carefully noted: To successfully raise a check or draft requires so much less skill or art than to accomplish a forgery that it has of late become alarmingly prevalent. Often where a check or draft is printed on ordinary paper the original figures are removed by some chemical process so skillfully that no alteration can be detected, even with a strong magnifying glass.

It is not uncommon, when filling up checks or drafts, to take another pen, and with red ink write the amount across the face of the paper, and again make the figures in and through the signature. All these precautions may make tampering with the amount more difficult for a clumsy novice, but it only imposes a few moments more work upon the accomplished manipulator. He takes his strong solution of chloride of lime and rain water, or other prepared chemicals, and with a pen suited to the purpose, by neutralizing and abstracting the coloring properties of the ink, he carefully obliterates such portions of the lines in the figures and written amounts as suits his purpose, then easily makes the alteration he desires, the red ink coming out as readily as black. And if the tint or coloring of the paper should have been affected by his cautious touch, he takes the proper shade of crayon or watercolor, and carefully replaces the original shade.

Now, the signature not being touched, but remaining genuine, and the payer not being supposed to know who wrote the check, but only who signed it, pays the amount specified, and the law holds the " maker of the check responsible when there is nothing in its appearance to excite suspicion, and the signature is proven genuine."

It is probably a fair statement to make that any draft issued can be raised, but it is unquestionably true that some can be much more easily altered than others, and as in the last ten years additional safeguards have been thrown around the bills of exchange of banks, so the forger has become more and more expert and proficient, just about keeping pace. As the question of armor that can not be pierced and projectiles that will pierce anything are first one and then the other a little ahead, so it is with the bank forger and the banks.

Admirable as some of the work unquestionably is, if anything so disreputable can be called admirable, there is even yet a something about either the work or the operator that should arouse the suspicions of the teller or cashier who is on the alert; and a teller or cashier without suspicion, and who is not on the alert, may be a comparatively good man, but is certainly in the wrong place.

The presenter of a counterfeit bill at the teller's window may have no knowledge of the character of the bill that he is presenting, but he who presents a forged draft, in addition to presenting a bad bill, has a consciousness himself of the fraud that he is attempting, thus giving the teller not only the chance of scrutinizing the bill, but also to judge of the appearance, whether nervous or otherwise, of the man who is laying the trap, and these two facts should inure greatly to the advantage of the teller.

As the news of the many successful depredations is scattered, we see banks trying different methods of protection, many of which at first glance are admirable, but which it will be seen on a little careful study simply require but slight change of method on the part of the professional forger to successfully evade. For instance: Many banks are daily advising their correspondents of the number and amounts of drafts issued, either in the course of the mails or otherwise. This at first sight would seem to be a most absolute protection, but it really may prove a trap to the bank so advised, as may readily be seen. Let us suppose that Mr. Forger steps into a bank in Cleveland, buys a draft for $5; a day or two later, or the same day, he buys another draft for $5,000. The first draft is successfully altered to $5,000, but would not of course be paid by the correspondent bank for this amount, because the advice they have of this number is that it was issued for $5; but it was a simpler matter to change the number of the draft to correspond with the $5,000 draft, the number of which the forger has, than it is to make the other alterations necessary to raise it from $5 to $5,000. After making these alterations it goes in for payment, and on reference to the advice sheet it is found that this apparent number was issued for $5,000 and paid accordingly. Then the forgers have simply the problem on hand to avail themselves, either directly through the bank of issue or elsewhere, of this genuine $5,000 draft, which is certainly not a hard task for the men who have successfully performed the harder one.

CHAPTER III.

ALTERING BANK NOTES.

Bankers Easily Deceived—How Ten One Hundred-Dollar Bills are Made out of Nine—How to Detect Altered Bank Notes—Making a Ten-Dollar Bill out of a Five—A Ten Raised to Fifty—How Two-Dollar Bills are Raised to a Higher Denomination—Bogus Money in Commercial Colleges—Action of the United States Treasury Department—Engraving a Greenback—How They are Printed—Making a Vignette—Beyond the Reach of Rascals—How Bank Notes are Printed, Signed and Issued by the Government—Safeguards to Foil Counterfeiters and Alterers of Bank Notes—Devices to Raise Genuine Bank Notes—Split Notes—Altering Silver Certificates.

A dangerous game, and one too often successfully perpetrated, is the raising of bank bills from a lower to a higher denomination. Counterfeiters have often been detected making ten bills of nine by the following operation:

A counterfeit one hundred-dollar bank note is cut into ten pieces; one of these pieces is pasted into a genuine bill, cutting out a piece of the genuine of the same size. In pasting nine genuine bills in this manner, nine pieces are obtained, which, with one piece of counterfeit, will make a tenth bill, which is the profit. This operation is not a very successful one, as the difference between the counterfeit and the genuine will be very evident to any one who examines closely.

Every business man should know how to detect altered bank bills, and a close scrutiny of all money offered, bearing in mind the suggestions here made, will prove a safeguard. Bank notes are sometimes altered by raising from lower to higher denominations, or replacing name of broken bank by name of good one. This is done either by erasing words and printing others in their place, or by pasting on the original bill a piece of counterfeit work or a piece taken from some genuine bill. If the former, the new counterfeit piece will always differ from the surrounding genuine work. If the latter, the fraud will be revealed by holding the bill up to the light, when the portion pasted will look darker than the surrounding portions.

Another method employed is to cut ten-dollar bills in halves, also five-dollar bills, then join them, and raise the five part to a ten by the blue paper dodge. This bill can be successfully worked off in a roll of other bills, owing to the workmanship, and sometimes a gang will visit a certain locality and flood it with doctored bills. Fifty-dollar bills have been often raised from a ten. This fraud is generally neatly executed, and is well calculated to deceive the unsuspecting, and a banker, in hurriedly counting money, is liable to be taken in on one of these.

A recent scheme to defraud with raised bills is to raise a two-dollar bill to a five. In order to accomplish this feat rascals cut out the figure five in the left-hand corner of a "V" and paste it over the figure "2" in the upper right-hand corner of the two-dollar bill. The pasting is done so neatly that not one person in a hundred, or even a thousand, unless an expert, would notice the difference. The very small $2 marks in the scroll-work surrounding the large figure are blotted out with a pencil and are not visible. The figure "2" in the lower right-hand corner is erased with acids, and the bill is in all respects a first-class imitation of the genuine article. Treasury officials say that this is something new in the way of bill-raising, and is very dangerous.

Many people who are not used to handling money have

been swindled by what is known as " Imitation Money." The United States Treasury Department is making strenuous efforts to break up the practice of issuing imitations of the national currency, to which many commercial colleges and business firms are addicted. This bogus currency has been extensively used by sharpers all over the country to swindle ignorant people, and its manufacture is in violation of law.

So vague is the general idea as to how a bank note is made that we give an explanation of the various processes it goes through before it is issued as a part of the " money of the realm," saying, by way of introduction, that this country leads the world in bank-note engraving. Unfortunately, the first consideration in making a bank-note is to prevent bad men from making a counterfeit of it, and therefore all the notes of a certain denomination or value must be exact duplicates of each other. If they were engraved by hand this would not be the case; and, another thing, hand engraving is more easily counterfeited than the work done by the processes we herewith describe.

Every note is printed from a steel plate, in the preparation of which many persons take part. If you will look at a $5 " greenback " you will see a picture in the center; a small portrait, called a vignette, on the left, and in each of the upper corners a network of fine lines with a dark ground, one of them containing the letter " V " and the other the figure 5. These four parts are made on separate plates.

To make a vignette it is necessary, first, to make a large drawing on paper with great care, and a daguerreotype is then taken of the drawing the exact size of the engraving desired.

The daguerreotype is then given to the engraver, who uses a steel point to mark on it all the outlines of the picture. The plate is inked and a print taken from it. While the ink is still damp the print is laid face down on a steel plate, which has been softened by heating it red hot and letting it cool slowly. It is then put in a press and an exact copy of the outline is thus made on the steel plate. This the engraver finishes with his graver, a tool with a three-cornered point, which cuts a clean line without leaving a rough edge.

Now this is used for making other plates—it is never used to print from. It must be made very hard; this is done by heating it and cooling it quickly. A little roller of softened steel is then rolled over it by a powerful machine until its surface has been forced into all the lines cut into the plate. The outlines of the vignette are thus transferred to the roller in raised lines, and after the roller is hardened it is used to roll over plates of softened steel, and thus make in them sunken lines exactly like those in the plate originally engraved. The center picture is engraved and transferred to a roller like the vignette, but the network in the upper corners, and also on the back of the note, is made by the lathe. This machine costs $5,000, a price that puts it beyond the reach of counterfeiters, and its work is so perfect that it can not be imitated by hand.

The black parts of the note are printed first, and when the ink is dry the green-black is printed, to be followed by the red stamps and numbers. It is then signed and issued. For greater security one part of the note is engraved and printed at one place and another part at another place, when it is sent to Washington to be finished and signed.

But even after all this care and all these safeguards many skillfully executed counterfeits and raised and altered bank notes have been made and issued, some of them so good as to deceive the most expert judges of money.

Many devices have been resorted to by counterfeiters to raise genuine bank-notes, as well as to manufacture bogus ones, but one of the most novel has recently come to light. The scheme consisted of splitting a $5 and a $1 note, and then pasting the back of the $1 note to the front of the $5 note and the front of the $1 note to the back of the $5 note. The mechanical part of the work was excellently done, but the fraud could be detected the moment the note was turned over.

An effort had been made to change the "one" to "five" on the "one" side of the new combined note, but it was done so clumsily that the fraud would have been seen at a glance, and the only hope of passing the notes as fives would have been to pass them over with the $5 side up and trust to the man receiving it not to turn it over before putting it away. The doctored notes came to the notice of the writer through one of the Chicago banks, with the request that they be allowed whatever they were worth. The government always redeems notes at the face value, and as the faces in this case were of a $1 and a $5 note, $6 was allowed. It is not known whether the bank was caught on the split notes or not.

Another scheme for altering bank-notes is practiced with more or less success. It is to take a one dollar silver certificate and by means of powerful acids and fine penwork the large figure "one" on the reverse side is split into two "tens," and the intermediate portion transformed into a scroll. On the other side the "one" over the representation of the silver dollar is obliterated and "ten" substituted, but the "s" is left off the dollar. The single "1" figures in the corners are neatly eaten off and the figure "10" substituted. The small "one" is changed to an "X" and a new series number is printed in red upon the face. The bill would pass anywhere. None but an expert would detect the fraud.

CHAPTER IV.

TRAPS FOR THE UNWARY.

SCHEMES FOR DRAWING DOLLARS FROM THE POCKETS OF THE UNSUSPECTING—FAKES AND FRAUDS OF ALLEGED MEDICAL MEN—SCHEMES WITH CATCHY TITLES—PATENT MEDICINE SWINDLES—HOW PORTRAIT COMPANIES SWINDLE THE PUBLIC—MAKING PORTRAITS FREE OF CHARGE—A SWINDLE PURE AND SIMPLE—SAMPLE OF LETTERS SENT TO DUPES—"EVERY PORTRAIT MUST HAVE A FRAME"—SOMETHING FOR NOTHING—TOWN SITE AND LAND SCHEMES—PAPER CITIES AND TOWNS—INVESTING IN MINING STOCKS—THE GOLD BRICK SWINDLE—HOW THE SCHEME IS WORKED—THE CANCELLED STAMP FRAUD—HOW THE SWINDLE ORIGINATED AND IS WORKED—THE CLOTH SWINDLE—AN EASILY WORKED AND SUCCESSFUL GAME—SWINDLING TRICKS AT A CIRCUS—THE SHORT CHANGE MAN—STRIPPING NOTES—THE TOP AND BOTTOM WORKER—DON'T MAKE WAGERS WITH STRANGERS—AVOID ALL GAMES OF CHANCE.

Probably the most successful in the aggregate of all devices, as to the money to be made out of it, the extent and scope of operations, the ease with which victims are hooked and the entire escape of the operator from any taint of reproach or criminality in connection therewith, is worked under the guise of healing medicines, or cures for the sick. It is said that seven out of ten persons are sufferers from some form of chronic ailment. This terrible average indicates the field of operations open to the humanitarian labors of the good physician and the devilish practices of those who impose upon the suffering, to relieve them, not of their diseases, but of their money.

Mankind parts with anything rather than life or health. The ignorant, the careless, the unthinking and the frightened comprise the bulk of humanity after all. Some people, reasonable in other matters, seem to prefer to believe in a quack doctor's advertisement to the best attested reputation of a well established physician, and will pay such a specialist, for a dose of wind and water, ten times the price asked by the regular for a cure. Hence flourish these "Doctors," "Specialists," "Discoverers" of rare and wonderful remedies, "Medical Institutes," "Magnetic Physicians," "Electro-Therapeutic Baths," "Massage Treatment," "Ladies' Physicians" and "Faith Cures," and a hundred other schemes under catchy titles which adorn the advertising pages of the newspapers, attracting the attention of those out of health to an easy way of regaining it. All it takes is the selection of the proper "specialist," the payment of the fee, a medical examination—especially if the victim is a woman—and the patient is set down for a "Course of Treatment," which is limited by just one thing, the amount of money which can be safely absorbed by this bloodsucker from his helpless and ignorant prey. The medicine has nothing to do with it, and probably does not cost the "Doctor" a dollar a barrel. The technical medical terms used are merely for effect.

The inspection of the victim and the use of instruments of examination and the stretching out of the subject upon the examination chair are simply part of the process which impresses the object of these attentions with the wonderful resources and skill of the pretended physician, and if she is a woman of refinement, secures her as a permanent customer, for no lady will want to submit to the same treatment from others, and hence will always return to the "specialist" who has already made the examinations which it is pretended are necessary.

These victims of their wiles afford the rich rewards of their dishonest practices. These so-called "Doctors" do not, as a rule, associate together. They have no organizations, no comradeship. Their hands are against each other as well as against their fellow men, but if two or three of them on rare occasions gather together, no joke is enjoyed more than their experiences with ladies who are permanent customers, because of the hold they have obtained over them in this way. It is amazing how trustful women are toward any one who parades under the name of "Doctor."

Never pay attention to patent medicine advertisements. If you are sick or ailing employ a reputable physician. Patent medicine nostrums and the "cure-all" mixture of quacks will do you, as a usual thing, more harm than good. There are many proprietary medicines of merit, and the manufacturers of them do not resort to questionable means in disposing of same.

One of the easiest worked swindles is that sent out by "portrait companies." The circulars are printed in imitation of typewriter, and certainly read in a harmless manner, and are cunningly worded. The country is flooded with circulars, mostly from Chicago, New York and other large cities. Some of them offer a portrait free, and then sell a frame for eight to twelve dollars, which costs them from seventy-five cents to a dollar; and others collect installments. Whatever form the scheme assumes, the customer is invariably cheated, as the "crayons" are only cheap fadable sun-prints with a few touches of crayon or India ink, and the frames are of the cheapest and most perishable molding and metal. Some idea may be found of the quality of the "art" from the fact that a young man employed in a "crayon studio" is expected to turn out twenty finished portraits a day. One of the worst features of this business is that it often succeeds by appeals to the tenderest and holiest emotions of the human heart. Small likenesses of the dead are copied, enlarged and framed, the temporary appearance being so good that the surviving friends do not hesitate to pay the price demanded, only to find in a few months that they have a faded print inclosed in a shabby frame.

The following letter is the first one sent and certainly reads smoothly, but is simply the bait to catch the unwary:

GREAT AMERICAN COPYING HOUSE, 181 and 183 W. JONES STREET,
Rooms 96 and 97.

DEAR SIR:—If you will send us a photograph of yourself, or any member of your family, we will make you a full life-size crayon portrait, free of charge.

The only consideration imposed upon you will be that you exhibit it to your friends as a sample of our work and thereby assist us in securing other orders. Also, that you promise to get it framed in a suitable frame for a fine portrait, so that the work will show to advantage. Of course, you would not allow a fine portrait to stand around unframed, and have it ruined.

We trust you will not consider this a "scheme," as it is not, but an excellent manner of placing a specimen of our work in your vicinity.

A guarantee for the return of photo is assured, so have no fear of losing it.

This offer is good for ten days. This will be a "Sample Portrait," worth $35, and as fine as can be made.

Send your full address, plainly written, with photo., as that will assure its identity.

Hoping that you will kindly oblige us and use your influence in furthering our interest, I remain,

Respectfully yours,
JAMES R. BROWN.

Here is a firm who proposes to make a life-size portrait of any photograph sent on. This it would do free of charge—wouldn't charge as much as a five-cent piece. Usually a person bites at this bait because it is so cheap—costing only the loan of the photograph. The reason given by the firm for giving away these portraits is that it desires to introduce its superior class of work throughout the country.

Now the facts in the case are that the firm makes over a hundred per cent. and that, too, off of the person who gets the portrait for nothing. After receiving the photograph the victim is informed by return mail [copy of which letters we reproduce following this paragraph] that the crayon would look very much better in a frame than if tacked on a wall or pasted over the fire-place. Of this the victim has no doubt, and then he reads that the firm also deals extensively in picture frames which it is selling at unheard of prices. This is where the rub comes in, and if the gullible fellow does not order one of these frames—and they are of the very cheapest material—he loses his photograph. Sometimes this photo. is a relic of a departed mother, sister or wife. Of course, there a hundreds of people who order a frame rather than lose the picture or apply to the police

GREAT AMERICAN COPYING HOUSE, 181-183 W. JONES ST., ROOMS 96 AND 97.

DEAR SIR:—The photo sent to us received and will be returned safely. We have completed a very fine life-size 20 x 24 inch bust from the same, which we guarantee to be POSITIVELY A FREE HAND CRAYON. No finer portrait ever went into your vicinity, and is worth $35. It is an exact copy in every particular; will never fade, and will always keep its effect. By close examination you see that it has not a rough finish as is common with artist work, but has as soft a finish as at a distance. These are honest statements which we absolutely guarantee. We are laboring to build up a business that will be permanent.

The portrait is actually worth $35, and we trust you will exhibit it to our mutual advantage when received. You understand the Portrait is sent to you FREE, provided you exhibit it, but no portrait looks well without a frame; in fact, does not "show off" at all. We are sending out many portraits to different parts of your State, in the hope of building up a large trade, and in order to display our work to advantage must make it look as well as possible.

A portrait framed looks well, while one unframed looks unfinished. You can easily see how it is; we might ship a car-load of the very best portraits to people, who will wait their own time in getting them framed (and a great many people live in out-of-the-way places and have no opportunity to get them framed), and when they do frame them it is with a cheap, narrow, inferior frame, that would not show a chromo off to advantage, much less a Hand Stippled Crayon portrait, for which any reputable artist would charge $35. This is not a scheme to sell a frame, but is a sure way of exhibiting our work to the best advantage so that benefit will return to us. The better the portrait looks, the better it will please you and the more good it will do us. You will see how easy it is for people to send us photos and get a valuable portrait free, and never endeavor to do us any service, but if we ship the portrait from our studio in first-class order, we know we are safe, and you are satisfied, and the work itself will advertise us. We pack the portrait securely, placing heavy backing and cover on it. The glass is of triple strength and French plate, and the portrait is as good as can be produced at any price. It is not hurried through but the greatest pains taken with it, so as to give a perfect likeness. Being a sample portrait it is necessarily a valuable work of art. Be assured we mean what we say, and are not trying to sell you a frame, but must know that our portraits will be framed and then we are positive they will benefit us. We take the utmost care in finishing it up, but you can see that it will be impossible to ship portraits for samples without frames. We are handling but one style, and one size, 20 x 24 frame, and have the finest in the market for the money, at the very lowest retail price. There is not a frame in the city more suitable for a portrait than the one we are handling. It is 3-inch old gold outside, raised center 2 inches of elegant gilt, all handsomely ornamented, 1½ inch red plush, and 1 inch ornamented gold lining, making in all a 7½ inch frame. There is no copying house in the city but sells the same frame for $12.50, and our work is superior to any copying house work, and besides they are telling you that they are giving you a life-size picture, when in reality it is only 18 x 22. All we ask is $9.75 for the frame, that includes the finest French plate glass, backing and packing; we expect to be benefited by getting orders in the future through your influence.

We send the portrait and frame C. O. D., or remit by draft, P. O. order or express. A discount of six per cent. is given when CASH ACCOMPANIES ORDER, and you save return money charges. Please let us know by what express company to ship. Please place your order at once as we desire to get our work introduced to the notice of your friends.

Remit, or will send C. O. D., PRIVILEGE OF EXAMINATION ALLOWED. We gladly remunerate you for acting as our agent and will quote you agents' prices for future orders.

You can take many orders and thereby derive quite a revenue as everybody wants one when their neighbor has one. Remember we fulfill our contract to the letter, giving you a portrait FREE.

In conclusion, will repeat, we send with the privilege of examining before you pay one cent, and if it is not perfection in every particular, return it at our expense.

There can be nothing fairer than this; it is surely evidence that we have done you a piece of work that will benefit us in your vicinity.

Hoping you will appreciate our manner of endeavoring to please, we are, Yours Very Truly.

(Dictated.) JAMES R. BROWN.

Now, while it is readily discernable that the scheme is a swindle, the difficulty arises as to how to proceed against the fellows criminally. They have lived up to their agreement and do actually furnish a portrait free, but they make up profitably on the frame. They have violated no law, and are therefore not amenable to the statutes of either the city or state. There are hundreds of such schemes worked every day all over the country. Don't expect something for nothing or you will get swindled every time.

It is said that these out-and-out swindles of a petty kind do no serious harm and afford a good lesson at small price. The infallible recipe for getting rich which was sent in return for a two-cent stamp: " Work night and day and never spend a cent," and that for enabling a man to do without eating: " Take a dose of poison," were worth the money to any one except the man who could not laugh over the matter with his friends.

Always look out for town-site and land schemes. They are usually frauds. If you want to buy real estate where the land is located, don't take the word of any agent or promoter. An honest deal will stand rigid investigation. Land and improvement companies are a very common means of divorcing a man and his money, and not much to the satisfaction of the man. There is hardly a neighborhood in the United States where these companies have not been organized, and where they have not uttered their magnificent promises and then gone on to ruin, not only their dupes, but oftentimes their promoters. These schemes look perfect on paper, but imperfect and disheartening results may be be found scattered along the lines of railroad near all our cities and towns, and looming up by the seaside and lakeside, by forest and river, wherever a sanguine soul discerns the possibility of a hypothetical increase in value. The wrecks of these "paper cities" are quite numerous in all parts of the country, not because there might not have been good, solid foundation for them, but because they were too purely speculative, and started off on a basis of "great expectations" with forced and unnatural prices. The hundreds of flourishing suburbs near all cities are prosperous proofs of what wise and well regulated plans can accomplish. But as to these remote and intangible castles in the air, we can only emphasize the caution to let them alone, until there is more definite knowledge. Doubtless many will learn too late "that men betray," and that it is poor policy to trust to paper promises.

In making investments in mining stocks great care and discernment should be used. Because a company has a high sounding name and is capitalized at a few millions of dollars is no indication that stock offered is of any value. Where one mining company pays a dividend five thousand are worthless. Dealing in shares of unproductive and undeveloped mines is simply speculation.

A clever trick, and one that is continually and successfully worked, is what is known as the "gold brick" swindle. Some wealthy business man is selected by the swindlers, who approach him with a plausible story concerning a solid brick of gold which they have in their possession, and which they will part with for a very small sum, for certain reasons they don't care to have known. They give the impression that they have come by it in an underhand manner. The brick is taken to a bogus assayer who is in the deal, and the most rigid tests are made with satisfactory results, and a bargain is made at once. The money is paid, and when the victim takes the brick to a bank or the United States mint he finds his supposed gold brick is simply brass. A corner has been chipped off the baser metal and pure gold substituted. This is what is tested, and the intelligent and wealthy business man is out the amount he paid for the "gold" brick.

Now and then some one announces himself as the victim of the one million postage stamp hoax. It is announced that if 1,000,000 cancelled stamps are collected and forwarded to some one a bed will be provided for an invalid boy in some hospital or a home for an orphan. Christian churches have been the special victims, and there is hardly one in England, the United States, Australia, India, or any other country that has not had several members begging, borrowing, and even stealing postage stamps in order to make up the 1,000,000 that will go to clothe and feed some orphan.

This swindle originated in the fertile brain of a postage stamp collector at Stettin, Germany. He desired to get vast collections to sort out and sell again, and hit upon a plan to set the whole civilized world to go to work for him free of charge. He preyed on the sympathies of people by announcing that an orphan would be cared for in "the Syrian orphan home" for every 1,000,000 stamps sent to him. This worked well, and the next dodge was the starting of a mythical mission in China, the holy sisters of which agreed, for every 1,000,000 stamps sent to them, to save from the jaws of the crocodiles of the Yellow river at least one Chinese baby, and then educate and Christianize it. The stamps were to be sent not to Jerusalem or China, but to Munich or Stettin. The last claim on the sympathy of the world that has been made by this German is that for 1,000,000 stamps a home for an old lady or an old gentleman will be provided in one of three homes—one in London, another in New York, and the third in Cincinnati. For 500,000 stamps a bed will be endowed in a hospital and for 100,000 a home will be found for an orphan for one year. There are agencies in various cities to forward stamps to Stettin. It is estimated that this swindler has collected over 100,000,000 stamps in the United States alone, and that these were worth from $500,000 to three times that amount.

Few of the swindles that are almost daily practiced upon the farming communities of America are carried out more successfully than is that which is commonly known as the cloth fraud.

There is scarcely a township in any State of the Union where it has not been carried on, and thousands who are usually wide awake in driving a bargain, and are too worldly wise to be taken in by any new-fangled swindling device, have it to say that they are fooled by the cheerful cloth fraud, and that their notes in the possession of neighboring bankers or private note shavers and money lenders is conclusive evidence of their childish simplicity and neglect to keep pace with the current of events. This is the way the cloth swindle is worked:

A pair of smooth rascals drive up to a farm house in a stylish turnout and informs the people that he has been sent there by Mr. So-and-So, a friend of the family, who thought they would be delighted to take advantage of some great cloth bargains. They profess to represent the leading dry goods house of Chicago or New York and incidentally remark that the firm has been obliged to reorganize, and is on the verge of bankruptcy in fact. It was caught with an enormous stock of goods on hand, and has resorted to the popular plan of disposing of them. He continues that there were about three hundred salesmen in the great house, and these gentlemen have been sent out with goods, and instructed to dispose of them at the very bottom prices. He (the agent) is one of these salesmen; he has some goods he knows will please the farmer's family. This is the manner in which he paves the way to a sale:—

With this introduction he goes to his buggy, which is filled with dry goods, and brings in a large bundle, being assisted by the man in the wagon, who turns out to be a neighbor and acquaintance of the farmer whom the swindler has employed to ride about with him and endorse the goods. This neighbor's acquiesence in what the agent has to offer goes farther than anything else in influencing the head of the household to give the stranger a favorable hearing.

Now comes the nice part of the agent's work. Calicoes are displayed and offered for less than one-half than they can be purchased for at any store. Ginghams, delaines, muslins, sheeting, are thrown in at the same great sacrifice. The wife herself acknowledges that she cannot begin to purchase the goods for the figures the stranger offers them for. After the light goods, the swindler produces a piece of broadcloth. This he flaunts in the eyes of the farmer, assures him that it is the finest article to be had for the money, and that his house made a special importation of several thousand yards. On this cloth he puts a certain figure, which eventually proves to be about three times more than it is worth. Convinced that they have secured the calicoes, etc., at a bargain, (and they *are* sold for less than the market price) they will venture further.

Having, during the conversation, informed the farmer that he has been instructed by the house to sell nothing less than a $150 package of goods to any individual, he further conveys the intelligence at this point that payment need not be made under twelve months. He will take the farmer's note and wait on him for a whole year. The farmer has at last found an accommodating friend and a gentleman it is a pleasure to do business with.

The result is the farmer buys a bill of $250 and gives his note for one year. It isn't long before the farmer discovers that the broadcloth is shoddy—the very worst kind of shoddy. It is cloth pressed, not woven, and composed of the refuse of a woolen mill, held together by horse hairs. He finds he has been most thoroughly swindled and that his note is in the hands of his village banker and he must pay it. The only way to avoid being swindled by traveling merchants is to let them alone, unless you positively know them to be reputable. When you want anything go to your own merchant, pay him his price and if things do not turn out as represented he will make it right. Don't be caught by specious offers. No person is giving away goods without a good return in prospect.

It is a generally accepted fact that all traveling shows, no matter how honest the proprietors, carry in their wake a horde of thieves, who prey upon the public in rural towns under the guise of peddlers and sellers of nostrums. A large numer of small circuses carry with them as assistants a regularly organized band of thieves, whose business is simply to steal. In many cases they pay a percentage of their stealings to the proprietors. It is a fact, and can not be denied by any showman who will tell the truth, that many of these proprietors will not employ a thief, unless he is capable of stealing a certain amount per day. To gull the public these worthies are ostensibly employed as candy salesmen or "candy butchers," and general assistants around the tent. They are constantly on the lookout for victims, and will hesitate at nothing to gain their ends. Visitors to the show are called "guys," and if it becomes necessary to use desperate methods to get their money they are robbed by what is known as the "Johnny Armstrong" method, or in other words, actually garroting them.

The "holding out" trick is a neat one and seldom fails to succeed. The short change man has several ways to work, but "holding out" silver and "stripping" a pile of notes are the favorite methods. He may be a "candy butcher," an outside ticket-seller, a soap fakir, or even a peanut stand keeper. If a man whom he thinks he can work it on approaches, the short change man will perhaps quietly ask him if he has not a large bill, as he is anxious to get rid of some smaller notes or silver. The big note is produced, and if silver is to be "held out," the fakir counts the change correctly in his own hands, in full view of the intended victim. Then taking all the money in one hand, he pretends to drop it into the hand of his customer. He manages to "palm" two or three dollars.

"Stripping" notes is done by first counting them before the victim, allowing him to be sure that it is straight, and then to recount them, turning the ends of the notes over one by one. After three or four have been turned the crook "strips" them with the fingers of his left hand into the palm, and carefully rolling up the remainder, tells the man to put it away where no one can get at it. Sometimes the short change man counts at both ends, thus: "Fifty for the ticket and fifty is one dollar, two, three, four-fifty, and the fifty you have. Thank you."

The "top and bottom" worker sells boxes or packages of some kind that may be opened at the end. He has a corner of a bank-note placed just so that it can be seen. He takes a ten-dollar bill, folds it up in full view of the open-mouthed greeny, and pretends to put it under the lid of the package. But he don't. He palms the bill, and exposes the corner of a small bill, or perhaps a very small piece of a note torn off for the purpose, and asks:

"What'll you give for it?" He is pretty sure to get an offer and never refuses to sell.

What is known as the "push" is when a "guy" comes to the circus fakir to purchase some article and presents a ten-dollar note. The fakir takes the bill and commences to fold it, and while doing so asks the man if he has not got smaller money. The man then will for an instant lose sight of the bill. At that moment it is palmed or dropped and a one-dollar note folded in such a manner as not to show the number (which the fakir has already prepared) is held in his fingers and given to the victim, with any small article he may wish to purchase, and the fakir remarks, "Oh! pay me when you come out. Put your money in your pocket so you won't lose it." Then the "guy" goes off just nine dollars out. Later he discovers his loss but is told his pocket has been picked and the one placed in his pocket to disarm suspicion.

Under no circumstances make a wager on any game of chance, especially at a circus or country fair, and especially with strangers. Do not get any notes changed. Take the exact amount you intend to expend in small change, and above all mind your own business and keep your hands out of the tiger's cage. When you go to the circus see that your dwelling is not unprotected, for it is when the circus is in town that the "day worker" makes hay, whether the sun is shining or not.

All games of chance are against the player, 100 per cent., as all games are "faked." The long belt with its hollow tube, through which the belt is thrown off by a half turn; the wheel which pays 10 for one as the number bet upon, red or black; "sweat" or stud poker with dice, are among the other devices to entrap the unwary.

Never bet on another fellow's game.

CHAPTER V.

SCHEMES TO ENTRAP DISHONEST MEN.

GREEN-GOODS AND SAWDUST SWINDLE DESCRIBED—AVARICE OF DISHONEST PEOPLE—BUYING COUNTERFEIT MONEY—SENDING A SPECIMEN OF COUNTERFEIT MONEY FOR EXAMINATION—FLEECING VICTIMS—PAYING OUT GOOD MONEY FOR A BOX OF SAWDUST—HOW THE GAME IS WORKED—COPY OF LETTER SENT TO CUSTOMERS—INGENIOUSLY WORDED CIRCULAR—EVERYTHING MUST BE CONFIDENTIAL—THE RED INK MISSIVE—GIVING A PASSWORD AND NUMBER—CONFIDENTIAL INSTRUCTIONS—A FRAUDULENT NEWSPAPER CLIPPING—A QUICK AND CERTAIN WAY TO FORTUNE—A SCHEME THAT SHOWS INGENUITY AND PROVES TEMPTING—SELECTING A VICTIM—" KEEP THIS ENVELOPE"—ANOTHER RASCALLY LETTER—PROFIT IN GREEN-GOODS BUSINESS—THE BOGUS LEGACY FRAUD—FORM OF LETTER USED—THE CAPPER AND THE PART HE PLAYS.

The foundation on which every sharper works is avarice. The cupidity, stupidity and criminal avarice of thousands of ignorant people makes the green-goods and sawdust swindle one of the most profitable swindling schemes in the country. The man who bites at the counterfeit money scheme, and of course always loses his good money, is in no manner to be pitied, as it is simply a case of a would-be swindler being nipped at his own game.

The " sawdust " swindle is so called because the victim gets a box filled with sawdust instead of the counterfeit money he expected. A farmer or small storekeeper, living remote from New York or Chicago, receives a circular informing his prospective victim that he has a large quantity of " green-goods" (the word money or counterfeit money is never used) of different denominations, which he will sell at a great discount. A personal inspection and visit is solicited. Often a genuine, new and crisp one-dollar bill is enclosed as a "specimen." The victim thinks it over, concludes to spend it. It is readily taken by his home merchant, and he at once concludes he is leading too slow a life, and with visions of wealth dancing before his eyes, he sells some stock or mortgages his farm or business and secures a few hundred dollars and departs to meet his supposed benefactors. The circulars set forth that $3,000 in "green-goods" is offered for $200 in good cash; $5,000 for $300; $8,000 for $400; $15,000 for $600, and so on in proportion. Of course, if the person addressed be dishonest he at once makes haste to visit his benefactor. This he does and is shown what are said to be specimens of the counterfeits, but which, in reality, have just been obtained from the bank. If he has any doubts about being able to pass the money he and the "operator" take some of it and purchase articles at a neighboring store. It is accepted without a word and the countryman is satisfied. He concludes at once to take a certain amount. The counterfeits are to be sent by express to his home, "as it would be dangerous for him to carry so much money on his person." The victim goes away perfectly satisfied, with bright pictures of the manner in which he will enjoy himself when he gets home. A box arrives "C. O. D." He pays the charges and carries it to a quiet corner to remove his wealth unobserved. He opens the box and finds it filled with sawdust or some other worthless trash.

The country is being continually flooded with circulars, and although the wording is sometimes changed, they are all of the same purport. We reproduce but one to show the cunning ingenuity of these "green goods" swindlers. It is a strange thing that thousands of people bite at this bait every year, only to wake up thoroughly swindled. The letter reads as follows:

CONFIDENTIAL.

Friend:

This is the chance of your life and the one you have been looking for, and if you let it pass it will never come again. So read carefully and thoughtfully. I have a class of goods which *you* can handle and make money faster and easier with than you ever have in your life. They come in denominations of $1, $2, $5, $10 and $20, and will go anywhere and everywhere, and are as perfect as human skill can make them. My terms are: $300 for $3,000, $450 for $6,000, $650 for $10,000, $1,000 for $20,000 or more, and $40,000 costs $2,000; $3,000 for $300 is the very smallest amount I will sell. I will give you the *State right* if you take $20,000 or more of my goods. The *State right* means that I will not sell to any one else but you in your State, while you remain my customer. I warrant each and every one to be perfect as to *Paper Coloring*, *Vignette*, *Printing* and *Engraving*. The signatures are as perfect as the genuine, and when made to appear as having been used or handled much I defy the best *Bank Clerk* or expert to tell them from the genuine. It has cost a great deal of time and money to perfect these goods, and I have at last succeeded where many others failed, in producing the *genuine fiber paper*. These goods cannot be detected in the ordinary course of trade, and only at the Treasury in Washington, through the duplication of the numbers, and not then if the genuine bill of the number is still in circulation. Now, my way of doing business is as follows: When you come here I will show you my stock of goods; you can *examine them* and compare them with the genuine, and in fact submit them to any test you see fit before you *pay me*. Then, after you are thoroughly satisfied on every point, you can select whatever denominations you may want, and when the goods are in your possession *you pay me*, and if you feel disposed to carry the goods with you you may do so; if not, I will ship them by express or in any way you may desire, as I want to introduce my goods in your section of the country as soon as possible. I promise that if you do not find my goods as represented, and should you not be perfectly satisfied in every respect, I will pay your entire expenses to and from home and for loss of time. Make up your mind to come on at once if you wish to handle these goods. To do this business safely it should be done face to face. You can then see me, and I can judge the party I have placed confidence in; besides, it is absolutely necessary I should see you on our first deal in order to show and explain a simple method by which you can dispose of them in large lots, and how to make them appear as having been in circulation for some time. If you conclude to embrace this opportunity, send me a telegram, saying, "SEND ME INSTRUCTIONS," and sign your telegram with your *Pass-word and Number only*, as on the enclosed slip, then I will know who it comes from, and I will immediately respond by sending you instructions how and where to meet me, also a *sample of my goods*. Be careful that your telegram is signed with your Pass-word and Number, or else I will not be able to tell who it comes from. Enclosed you will also find a newspaper clipping, which speaks for itself. Your own good sense will tell you I can have no object in misrepresenting my goods and bringing you here on a foolish errand, for I ask no money in advance, and do business only in the manner above mentioned. If you have not the ready money to purchase my goods, I will make this proposition to you: I will consent to your taking some confidential friend in with you, provided, of course, he is trustworthy, and then you both can come on together; but you would be foolish to take any one in with you if you can in any possible way raise the required amount yourself.

In conclusion, I wish to say if you cannot come on here, or have not $300 to invest, and you think favorable of my business, send me a telegram saying, "WHAT IS MARKET PRICES?" and sign your Password and Number to it, or I will not know who it is from. I will then make you another proposition. Be patient, and be guided by my advice. If you do you will be sure of success. No such thing as fail. Act square! Be true and honorable! Do me no harm, and you will never regret it as long as you live. You can make money faster and easier by dealing in my goods than you ever dreamed of before in your life. Won't you try it?

CAUTION.—No other person is now authorized by me to correspond on this subject. Do not be deceived by shoddy imitations. I am the sole owner and proprietor of this enterprise. Communications from others offering similar goods for sale are absolutely unreliable and positively worthless. Pay no attention to them. Trusting I shall receive a favorable and immediate telegraphic reply, I remain

Yours confidentially,

N. B.—Telegrams from you must be prepaid or they will receive no notice. "I answer all telegrams." Except I give you permission, never write me a letter, as I will refuse to receive it, and then it will go back to the Post Office, and be returned to you, probably opened. So be cautious. I earnestly request that you will treat this matter confidentially; *mention it to nobody!* If it does not suit you destroy this letter.

The following letter always accompanies the above circular, and printed in red ink to attract attention. Both letters, however, are printed in typewriter, giving the inference that they have been specially dictated to each party receiving them.' Neither letter has any firm name, street number, or in fact anything printed, as is usual on a letter head from an honorable and legitimate business house:

Keep this for future reference.

Send your telegrams (no letters) to

JAMES BARLOW,

Easton,

Pennsylvania.

Your Pass-word and Number is "RYDER, No. 452." Do not sign anything else.

CAUTION.—Be sure you have the numbers (plainly written) on all telegrams after you sign the Pass-word "RYDER," otherwise your telegrams will positively receive no attention whatever. The "figures" are very important. All answers from me will be sent to the same name and address as written on the present envelope, unless otherwise instructed by you.

Above all things do not sign your name, only your Pass-word and Number, and send all telegrams over the Western Union Telegraph Company lines (if possible), to avoid mistakes. Also prepay all messages, as it is very important. Should the telegraph operator ask you for your name and address, refuse to give it; simply say, "My name or address is not necessary."

N. B.—Should there be any official notice stamped on this envelope, pay no attention to it whatever, as it is put there by the new administration to find out who has got the plates, as they are missing from the Treasury. Possession of the original plates is the foundation of my success, and as I have the plates the stamping of this ridiculous notice cannot injure me at all, unless to frighten off some timid agent.

In addition to the typewritten letters there is always a newswpaper clipping purporting to be cut from some leading paper, which is ingenious in its construction and calculated to impress dishonest men that they have at last found a quick and certain way to fortune:

A COUNTERFEITER GOES FREE.

THE COUNTRY FLOODED WITH $2,000,000,000 OF COUNTERFEIT MONEY IN THE PAST YEAR, AND PRONOUNCED BY GOVERNMENT EXPERTS TO BE AS GOOD AS THE GENUINE GREENBACK.

The failure of the United States court to convict Joseph Reed, alias Banks, alias Moore, and many other aliases, one of the most skillful and expert counterfeiters in this or any other country, is a great disappointment to the chief of the Secret Service. He believed that he had a sufficiently strong case against him to warrant a different result than the one obtained. The District Attorney thought so too. The fault was due to insufficient evidence. Yet the story is one of the most extraordinary ever told, involving as it does the most remarkable credulity and no less unusual cunning.

About three months ago a prominent merchant of California received a letter from this same gang offering to sell him money printed from Treasury plates that could not be told from the genuine. The merchant by the barest accident happened to be an honest man at heart, and although the temptation offered him was a great one, one that not one man in a hundred could refuse, decided not to accept the proposal but to inform United States Marshal Moore, who answered the letter under the merchant's name who had received it, and wrote to the counterfeiter and informed him that it was "just the stuff he was looking for," but stated that owing to the pressure of business it was impossible for him to visit New York and suggested to Mr. Counterfeiter that the mails were a safe medium through which to transact business, and stated that if this was satisfactory, he would order $300 worth to start on.

The reply came back that on no account would he do business through the mails, that it was absolutely necessary that he should see his customer and do business *face to face only*, being the safest, surest and most satisfactory way to transact a business of this nature, and promising if the goods were not as fine as represented, reimburse him for all expenses of the trip and forfeit $1,000 in gold.

In consequence the marshal wired for "instructions" how to know and where to meet the counterfeiter, and in due time arrived at place of meeting, the Grand International Hotel, New York City, and was called upon by an old man who brought with him a valise, which he opened in the room, displaying packages of money amounting to $100,000. The detective examined the money carefully, said it would suit him, and put his hand in his pocket as if to bring out the money to pay for it; but in the place of money he drew a pistol, and placing it at the counterfeiter's head made him a prisoner, and took the contents of the bag into his possession. Upon being arraigned upon the charge of offering and selling what was supposed to be counterfeit money, the prisoner apparently became indignant and stoutly denied that he ever had a counterfeit bill in his life, and he demanded that the experts employed by the Treasury Department at Washington be sent for.

His demand was complied with, and on arrival of the gentlemen they at once set about making a thorough and critical examination of the supposed counterfeits; then submitted their sworn report, which was as follows: That all these United States Treasury notes were printed from genuine plates used by former workmen in the Printing Bureau, and were perfect and exact duplicates of genuine bills issued by the Government. They further added that they had long been aware that some person had possession of a set of plates supposed to have been furnished by one of the engravers in the Engraving Bureau, and finally that the only difference between the notes found on the prisoner and the genuine, lies in there not being so much silk fiber interwoven in the paper. The prisoner's counsel asked the Government experts if they would swear that the bills examined by them were counterfeits. To the astonishment of every one in the court-room, they replied that they would not, in fact could not, as they were positive the bills were as good as any issued by the Government, and added that the fault lay in the careless manner observed in the Treasury Department in allowing workmen to handle Government plates, printing inks, dies, etc., as they wished.

The judge had no other alternative than to instruct the jury to discharge the prisoner, who thanked the jury and quickly skipped out of the court-room, valise in hand, that contained a cold $100,000 of money that was good enough for the writer at all events. The reporter was not alone in his envious thoughts, because from the expressions and suggestive remarks of some of the members of the jury at the departure of the prisoner, it seemed that they would like to have a few thousand of the so-called counterfeits themselves.

To give our candid opinion we could see no difference in the bills as the notes were printed from genuine United States plates, obtained from the Engraving Department at Washington, by whom it is not known, and perhaps never will be. As the case now stands some one is getting rich in a safe, fast and sure manner at the expense of the Government.

The Secret Service detectives say that the only way to effectually stop the circulation of this money is to capture the plates now in possession of this gang. The presumption is that the plates are not in this country, but in Canada, and that the printing is being done there. There is no possible way of tracing the bills to any of the agents circulating them; to do so, it would be necessary to have a Government expert in every store, in every town and city in the United States, as these bills are sold by the wholesale to trustworthy farmers and country merchants, in sections of the country where not one man in ten thousand knows anything about money (its genuineness, etc.), and are readily passed from hand to hand in the ordinary course of trade without their true character ever being discovered or even suspected. When large bills are offered by a purchaser, they are given out in change, and the latter innocently passes the bills upon some one else and thus they go through thousands of hands without any fear of detection or any possibility of their being traced to the agents circulating them.

The District Attorney, in conversation with the reporter, casually remarked that it was astonishing how eagerly the average citizen, that is, those who are apparently honest and fairly well off, are willing to engage in the business. The race for wealth predominates over every other consideration. All a person wants nowadays is money, it don't seem to make any difference, either, how they get it. The advice of the poet to his son is followed by all classes of the community: "Get money, my son; get money, honestly if you can; dishonestly if you must."

As the Government only is the loser, and is so well able to stand it, the average citizen has no conscientious scruples whatever in taking advantage of the offer made by these men, especially as there is no risk or danger in handling these bills if they use proper precautions and keep their business to themselves. A close mouth, as they tell you, is the secret of success in this nefarious scheme.

This is the manner in which the "green goods" business is worked, and it goes without saying that only dishonest men will attempt to do business with these frauds and swindlers, and if they are caught at their own game they are but served right. There is in fact but very little counterfeit money in the country, and those who make it do not by any means hawk it about the country for purchasers.

A scheme that shows ingenuity and a phase that proves tempting, is a new and catchy "green goods" swindle that has made its appearance in many sections of the country. Look out for it.

A stranger comes to town and selects his victim, usually a saloon keeper. He makes the saloon his hangout and spends money freely. The proprietor soon notices, if he is at all observant, that every time the stranger pays for anything he passes out a crisp, unwrinkled bill. The stranger becomes very friendly with the proprietor, and one fine day he says:

"Well, I must say good-by to-morrow. But before I go I wish you would give me back those new bills. I will give you other money for them."

"Why, what for?"

"Well, I'll tell you. That money I've been spending here is not right, see? I've grown to like you, and I don't want you to get into trouble."

The victim is astonished. Probably goes to his cash drawer and examines some of the money. He swears that it is real, but the stranger laughs at him.

"Real? why, I'll sell you cords of that stuff for $30 a $100?" Then the stranger goes on to explain the same old story, but with this addition:

"You've seen this exposed in the papers a hundred times, and how a man is bound to lose his money if he runs up against the game. Well, if you'll do business with me I'll put the money right into your hands before you pay me a cent."

That certainly looks reasonable, and let us suppose the victim bites. He agrees to "do business." He says he will buy $100 worth. The sharper then tells him to meet him the next day with $100 in $5 bills. They meet. The sharper produces a large envelope. They count the money and place it in the envelope. The victim is directed to seal the envelope. The stranger then says: "Now, I will mark this envelope in your presence." Suiting the action to the words, he takes out a stylographic pen, spreads out a newspaper on the bar to write upon, writes a number across one end and three initials in the middle, then, as he blots the writing with the envelope with the newspaper, says: "Now you keep this envelope with your money in it; and when our agent calls on you to-morrow he will count the 'goods' into your hand. And when you are convinced that it is just as represented, not before, hand him this envelope. He will recognize the number and initials and receive it as payment."

With these words the stranger hands the victim his

envelope, bids him good-by, and takes his leave. It is needless to say that he immediately leaves town, and that when the agent fails to arrive the next day and the victim opens the envelope he finds it filled only with pieces of blank paper cut to represent the $5 bills !

A few words will suffice to explain the trick, for it is as truly a sleight-of-hand trick as any legerdemain artist can do on the stage. The crook has two envelopes precisely alike. One he prepares by marking it with a number and initials and filling it with the required number of blank sheets of paper. This he folds inside of a newspaper and puts it carelessly in his pocket.

The other envelope he keeps in readiness to produce at the right moment to receive the victim's money. When he has seen the "bundle" safely inside and sealed, he takes out his newspaper, spreads the envelope upon it, writes on it, opens up one corner of the paper, and puts it underneath and blots it. Then here comes the change, which is simple enough. He takes out the dummy envelope and hands it to the victim. It is all so natural that anyone might be deceived. The victim thinks that his money does not go out of his sight for a moment, but it does, very much so.

Here is another form of letter these "green goods" frauds send out. These smooth rascals know that only those willing to be rascals will treat with them. They are too wide awake to have any counterfeit money at all—not a dollar. Their whole object is to get hold of the good money of foolish knaves by promises, and give nothing in return, knowing their victims dare say nothing, as by so doing they would expose their own rascality. The letter reads as follows:

My Dear Sir: I wish to secure the services of a reliable person in your county to push the sale of a certain class of goods which I manufacture. I guarantee one hundred per cent. profit and over according to the amount of capital invested. The goods are used by every one, and the business is *strictly confidential*, as it is the same as all other large-paying enterprises; it is not exactly legitimate; possibly you can guess its nature. Should you be willing to engage let me know as soon as possible, and I will send you full particulars.

I am yours in confidence,

New York City, N. Y. A. J. K., Bowery.

There are in Chicago and New York firms who are sending out circulars proposing to sell cigars in imitation of real Havanas, so that they can be sold at such a profit as to realize a fortune. It is obviously intended that counterfeit money should be read in place of cigars. The circular reads:

"They are made in brands of Ones, Twos, Fives and Tens, of green tobacco, and the most experienced smoker cannot detect them, even if that smoker be a banker. They are made by skillful men who served their apprenticeship in Washington."

This is an artful means of suggesting that counterfeit money is really meant, although if you are tempted to invest you will get nothing in return but bitter experience.

Pages could be filled with recitals of these swindles; the entries in the books of one of these frauds recently arrested in Chicago shows that he had done a business of over ten thousand dollars in about six months. It shows an incredible amount of folly and dishonesty, for every one who enters into serious negotiations with these sharks does so with the full expectation of receiving counterfeit money which he intends to pass as genuine. Disappointing as it may be to receive packages of bricks, sawdust, or blank paper, it would be still worse to get counterfeit money, the use of which would end in long imprisonment.

The heads of the sawdust gangs have devised a new scheme to defraud, and are flooding the mails with letters and circulars. Instead of the old circulars which offered counterfeit money for sale they have had prepared a circular in which it is stated that money has been left to the person to whom the letter is sent by a distant relative, and that the legacy can be secured by the payment of a certain sum of money to an agent named. The circulars are printed on the cyclograph, and one of the forms is as follows:

NEW YORK, May 10, 189...—*Dear Sir:* A distant relative of yours has died in this city and has left $3,000 to you. The money is deposited in the bank and awaits your order. We have been given charge of the estate, and as soon as you can establish your claim the $3,000 will be paid to you To do this you must come to New York and let us see that you are acting in good faith. Of course, before you can get the money you will have to pay the legal expenses, which will amount to $250. This amount it will be necessary for you to bring with you. It would be well for you to act quietly about the matter, for fear some one may hear of your good luck and cause you trouble by laying claim to the money. We are your friends, and you can trust us implicitly. Before you start for New York you had better telegraph us along the line and we will have some one to meet you. You should come by the New York Central Railroad. When you arrive in New York take the elevated road at the station (fare five cents) and ride down to Fulton street. Go to the United States Hotel and register, and remain in your room until our agent calls. Inclosed you will find half of a card on which is marked F 116 a. Keep this, and when the agent calls on you he will present the other half of the card; so that you will know that he is all right. Be mighty careful who you talk to for New York is a wicked city and full of pitfalls and bad men. Hoping that you will be able to prove everything satisfactory, we remain, yours truly,

B. BROWN, No. 183 ——street, New York.

N. B.—Return this letter when you send an answer.

The name and address are on a separate slip of paper, the same as the old-style sawdust letters. When the victim arrives in New York he is met at his hotel by the "capper," who conducts him to the office of the principal swindler. There the countryman, after he has shown his credentials and proved that he has the money to pay the commission with, is shown the $3,000, which is done up in packages and consists of crisp new bills. These are counted out and put in a box, and the victim is instructed to send the money by express to his home. Before the box is taken from the room a duplicate one, containing brick and waste paper, is substituted. The latter box is shipped by express, and when the victim arrives home he finds that his " legacy" consists of rubbish.

CHAPTER VI.

SNEAK THIEVES AND THEIR METHODS.

Robbing Banks in Daylight and During Business Hours—Skill, Address and Daring—Familiarity with Banking Business—Tools and Equipments Used—How Money is Concealed—How Sneak Thieves Enter a Bank—Confederates who Engage the Attention of the Cashier While the Safe is Rifled—How the Scheme is Successfully Worked—Abstracting Money from Behind Railings—An Accommodating Cashier—Working a Bank President—A Very Sharp Practice that Usually Works—Calling for the President or Cashier with a Carriage—The Invalid Game—Bank Clerks who are Victimized by Thieves—How a Country Bank is Worked by Sneak Thieves—Preventing a Bank Door from Locking—Entrapping a Paying Teller—Picking up all the Cash in Sight—Use of the Iron Hook—"Is This Your Money, Sir?"—Robbing Bank Customers—How to Guard Against Sneak Thieves—The Latest Sneak-Robbing Dodge—How to Tell a Thief—Inspector Byrnes, of New York, on Thieves—How to Distinguish a Thief from an Honest Man—Should Bankers be Armed During Business Hours?—Schemes of Till Tappers.

The most dangerous class of thieves is the sneak. There is no thief in the world so much feared by banks and business houses as the wily sneak. For the burglar they have the natural dread common to all persons who fear a combat in the dark. For the sneak, who has made the robbery of banks by daylight and during business hours a study for years, they have more fear than for all other classes of criminals put together.

No other branch of criminal life requires such address, such consummate cunning, such adroit skill, and almost incredible daring. The stalls, or men who do the preliminary work, or, in other words, who direct attention from the sneak, who is doing the stealing, must not only be gentlemanly in bearing, dress and behavior, but must of necessity, to carry out his discreditable work, have an intimate knowledge of all that pertains to banking. In fact, the large majority of them have been engaged during the honest period of their lives in the banking business. Their entrance into a banking institution occasions no surprise or suspicion, and cashiers and clerks afford them desired information with as much consideration and politeness as they bestow upon their well-known and responsible depositors and customers. The sneak, however, need not be so well favored, although he frequently is as much of an apparent gentleman as his associate.

Before describing the movements of this class of criminals it may be well to mention a few of the articles which are considered essential for successful operation. The most important thing is that the sneak shall be supplied with a pair of shoes or slippers that will make no noise—a creaking shoe being considered as a sure producer of detection—with very little heel, or a pump sole. In the winter time rubbers are worn. The low heel is a wise precaution, for almost every bank vault has an iron step or a bar on the floor, against which the doors close, and there would be great danger in striking against this if the heels were high. The slightest noise in the direction of the bank vault is certain to attract attention, and then detection is sure to follow. The sneak is also provided with a large bag in which to conceal his booty; it is generally made of muslin, and is furnished with a drawing string in the top, much after the fashion of the bags usually carried by lawyers. This bag is large enough to hold one or more tin boxes such as are usually found in the vaults of banks, and in which valuable papers, bonds and money are kept. Sometimes the pockets in the coat worn by the sneak will extend around the entire inside lining, which makes the inner lining of the coat one immense pocket precisely similar to that used by male pickpockets. This is used when the bag has been neglected, or where a sudden opportunity occurs to perpetrate a robbery for which no previous preparations were made.

Another part of the sneak's outfit is a bunch of skeleton keys, so if he have time he can quickly open the strong boxes in the bank vaults without the dangerous and troublesome task of lifting out the boxes themselves. In case a box is lifted out it is held perfectly level for to tilt it would cause it to rattle and attract attention.

For the purpose of illustration we will select a bank in which, as is frequently the case during business hours, the vault doors are open and the strong boxes are unlocked. The vault, we will assume, is at the rear end of the banking room, and the clerks, as they stand at their desks facing the customers, generally have their backs toward the vaults. Should this be the case—and it frequently is so—there is generally a passage-way, or small gate at the end of the desks by which the clerks enter, and through which, also, the sneak can readily work his way. This is one of the most simple operations for the sneak, and in which he is almost uniformly successful.

One or two sneak's confederates or stalls will enter the bank, and in the most business-like manner possible, engage the cashier in conversation upon some question of banking business. Information is wanted about opening an account or drawing a draft—and it is a very easy matter to prolong a conversation of this character sufficiently long to enable the sneak to step into the vault or safe and to hastily pick up all that he can conveniently carry away, and then to make his way again to the front of the bank. This style of robbery is generally attempted in country banks where there are but few clerks, and where the number of customers is small; but the number of country banks is far greater than the apparently well-guarded city banks with their army of clerks and watchmen. For this reason country banks are more generally selected by watchful thieves. Notwithstanding the precaution taken by city banks, they are often easily robbed by sneaks. Money should not be kept in snatching distance. A thief recently walked into a bank in Montreal, placed a soap-box on the floor in front of the teller's window, stood on it, and reaching over the railing, snatched about $6,000 in bills and escaped. Dozens of other cases could be cited. If bankers will profit from reading this work, the bank sneak will find his occupation gone.

Again, should the safe or vault in the bank be so arranged—being placed at the end of the counter and at the side of the cashier—that any person entering it would be instantly discovered by the cashier, the stall then takes a prominent part in the transaction.

Entering the bank, he addresses the cashier, and engages him in the calculation of the interest due upon a draft which he has in his possession, or consults him about the collection of some coupons, inducing him by degrees to perform the necessary task of figuring up the possible results. The stall is meanwhile so placing himself, that the back of the cashier will be turned toward the open door of the vault. With a natural desire to see what the cashier is doing, he will turn the paper in one direction or the other, so that that gentleman will be obliged to shift his position in order to accommodate his visitor. The ignorance of the visitor is quite surprising, and the questions asked are propounded in such an affable, insinuating manner, that the good-natured cashier, all unconscious of what is transpiring behind him, will exert himself to the utmost in order to fully enlighten his gentlemanly but decidedly ignorant visitor. Occasionly the stall will be very deaf, so the cashier will have to stoop over to speak in the deaf customer's ear to be heard.

When the cashier has been sufficiently engaged, and has been turned around to the proper point of obliquity, the sneak will dart into the vault, and in a few minutes will emerge with all the available plunder concealed beneath his coat, while the time the sneak is at work, another stall will come in with heavy creaky boots, and pace back and forth, drowning all other sounds. Not only is the vault the point of attack, but very often there are large amounts of notes piled up on the tables or counters behind the railing which surround the cashier or clerk, and if these can be safely taken, the labor of the sneak is made much more easy and more profitable than if he is required to enter the vault. Suppose the bank is duly opened for business—the vault doors are open and the clerks at their desks; that they would not be able to see any one who entered or left the vault, and that the only way to get behind the counter is through the room of the president, which is in the rear of the building. The president will of necessity perceive any person who comes into his room, whether to engage him in conversation or to pass through into the banking room in front. It would seem an impossible task to pass this watchful officer unseen, but to the professional sneak thieves it is an easy job.

The plan of operation to effect the object is as follows: Two of the stalls will enter the president's room for the purpose of consulting him upon some matters of financial import. If the president is sitting in such a position as to control the entrance to his rooms, this is all the better for the success of the enterprise. One of the stalls advances to the bank official's desk and announces the nature of his business, while the other quietly takes a seat, and draws from his pocket a newspaper—and then opening it fully, under the pretense of looking over the stock reports, holds it so as to entirely screen the view of the front door of the president's room. This will enable the sneak to enter the room ; then the stall will quietly change his position so as to cover the doorway leading into the banking room and behind the counters. It will be noticed that the sneak is shielded by the newspaper from the moment it is opened until it covers the door which leads to the vault or safe. Once past the door, he quickly glides into the banking rooms. If the money is handy he takes it ; but if necessary he enters the vault or ransacks the safe and takes everything valuable within his reach. When he has completed his operation, the same manipulation of the newspaper is gone through with by the stall, and the sneak quietly and safely makes his escape. The whole operation does not occupy more than three or four minutes' time, and this is generally the longest period that is required for successful work. Immediately upon the sneak taking his departure, the interview with the president is quickly terminated, and the thieves, politely thanking the bank official for his kindness and courtesy, take their leave.

When this arrangement cannot be safely carried out, another method is for one of the stalls to procure a carriage, and driving up to the door of the bank request the president or cashier to come and transact some business with an invalid who cannot leave the vehicle. In such cases the name of the president or cashier is first obtained, and being addressed by his proper name when the request is preferred, he is entirely unsuspicious of danger, and emerges from the bank to await the orders of his invalid caller. Clerks and cashiers have also been called out in this way, during the dinner-hour, when they would be left alone in charge of the bank. Of course the sneak is on hand, and while the president or cashier is engaged in conversation on the sidewalk, he quietly enters and robs the bank. At other times the stall will approach a pigeon-hole of one of the desks in front and request to speak to the president, who is in his room in the rear, and that gentleman, being thus called suddenly, upon the impulse of the moment will answer the summons and thus leave the way open for the hiding sneak.

Clerks whose positions are such as to prevent the entrance of the sneak to the vaults have been often called by name to some pigeon-hole in the desk opposite to him, and there held long enough in conversation on some real estate held by a man of a similar name for the thief to accomplish his purpose. The manner in which the stalls acquire the names of the employes of a bank is very simple. They present themselves at one of the pigeon-holes at a distance from the clerk whom they desire to call, and pointing out the individual, inquire:

"Is that gentleman opposite named Brown? He looks like a man I used to know down town several years ago." In most cases the clerk will say, "No, his name isn't Brown. It's so and so."

The information thus obtained is conveyed to another stall, and shortly afterwards this confederate enters, and going directly up to the pigeon-hole, calls the name of the clerk in a very decided tone of interest and acquaintance.

The first and governing principle of the sneak is not to allow himself to be seen by any one, for if any employe of the bank has noticed his presence he will naturally feel uneasy and suspicious, because he is aware of the fact that there is a strange man in such a part of the building, and his movements should be watched. To overcome this difficulty, therefore, the sneak enters the bank first and endeavors to get a good position, where he will not be noticed, and there he will sit or stand, apparently engaged in some intricate financial problem, with paper and pencil. Sometimes he will enter the president's room, which may be empty at the time, and if discovered before his confederates enter he will excuse himself by saying that he is either waiting to see the president or is expecting his mother or sister to come for the purpose of making a deposit of money or to invest in some securities for which the bank is an agent, or he may enter the president's room with one of the stalls and then trust to the adroitness of his companion in engaging the attention of the president long enough for him to get to the safe or vault quietly, get what is convenient to his hands, and return without his absence being noticed by any one in the bank.

In a country bank, where there is but one man in charge of the bank at noon-time, and the position of this man is such that he can see any person who may enter, the two stalls will enter the bank, and while one of them is engaging the clerk by changing a large note or in answering some question of a financial nature, the other will hold up a newspaper, and under the cover of this the sneak will make his entrance, and walking quietly as far as the counter, crouch down in a stooping position, and thus sneak towards his work, without his presence being known or even suspected.

These modes of operation are among those most frequently used by sneak thieves in robbing banks whose vaults and safes and the doors and drawers to the money departments are open during business hours. The entrances to the interior of the bank—that is, that portion of the building reserved for the clerks—are frequently supplied with doors which are always locked; and every clerk and messenger who passes through this doorway is required to unlock this door before he can be admitted. In the first case all the employes are provided with keys that will unlock this door, or there is a spring latch upon it which can be worked from either side. The sneak, under such circumstances, will place himself near this door and wait until some one comes who unlocks the door to obtain entrance. As a rule, the locks on this door are spring locks, and as soon as the clerk has passed in he will shut the door violently behind him, which will insure its locking without further attention on his part. Directly behind him, however, is the sneak thief, and as the door bangs to he inserts a wallet or a wedge of wood between the frame and the door, and this prevents its locking. To enter through this door is the work of a moment, and with the stalls at work in front the robbing is consummated.

A sneak will enter a bank with a confederate, and stepping up to the paying-teller or cashier, and holding a genuine ten or twenty-dollar note in his hand, say:

"They told me in the hotel that this note is a counterfeit; and it being such a genuine-looking note, I thought I would just step in and let you and the receiving-teller look it over. Will you call him over?"

The cashier or paying-teller takes the note, and surprised at the genuineness of its appearance, calls the receiving-teller over to look at it. As the receiving-teller leaves his position the confederate begins his work. He has with him a small folding camp-stool. He has been standing at a desk outside, busily engaged in counting some money. No sooner, however, has the paying-teller answered the call of his associate, than the confederate noiselessly carries the stool to the counter, and putting it on the floor, leaps upon it, and in a twinkling has taken all the money within his reach which he can readily grasp. Stepping down quickly, he walks out of the door, carrying his stool along with him. He does this in order to leave nothing behind which would give a clew to the officers, who would seek out the storekeeper who sold the stool, and thus obtain a description of the individual who purchased it. When the money is placed a short distance from the window, too far away to be reached by the hand, a cane, and sometimes two joined together with a screw, with an iron hook at the end, is used. It is astonishing how successfully the thieves have worked an operation of this kind, and frequently hours have elapsed before the loss is discovered, and then too late to determine how the money disappeared or by whom it was taken.

Those persons who transact business with banks, safe deposit companies and other financial institutions of the country, are especial objects of attack from the sneak thieves. The manner in which this fraternity operate upon a gentleman who is either making a deposit or drawing a check at a bank is at once simple and generally successful, and many sharp business-men have been robbed of large sums of money by a process which would seem to be almost impracticable. Thieves call this a turn trick, or the act of turning a man away from his money, in order to enable the thief to make off with it.

This is the way it is done: A man receives a check for a certain sum of money, and to get it cashed he goes to bank. It is but natural that the receiver of the money should recount it.

In all banks desks are provided for this purpose, and the gentleman carries his money over to the desk and proceeds to verify the count of the bank officer. Of course the thieves have watched this transaction very carefully, and when the gentleman lays his money upon the desk they are prepared for action. Say the gentleman has received five thousand dollars in twenty dollar bills, and that they are in packages of one thousand dollars each. Placing the money in front of him, he takes one of the packages in his hand and proceeds to count. This is the thieves' opportunity. The sneak immediately takes his position behind the man and in such a manner that he will not be seen on either side. Then the stall appears, and dropping a bank-note upon the floor on the opposite side from where the money is lying on the desk and about five feet in the rear of the victim, who is politely touched upon the shoulder and asked, "Is this your money, sir?" The victim will instinctively turn around, and seeing the note on the floor will stop to pick it up. As he does so the sneak behind him reaches forward and abstracts about three-quarters of the pile on the desk and beats a retreat. The reason he does not take all the money is because if the victim noticed the entire disappearance of his funds he would immediately rush for the door and seize the first man going out. If, however, he finds part of his money remaining he may not, at first glance, notice any diminution of it, or if he does he will naturally desire to see how much is gone.

To guard against the ingenuity of the bank sneak thief, who of all others is the most dangerous man in the criminal classes, a constant, unceasing vigilance must be maintained. As to the mechanical contrivances for foiling this class of thieves, good doors, securely locked, wire fences and wire partitions, so all parts of the bank can be seen; modern office appliances, good safes and vaults, and, above all, care in dealing with strangers.

A very slick trick by sneak thieves was perpetrated upon a New York bank not long ago. A well-dressed young man entered the bank and reaching his arm deliberately through the paying teller's window grabbed $4,000 and walked out. A cry was raised and the young man was apprehended at the door. A police officer stepped up and arrested him. The teller demanded the money. The police officer said to let the thief keep it until he arrived at the station, as the captain would find the money in his possession and thereby easily convict him. Neither police officer or thief were ever seen again, the wretch who personated an officer being a pal of the money grabber.

There is always something that distinguishes the thief from the honest man and woman, says Inrpector Byrnes, of New York City. It is hard sometimes to say just what that something is, but it is always there. I suppose the quality to which I refer is, in its essence, the self-consciousness of innocence which the Almighty has intended for the protection of the guiltless.

In the first place the conscious thief is invariably furtive in his or her glance and more or less nervous in movement. Accomplished thieves are able to assume a veneering, so to speak, of innocence, but it is a moral impossibility for them to successfully counterfeit it for any length of time if put to any proper test.

Take a thief in a crowd. He invariably gives himself away to the experienced eye. An honest man plunges along the street and does not care much whether he runs into somebody else or not so long as he dces not get hurt himself or hurt the other man—provided he is polite and considerate, of course. He swings along, his eyes straight ahead, bent on getting to his destination as soon as possible if he is in a hurry.

On the other hand, the crook is in constant fear of apprehension, and to save his life he can't help showing it. Even when he is not out for business he manifests by his furtive air, his glancing, suspicious eye, his general manner of being watched and under surveillance, that his conscience is not clear and that he fears that he may be pounced upon at any moment by the officers of the law.

In view of the fact that desperate men are walking into banks and demanding money of the president or cashier at the point of a gun, the question has arisen if it is not part of a banker's duty to go armed during business hours.

A favorite and successful till tapping scheme is for three or four half-grown men to enter a store, one after the other, being careful to select an hour when some of the clerks are absent. One or two of the party make a pretense of purchasing some small article, while the third, who, it has been arranged previously, shall secure the contents of the till, will probably ask for a pin to fasten a button on his coat. Sometimes one excuse is made and sometimes another, but if it is sufficient to turn the attention of the clerk, who is usually alone when the trick is worked, for a moment or so, the trick is done and the thieves are off. Occasionally a till tapper will work alone, creeping in an open door on his hands and knees behind the counter, rob the till and make a bold dash for the street.

CHAPTER VII.

BURGLARIZING BANK SAFES AND VAULTS.

BURGLARY AS AN ARTISTIC PROFESSION—THE ORIGINAL SAFE—ANCIENT MANNER OF PROTECTING SAFES—PERFECTION OF AMERICAN INGENUITY—POPULAR IDEA ON THE SUBJECT OF BURGLAR AND FIRE-PROOF SAFES—POSITION OF SAFES IN BANKS—HOW SAFES ARE ROBBED—NUMBER OF PROFICIENT BANK BURGLARS IN THE COUNTRY—HOW BURGLARS KEEP PACE WITH IMPROVEMENTS—THE MODERN BURGLAR AND HIS METHODS—AMUSING PRECAUTIONS TO CIRCUMVENT BURGLARS—WHERE BURGLARS GET THEIR TOOLS—TOOLS USED—SUPERIOR INTELLIGENCE OF THE MODERN SAFE BREAKER—CONSTRUCTION OF A FIRST-CLASS, MODERN SAFE—SEASON OF YEAR BANK BURGLARS WORK—BANK BURGLARS' HARVEST TIME—PICKING OUT A BANK TO ROB—STUDYING THE HABITS OF THE PRESIDENT AND CASHIER—ASCERTAINING THE DEFECTS OF A COMBINATION LOCK—HOW THE DIAL IS MANIPULATED WITH TIN FOIL—TOOLS REQUIRED BY MECHANICAL BURGLARS—HOW A SAFE OR VAULT IS QUICKLY WRECKED WITH THE SCREW AND SECTIONAL JIMMY.

Burglary, as an artistic profession, has made rapid strides of late years, but it is yet in its infancy. Fortunately, it is seldom that anything like real talent, mechanical or otherwise, is degraded to the service of the lawless, burglarizing craft. If such were the case, it would go hard indeed with the law-abiding citizen, and the detective would be left far behind in the effort to keep pace with the clever criminal fraternity.

The original safe was a crude affair and was manufactured in England about two hundred years ago. It was made of boiler-iron, put together with heavy rivets in almost the same manner as the modern boiler, and possessed a crude lock combination, the whole being opened by a ponderous key of very simple make. With an ordinary ratchet drill it could have been opened in half an hour, but proved all-sufficient to baffle burglars for a time.

Not to go back to ancient history, the old safe, known to many people who are still in business to-day, was nothing but a heavy iron box, with a heavy iron door and a big, heavy or brass key. The security of the safe was presumably increased as the key was larger and heavier. It was for all the world like the big, heavy door-key which a store-keeper formerly had to cart home with him, and which was at once a key and a weapon, as he could easily fell a man with it. The lock into which it fitted was more or less complicated in design, but it, too, was big and heavy and offered the burglar abundant opportunity for picking it. The manufacturer of these safes should also have had a regular dog farm for the breeding and training of fierce watch-dogs, one to go with each safe. In fact, bankers resorted to the use of dogs to such an extent that the name was given to the safe. The animals were trained to hold a position directly in front of the safe and to allow no one to approach except their masters. More faith was put in a good dog than in the cumbersome iron box, lock and key.

Gradually evolved from this crudity came the first real safe, that, too, made in England, some fifty years later. The builder had conceived the idea that a safe was a possibility that would resist fire as well as the burglar, but how to do it was the puzzle. At last it was devised with an outside shell of heavy iron, next to this a six-inch wooden lining, and then this covered by an inside iron shell, thus making really the first double safe. The object in using the wood was that in an intense heat it would simply turn to charcoal, and by thus becoming a non-conductor would preserve the valuables within. In this connection it may be said that very little improvement occurred in this style until 1840, when safe-building was first introduced into the United States. Then American ingenuity took a hand, and the result is the simple, yet elaborate, safes and vaults of the present, which are in demand the world over.

It was soon discovered that the ingemuity of the home-made burglar was keeping sharp pace with the safe-maker, and then a struggle began that has continued without intermission for half a century. But, after all, it is to-day, as in the outset of the fight, simply a question of time. There are experts who can open any safe made, provided they are given time enough, and why should not an expert burglar do the same? A burglar, however, has generally but a few hours in which to accomplish his work, and therein consists a great advantage and one which it will never be possible to overcome.

In the early development of safe-making in this country, the wooden lining was abolished, and a substitute consisting of dry plaster and alum adopted. These now are virtually abandoned. In case of fire the alum, which consisted of about ninety per cent. of water, generated steam, and that was supposed to be an almost certain preservative and protection. This was the general idea of the fire-proof safe.

But it was soon discovered that this yet was not proof against the flames. There was still another discovery. It was that an air space between walls was a necessity, and that in place of dry plaster and alum concretes should be used, as they contained a large amount of water. In this way safes are lined to-day.

There is one popular fallacy on the subject, and that is that all safes are both burglar and fire-proof, and when one is occasionally cracked the statement is almost invariably published that it was of the latest improved pattern. The strictly fire-proof safe of to-day is far superior to that of ten years ago, but any burglar can open one if given sufficient time.

American ingenuity having proceeded thus far and secured a reasonably perfect combination lock, the safe-builders directed their attention to the discovery of some material or composition that would be absolutely impenetrable by the drill. Immense sums of money were expended in this direction, but it was not until a few years ago that their efforts were successful. The United States leads the world in safe-making, and many safes are made upon which a burglar might wear away his life and not thoroughly enter.

The time lock was invented in 1870, and was a valuable acquisition to the safe-making industry. It is probable that more ingenuity is being expended just now upon the invention of bank locks and burglar alarms than upon any other branch that comes before the patent officials.

Next to this there is a generally received idea that a safe, say in a corner room where the lights are kept burning all night and where people are constantly passing, affords comparative immunity from the industrious burglar. Many bankers keep their funds in this way, but care should be taken to set the safe away from all walls, and yet then, by the aid of screens, burglaries have been effected.

The popular idea of a safe robbery seems to be that on a dark night, when not even a policeman is near, several big, strong men break into a place, and, drilling holes into the safe, they insert powder or dynamite and blow the door off, afterward setting fire to the building to destroy all traces of the crime. As a matter of fact, in a really "fine" job an explosive is rarely used; the tools can be carried in an overcoat pocket, and many weeks are often spent in planning and arranging for a single job.

There are in this country just about an even score of men

whom no bank vault or safe, however strong, can resist. To reassure society it might be stated that over half of these are safe behind prison bars. It is an adage among crooked people that they must go to New York for highwaymen, Philadelphia for thieves, Chicago for bank and safe burglars, and Cincinnati for pickpockets.

Safe-breakers have more than kept pace with improvements in safes, including time locks, chilled steel chests of eight or nine thicknesses, and electric protective attachments. Their tools are made by some of the finest mechanics and inventive geniuses of the world. A full kit of the most approved modern safe-workers' tools costs about $5,000.

The modern burglar is like love in one respect, he laughs at locksmiths. Yet he is not much of an artist, although he is rapidly improving. The simple tools of the burglars' trade indicate how easy the contrivances made to bar his progress are overcome. Yet these tools give no mark of great mechanical genius. They are as crude as the average burglar is. They are in keeping with his practices of force and brutality. The destructive power of the best pieces of handiwork is their main advantage, and doubtless an illustration of the housebreaker's stunted idea, that the best way to overcome obstacles is in all cases to break them down.

The tools used by the burglar are supplied to him. They are made by men after his own heart, and who make for him what is most effective in his hands. No doubt there are smart men engaged in the business of defying law and setting the rights of honest people at naught. Some of the methods they employ might be used to their credit in a commendable industry

There are places where the jimmy is absolutely indispensable to the burglar. Front doors, which a house proprietor usually has doubly bolted and barred and supplied with improved locks, are the last appertures in the world a night marauder would seek to enter.

It must be an amusing thing to the burglar to note the precautions taken to prevent his entrance by the street door after he has walked through the skylight on the roof without the slightest resistance, or dropped through the coal-hole leading to the cellar from the sidewalk, to find that no doors bar his passage from there to the rooms above. These are the popular ways of getting into many banks and business houses. The basement door, at the rear, if there is one, is another. In each case the jimmy is the magic wand that opens the way. It is more useful to the burglar than any half dozen of his other implements, and is the first thing he purchases when getting an outfit.

"How do safe burglars get their tools?" was recently asked a well-known New York detective. "Why, every man of any account in that line," was the reply, "has what he calls, 'his man,' who is a practical mechanic, and makes everything in the shape of jimmies, punches, etc., that the burglar uses. A safe-blower's outfit consists of many curious tools, some of them being of special design for some particular class of work of which the owner is the originator. Scarcely any two men work alike, and some of the clever ones invent instruments to do a certain part of their work. When a well-known notorious crook was arrested several years ago in his room, the officers found one of the finest kits of burglars' tools that was ever brought into police headquarters. Talk about ingenuity—if that man had applied but one-third of the intelligence to a legitimate business that he had spent in devising tools for robbery, he would have been a millionaire to-day."

Twenty years ago when burglars started out to rob a safe they filled a carpet sack with highly tempered drills, copper sledges, sectional jimmies, dark lanterns, powder and a fuse.

On the way they stole a horse and wagon, filling the latter with the greater portion of the tools of a country blacksmith shop. They would work on the safe from four to six hours, and finally blow it open with a fine grade of ducking powder. Usually the shock would break all the glass in the building, arouse the town, and the burglars would often have to fight for their lives. In those days the men had to be big and powerful, because the work was extremely laborious. If the burglar was an ex-prize fighter or noted tough, so much the better, for he could make a desperate resistance in case he was caught in the act or immediately after it.

With the modern safe burglar it is almost totally differerent. Although much more skillful and successful than his predecessor, he is more conservative. He seldom runs his own head into danger, and therefore seldom endangers the head of a law-abiding citizen by permitting his head to come into contact with him or the job while it is under way. Every precaution against being surprised is taken, and it is seldom the robbery is discovered until the cashier's appearance the next morning. The modern safe burglar is an exceedingly keen, intelligent man. He can open a safe having all modern improvements in from ten minutes to two hours without the aid of explosives and by only slightly defacing. Sometimes he leaves scarcely a mark.

A first-class modern safe, whether large or small, generally has double outside and inside doors, with a steel chest in the bottom, forming really a safe within a safe, the inside being the stronger. The outside door is usually either " stuffed " or " skeleton." The inside one is made of eight or nine sheets, of different temper, of the finest steel. These sheets are bolted together with conical bolts having left hand threads, after which the heads of the bolts are cut off, leaving what is virtually a solid piece of steel, which no drill can penetrate. The best locks are of the combination type, with time lock attachment. In many cities and towns safes containing the most valuables have an electric alarm attached. Any tampering with it will communicate the fact to the owners or the safe's guardian, which in cities is either an electric protective bureau or a central police station. A recent invention in France is a photographic attachment. As soon as the safe is touched this device will light an electric lamp, photograph the intruder, and give the alarm at the electric protective company's office. As a consequence safe-breaking is going out of date in France, as the cleverest criminals have so far failed to find a way to circumvent the camera.

The first thing considered by a gang of the finest experts is a bank's desirable location and the chances for getting safely away with the plunder. Every transportation facility is carefully considered. As the work is almost invariably done at the season of the year when wagon roads are impassable, railroad time tables are carefully considered. In these days of the telegraph and telephone the gang must be under cover in a large city or concealed with friends by the time the crime is discovered, which, at the utmost, is about six hours after the crime has been committed. From November 1st to March 1st is the safe burglar's harvest time, because then the nights are longest and the chances of detection less, as fewer people are on the streets, and houses adjoining being tightly closed to exclude the cold, exclude noises also. A man can furthermore carry tools in an overcoat without attracting attention, that he could not wear with a summer suit. The remainder of the year is spent in "marking" the most desirable banks for future operations. Four men, who compose the ordinary safe mob, will put up from thirty to forty "jobs" for a winter's work, allowing for all contingencies. From six to ten of these will be carried out. A bank safe will be broken into in a small town in Maine, and in ten days the gang will be operating in Texas.

Having decided on a bank, the habits of the cashier and other chief employees are carefully studied, above all of those who visit the bank after working hours, chief of whom is the watchman, if the bank has one. If the watchman drinks, or spends time visiting women when he should be at the bank, he is an easy prey. Weeks and sometimes even months, are spent in putting up a job of magnitude, and a number of smaller jobs are done to carry out one where the proceeds may run into the tens of thousands of dollars.

Men visit the town who have a legitimate business as a "blind." They make all preliminary preparations. The greatest ingenuity is employed to obtain exact information, such as the evenings the cashier or teller is likely to visit the bank and the exact time.

Burglars whose chief qualification is the mechanical ability to open bank vaults and safes, and steal thousands of dollars in bonds or cash, cannot be classed with those who break open a store door and filch a lot of buckets, brooms or dry goods.

The man who makes the defects of a combination lock, safe or vault a study, must have intelligence and mechanical knowledge equal to that of a man who draws a big salary for what he knows. Whenever any new combination lock is brought in the market for vault or safe use the scientific burglar obtains one, and by patient study discovers its weakness or defect, something which every safe or vault has. The combination of a safe or vault has often been learned by these burglars by obtaining an entrance to the banking house after banking hours, removing the dial of the combination and placing a sheet of tin foil behind it. Then replacing the dial, the turning of the combination in opening or closing makes the impression of letters or numbers on the soft foil, which is removed by the burglar at the first chance he has to get into the banking house. Having the combination impressed on the tin foil, he and his accomplices open the vault or safe, secure the contents, and then often change or put out of order the combination, so the doors of the vault or safe cannot be opened for some hours after the regular time for opening, and then only by an expert of that particular safe company. This of course gives the thieves several hours of valuable time in which to effect their escape.

The tools required by the mechanical burglar who forces open safes are the air pump, putty, powder, fuse, sectional jimmy, steel drills, diamond drills, copper sledges, steel faced sledges (leather covered), lamp and blow pipe, jack screw, wedges, dynamite and syringe, brace with box slide, feed screw drill, steel punches, small bellows, blank steel keys, skeleton keys, nippers, dark lantern, twine, and screw eyes. The latest and most dangerous set of tools manufactured is the second power in mechanics—the screw.

The method of work with the screw is to first rig a brace, and then drill a hole in the safe, cut a thread in the hole and then insert a female screw. Then with a long steel screw with a handle so long that two men can turn it, the screw is inserted in the female screw, and by turning it goes in until it strikes the back of the safe. Then either the back or the front must give way. In nearly all cases it is the latter, as that is the weakest, and it gives enough to insert the sectional jimmy, which the screw handle is part of. The jimmy is then inserted in the part forced out, and the safe is then torn asunder and its contents easily appropriated. This work is accomplished without much noise.

CHAPTER VIII.

BURGLARS AND THEIR MODE OF WORK.

Effecting an Entrance to a Bank—How the Outside Watch is Stationed and Communicated With—Important Part Beans and Sand Play—Fitting Keys to Street Bank Doors—Forcing Safe and Vault Doors Open Without Noise—Stripping Inside Steel Chests—Tools no Safe Can Resist—Mastering a Combination by the Ear—Bankers Should be on the Alert—What Examination After a Robbery Reveals—The Skill of the Expert Bank Burglar—Tools that Are Marvels of Expert Workmanship—Devices and Expedients of Burglars—Entrapping a President or Cashier—How Banks Throughout the Country are Examined by Burglars—Placing Pins in the Casing of a Door—What it Means—Getting Away Safely With Money—Where it is Usually Planted—A Police Superintendent's Advice to Bankers—Use of Skeleton Keys—A Well Equipped Burglar—Burglarizing a Residence—The Use of Steel Nippers—Tools Used by Cracksmen—Work of the Spreader and Drill—Use of Fuse and Powder—How Sound of Explosion is Deadened—Best Means of Protection Against Burglars.

The use of twine to the burglar is just as important as the telegraph is to the public. One of the first steps taken by the burglar after effecting an entrance into a bank is to fasten one end of the twine to something near the safe, and run the twine out to a confederate on the outside, who watches to give signals by pulling the twine when any one is passing the bank for the burglar to stop working. The outside man is generally in a room in an opposite building where he can command all approaches to the place where his pals are operating—sometimes on the roof of a lone building close by. They never station the outside man in the street, as the fact of a man stationing himself at night in front of a bank would attract attention, and might cause the arrest of all the burglars.

Beans or sand have been scattered along the pavement for some distance near the place of operations, so no person could walk toward the bank without being heard by the outside man. In cases where a watchman is in the way, two of the burglars will probably secrete themselves in the rear or alley-way where the watchman has to pass, and there stun or catch him, so he can not make an outcry. Then they tie and gag him, and leave him in the bank. Desperate burglars have been known to encase their feet in rubbers or heavy stockings (in small towns where there are not many policemen, and who can not be approached in the ordinary way), and to sneak and jump on the one on duty, so he cannot interrupt them in their burglarious work.

After all the preliminary work is perfected keys are fitted to every door which stands between the street and bank vault, by means of a thin sheet of brass, as near as possible the same size as the keyhole, and covered with a thin coat of carbon, which may be applied with a match. A dozen entrances may have to be made to the bank before it is finally robbed. A key is fitted first to the outer door. It is opened on a favorable night and a key is fitted to the next door. This course is continued until keys are had of every door leading to the vault. Having the watchman and officials of the bank down fine, one of the last things to do is to select a favorable night. The men who have done all the preliminary work then take their departure, and have no further part except to receive their shares. Saturday is the best night, if the trains suit Sunday night, because the safe-blowers have all of Saturday night, Sunday and Sunday night to work.

Then the bank burglar proper appears. He has usually

three assistants. The gang never appears until the night of robbery, and then not until 11 or 12 o'clock. If there is a watchman, his habits and disposition have been carefully noted, and having access to the bank by keys, it is an easy matter to surprise and overpower him. A "crow" is next planted outside, or in an upper window, if there be one, to give notice, by means of signals or a cord reaching to the workers, of the approach of a patrolmen or chance passer-by. A regular code of signals is used, telling when to cease operations and seek cover, and when to resume work.

Next is brought into use the simplest and yet strongest and most complete tool for the purpose. It is six inches in length and two inches in diameter at one end, tapering to nothing at the other. It is pear shaped, and a thread extends from end to end. It is made of Muchet's tool steel, the best in the world. A second wedge-shaped tap works inside this tool. When this tap is screwed home it exerts a spreading force of many tons. This tool, the persuader, is inserted in the most minute crack or drill-hole, and, properly blocked at the right time, will force the strongest safe door open with a sound no louder than an ordinary fire-cracker will make. The outer and inner doors open, if there be a time-lock on the chest, a small dynamite cartridge is placed opposite, a detonating fuse lighted, and the outer door closed. The jarring caused by the explosion, which makes a noise scarcely as loud as a pistol shot, disarranges the works of the time lock, which runs down and is useless, the lock running down with exactly a clock's sound when it is doing the same. The heavy outer door of the vault being closed, scarcely an audible sound reaches the street.

When drilling is necessary a light, compact machine, which fits the combination handle and which rapidly drills a small hole above the water rim of the combination dial plate, is used. A small steel broach is then inserted and the combination knob turned until the tumblers are brought into position, thus permitting the "dog" or bar to drop. A turn of the handle shoots the bolt back and the door swings open.

If the operators find on entering the vault that the steel chest is an improved one they then proceed to strip it. Sheet after sheet is taken off until the works are exposed. This is done by using a crow, which is sectional—that is, it may be extended or contracted, as may be necessary. To an ordinary observer the crow looks like the bar which holds the manhole plate of a steam boiler in place, and is worked on precisely the same principle.

Should it be necessary to "wedge" a safe open, a modified form of the old "drag" is used. It is a light but rigid and strong steel bar, sectional, so as to suit different sized safes and for ease in transportation, which clamps the outer side of the safe. Through the bar is run a screw-threaded bolt, with a ball joint at one end for a receiving wedge. On the other end is worked a railroad wrench, used by track hands for tightening rails, and which can be procured from any railroad section-house. With wedging and blocking no door can resist this instrument. Sometimes a miniature railroad "jack" such as engineers carry, is substituted. A heavy cleat is firmly fastened in proper position and placed on the floor. The wedge in the crack, the "jack" in place the result is but a question of time. This is a sufficient demonstration of how the money is procured.

Again, there are a few burglars who master a combination and manipulate its complex machinery with dexterity and precision by the ear alone. They have trained their sense of hearing and touch to such a degree that they can detect a false click of the ratchets within the lock, and mark the time of the drops, and if they are not disturbed they will master the combination, open the vault doors, and in a short time carry off everything that they can touch.

When, therefore, dishonest men have attained to such mechanical excellence, it behooves everyone who desires the safety of their valuable property to be doubly alert, and ever on their guard against the invasion of their premises by men who are as daring and unscrupulous as they are skillful and ingenious. Of course the cases mentioned above are rare, but that they occur is beyond doubt, and every succeeding year but adds to the increasing knowledge of the criminal, and makes absolute protection a matter almost impossible of attainment.

It must not be supposed that the robbery of a bank vault is in every instance but the work of a single night, in which the thieves locate their premises, effect their entrance, demolish the safe and carry off their booty, before the sun comes peeping over the hills, for such is not, and has never been the case.

Indeed, investigation has always shown that weeks, and frequently months have elapsed between the conception of the plot and the actual robbery. Examinations after a robbery has been committed reveal startling facts, and in almost every case traces will be found that prove beyond question that the thieves were as thoroughly acquainted with every movement of the bank officials, and with every portion of the despoiled premises, as the occupants themselves, and in many instances there are unmistakable indications of the actual presence of the burglars before the attempt was made to begin the active labor of breaking into the vaults. It is idle to decry, or to affect contempt for the skill of the expert burglar, for experience has demonstrated beyond question that he is possessed of more than ordinary mechanical knowledge, and that his energy and patience are phenomenal. Nor is there any reason why this should not be so. The burglar is trained to his vocation by the hardest discipline known to man. From his earliest and most primitive efforts until he has mastered all the intricate and difficult points of his rascally profession, there are ever present before him two startling alternatives. The somber walls of a prison and a long term of servitude, in case of failure, and in the event of success, the possession of fabulous amounts of money with which to gratify his every wish and desire.

Many of the tools used in forcing safes are marvels of expert workmanship. The air pump has attached a rubber hose, to the end of which is a small concave piece of tin, with a small tin pipe running through its center into the hose. The crevice of the door jamb—the safe door being closed—is puttied all around except for a space of six inches at the top and bottom of the door. At the lower opening is the tin attached to the hose and held firmly by the foot against the door. At the upper end is held a paper of fine powder. The air pump is then worked, draining all the air out of the safe at the bottom where the tin is applied. As fast as it is drawn out the air is sucked in at the top opening, and rushing in draws with it the loose powder in the paper, through which the air finds its way. After sufficient powder is put in a fuse is inserted at the top of the door, a light attached, the fuse timed, so the burglar can place himself in a safe place—which is generally in the rear of the safe—the two openings are puttied up, and the explosion follows, forcing the door out enough to enable him to use the jimmy.

That one is but another of the many ways used. In some cases it has been shown that the work of the burglars has been going on night after night for weeks; that during the dark hours, while the world was asleep, thieves were digging their way, step by step, to the hidden treasures; and while apparently secure from intrusion or interruption in an adjoining building, they removed heavy walls of masonry, and at last entered the vaults, and escaped with their plunder before anyone, even the watchman upon the premises, were aware of their presence. It may seem incredible, but the instances are not few where this very state of affairs has existed. The devices and expedients of burglars are indeed almost inexhaustible.

One of the methods resorted to by some of the more expert of this class of burglars, and where heavy robberies are contemplated, is to ascertain, by watching the residence of the cashier, and then to gain an entrance to his sleeping apartment by the measures resorted to by house breakers or hotel thieves. Wax impressions of the keys to the bank building, the vault and the safe have been so obtained while the cashier slumbered on, entirely unconscious of the presence of the burglar at his bedside. From these wax impressions exact duplicates are made, and the burglar is then ready for successful operation whenever the proper opportunity arrives to secure the greatest amount of plunder. In case this plan has been found impracticable, the cashier's house has been invaded in the night by a number of masked burglars, and everybody has been bound and gagged without ceremony. The cashier, in such cases, is compelled under threats of murder in case of refusal, to deliver up the keys to the bank, and in some cases to reveal the combination by which the vaults are opened. Leaving one or two of their number to guard the cashier and the other inmates of the house, the remainder of the gang hasten to the bank, and in a short time the robbery is successfully accomplished, and the burglars effect their escape before an alarm can be sounded. In committing these robberies the rascals exhibit as much mechanical ingenuity as they do reckless daring.

While making preliminary examinations of the banks throughout the country, burglars have a very simple but effective way of ascertaining whether there is a night watchman inside the bank without subjecting themselves to the danger and risk of being noticed in watching the premises. Here is one of the devices employed:

After the bank has been closed for the eveniug, pins are stuck obliquely in the casing of the door in such a manner that it cannot be opened without bending or disturbing them. If the pins are placed at 7 and found disturbed at 10 o'clock on one night, the "feeler out" comes back at 9:30 the next. He continues in this way until he ascertains on just what night or nights of the week and the hour regular employes who have keys are likely to visit the bank for inspection or to do extra work.

Now will be detailed some of the methods of getting safely away, which is really the hardest part of the work. Suppose the place of robbery is between Pittsburg and Philadelphia. A confederate—either male or female, the latter preferred—secures a lower berth of a sleeping car that will stop at the scene of the robbery or some point close by. The berth is always on the side of the car opposite the station. The car window is open on arrival at this point, and the "boodle" is passed through, thus leaving the thieves to escape unburdened. If caught, no evidence is found upon them, as the choicest tools are sent with the "swag" and the rest thrown away, and part of the proceeds can be used to effect their discharge if they are arrested.

Should the railroad scheme not be available, the plunder is secreted close by until it can be safely removed. Among the favorite places in which to do this are churches, school houses and graveyards. If a school house or church is chosen, the floor of the platform is cut in under the side,

Sufficient screws are counter-sunk to hold the board in place and the holes filled with putty of the same color as the surrounding surface. It was such a receptacle that held safely for months the millions of dollars in bonds stolen from the Northamptom Bank, of Northampton, Mass., in which the notorious "Red Leary" figured prominently. If a graveyard be the planting-place, a family vault which has not been used for some time is selected, keys fitted, a coffin. opened, the "swag" put in, the lid replaced, and the door reclosed until the time for the removal of the plunder. Fearful that some may think this last statement exaggerated, they are referred to the case of old man Yost, the king of "store workers" in his day, who robbed a jewelry store in Springfield, Ill., a few years ago, and hid the plunder in a cemetery vault, where it was found with an accomplice's assistance a few months later.

Mechanics have a maxim that "the best machine is the simplest." So in protecting a safe, the simplest means is the best. Police Superintendent Walling, of New York City, about fifteen years ago, when safe robbery was almost an every-night occurrence, instructed banks and business-men to place their safes and vaults in plain view of the street, and to have a light burning brightly in front of them. With this addition the plan is unsurpassed: Have a watchman visit your bank every half hour, thoroughly investigate, and signal some centrally located point. Should he fail to do so at the exact and proper time, let the central protective or detective bureau send out an alarm, surround the last place he was heard from and the place he was next due at, and safe-robberies will be few and losses slight in your city or town.

Skeleton keys are remarkable only for their simplicity. They are carried in bunches. Each pattern is made into all sizes. Those that are hollow at the end are used for pin-locks, with which bureaus are commonly fitted. The others are capable of twisting the spring of any common door lock. When the burglar starts out well equipped, several bunches of those keys rest conveniently in a compartment pouch under his coat. The pouch is attached to a belt that girds the waist. On this belt, beside the pouch, hangs the "bull's-eye,' whose light can be flashed and cut off at will. On the other side, a leathern bag is attached to the belt. It is used for carrying sections of a small jimmy and various other things. To lighten the load the belt or "harness" hangs depended from a strap which crosses the shoulder.

What robbers term a "soft snap" is the finding of a key inside of a locked door. It is just as handy to them there as if it were on the outside. The fine steel nippers can be inserted in the keyhole, gripping the key at the end. A single twist of the wrist, and the lock spring flies back. If it be then found that the door is held tight with a bolt, the key is pushed out and allowed to drop inside on the floor. A moment is waited to see if the occupant of the room is disturbed, and if so the intruder waits a while longer to allow the victim to settle into another sleep. This he will probably do after listening a minute, maybe with the mental philosophy that his ears have deceived him, or that the rats are prowling around. When the slumberer's heavy breathing betokens a clear coast, the robber runs the "finder" through the keyhole, feels around inside until the bolt is touched, and then slides it noiselessly out of the socket. This last implement is of pliable wire and can be twisted with ease into any shape required.

Frequently the robber is possessed with a grim humor. In such cases he puts the key back in its place and locks the door before departing with his plunder, leaving the victim to wonder how the thing was done.

So much for the tools used by cracksmen of the common class. Those used by experts are of a higher mechanical order. All entrances to banks, or places where a quantity of valuables are stored, are guarded by iron gates or bars, if proper precaution is observed. To get by these is the first thought of the cracksman. The "spreader" does the business for him. It consists of a power-steel screw, having two grip nuts of hard steel at one end, and an immense, hub-shaped one at the other. The latter is gripped with a wrench, and as the strength of powerful arms move the large nut along the bolt, the iron bars give way on either side sufficient to allow the passage of a body.

The "drill" is used principally for opening safes, but it can tear its way through brick or stone just as effectively. When at work before a safe door, a "diamond drill" is fitted into the socket at the top. A lever is often made of a six-foot jimmy, which a half dozen pairs of ponderous hands may grasp. A hole is bored in the safe, near the lock, then the "diamond drill" is taken out and in its stead is put a large bit for rimming out. Through the aperture thus made the "gripper" at the bottom of the drill-frame is pushed. The flat side of the "gripper" is perforated with holes, so that it can be pinned at any desired length. When it clutches the inside of the safe door it is made fast. A powerful screw is then set at work above, drilling another hole. The inward pressure from that operation causes an outward pressure from the "gripper" and the result is that a portion of the safe front is literally torn out. This is the method generally employed when it is essential to the success of the undertaking to be noiseless. When a little noise is not deemed dangerous, a much quicker and easier way of accomplishing the same result is adopted. The first hole is filled with powder, a lighted fuse is attached and a blanket thrown over the safe to deaden the sound of the explosion. If this does not succeed in tearing the lock away it will at least make a whole large enough to admit a wedge, and a few blows on this, with a sledge, finishes the job. The sledges used for such work are made of copper or lead from which no sound vibrates.

Keen witted, trusty watchmen, are the best means of protection against the burglar, and short shift for him when caught, for he knows he is playing a desperate game, and will take great chances before surrendering.

CHAPTER IX.

SWINDLES WORKED ON FARMERS.

DESIGNING MEN WHO PREY UPON THE RURAL SECTIONS—SWINDLING FARM PURCHASERS—LOCATING A POT OF GOLD—HOW FARMERS ARE FLEECED BY BOGUS BUYERS—WORKING THE COUNTY HISTORY FRAUD—SCHEMES OF SMOOTH TALKING RASCALS—SIGNING A CONTRACT—FRAUDULENT NOTES—FORM OF SWINDLING CONTRACT—BE CAREFUL IN SIGNING FOR STRANGERS—GIVING A RECEIPT FOR A PURCHASE—BOGUS CATTLE BUYERS—THE FARMER'S SAFEGUARD—A FAVORITE MODE OF SWINDLING—DON'T BUY PATENT RIGHTS—THE CORN BINDER SWINDLER—THE LIGHTNING ROD FRAUD—PURCHASING A FARMER'S ENTIRE CROP—TAMPERING WITH A NOTE—BOHEMIAN OATS AND SEED WHEAT SWINDLERS—WELL-DRESSED, PLAUSIBLE, TRAVELING SWINDLERS—BOGUS COMMISSION MEN—NEW SCHEME OF FARM SWINDLERS—THE MEDICINE FRAUD—FRAUDULENT ADVERTISEMENTS IN NEWSPAPERS—METHODS OF AN ARMY OF FRAUDS—SIGNING A HARMLESS PAPER—SCHEMES FOR ENTRAPPING THE UNWARY AGRICULTURIST.

Farmers seem to be the legitimate prey of a great army of oily tongued sharks. For years designing men have preyed upon the rural sections of the country, draining it of a large proportion of its wealth, as tribute to cunning frauds, lazy canvassing agents, and downright criminal swindles of all kinds. These men have become adepts in the business of hatching schemes and setting traps, that are so shrewdly manipulated that their victims are in every agricultural community and almost every household in the land. When one project fleeces the people until it is exposed and cannot be worked any longer, they have another to take its place. Every day might be heard the wails of regret and threats of vengeance from duped men and women, who had been made to give up their hard-earned money to pay for something they had no use for, because they did not know the "tricks of the profession."

Every farmer is anxious to sell his farm providing he is offered what he considers a good price; the same with his stock or anything else he may own. But you must look out for the stranger who drops on you unannounced to purchase your farm, offering a large cash price. He wants the farm for his brother-in-law, his son, or brother. Has been referred to the farm of the man he addresses.

After being shown carefully over the farm he is invited to remain all night. The stranger is taken suddenly ill in the night and remains for four or five days in an apparent stupor, eating lightly, but keeping his eyes and ears wide open. The kind hearted farmer has too much feeling to put the sick stranger out and nurses and cares for him in the same careful manner he would a member of his own family. He recovers and informs the farmer that during his illness and while apparrently unconscious he dreamed for three nights in succession that he had discovered, in a certain ravine in a remote place on the farm, an earthen jar buried in the earth, containing a large amount of silver. At this the farmer usually expresses surprise and refers to it as a most mysterious dream. The stranger finally agrees to take the farm at a stipulated price and is to go to some near-by city and get his cash and bring the party along who is to occupy the farm. As it is some time before train time the stranger suggests a walk over the farm and points out improvements he will make. They take a walk in the section covered by the dream, and the farmer's curiosity is sharpened, and "just for fun," to see if there is anything in dreams, gets a shovel and digs for the hidden treasure. A rock is struck, the dirt carefully removed, and when the rock is lifted there is revealed a large earthen jar brimming full of shining silver dollars. It is quietly carried to the house and the farmer thinks an equal division would be fair. There is usually from ten to twelve hundred silver dollars in one of these "finds." The stranger would consider it a favor if the farmer would give him a check for his half, or get the currency for him, as the silver is too much of a load. The farmer is of course willing to do anything for his friend. He discovers too late that he has been cleverly swindled from beginning to finish, and that his silver is simply a composition of some base and worthless metal.

The county history and county atlas scheme is one of the most plausible and successful enterprises worked by oily tongued rascals. It is well enough to preserve historic facts and incidents in permanent form, if honestly and properly executed. But as the prime motive is to get money without regard to accuracy of fact or honesty in construction of maps, it would be well for all people to withhold money from any of these "agents" until the actual work is performed, delivered and proven to be as represented and entirely satisfactory.

This is the way the county history business is worked up: An agent of the publishers visits the leading towns of the county they propose to write up, and ascertains if any history has ever been issued. In case he finds a productive field, he arranges with all the local newspapers in the county for advertising, and usually at a good rate, for it is necessary for these agents to have the newspapers of the county they are working with them. The "agent" booms the proposed history, and it appears in the county papers as original editorial, and as the history has the sanction and approval of the press, it is easy to reach the people individually. Then comes the historian to take facts and figures for the publication. A large volume is promised, giving the history of the county from its formation to date.

A genial, smiling but business-like man enters the store, office or residence of an intended subscriber. He draws forth a little paper-covered book and says, with an air of great respect:

"How do you do, Mr. Jones? I suppose that you have heard that the World's Historical County Publishing Co. are thinking of publishing a history of your county? They have sent me here to gather a few historical facts, and if you will be so kind as to give me a very few moments of your time, I will thank you."

"Certainly," answers the obliging gentleman.

"Where were you born? (Takes down the answer of this and each subsequent question as though the fate of nations hung on the reply.) What were your parents' names? When did you move to this section? When were you married? To whom; and your wife's name? How many children have you? What are their names and ages? What business enterprises have you engaged in?"

By this time the susprised Mr. Jones asks the urbane gentleman what he is driving at, and is told that he is merely gathering information for the county history now in process of compilation. Mr. Jones naturally asks certain questions, but is firmly and politely told that these inquiries can better be answered when the biography is finished. The glib-tongued agent again proceeds:

"Have you ever held public office? What important events have occurred in your life?"

Then the agent returns his biographical note book to his pocket, explaining what a valuable publication this will be. He informs his auditor in a very confidential manner that the plan of his company is to bring a copy of the history to anyone in the county when published; and the price is only $7.50, if you want a copy of this work, Mr. Jones, when it is finished. And Mr. Jones is so taken off his legs by the prospect of having his biography in a book, that he is almost persuaded. If he shows the least inclination to sign, the agent pushes the little book and a pencil before him and utters these fatal words: "Sign right there, Mr. Jones." The name is written before a serious thought is allowed to be given the matter.

The contract that is signed reads like this:

WORLD'S HISTORICAL COUNTY PUBLISHING CO.

GENTLEMEN:—Please bring to me one of your Histories of ———— County when published, for which I agree to pay you on delivery the sum of $7.50. I base this subscription on what you say in your prospectus, a copy of which has been given me by your agent.

————————

The law emphatically says a man must read what he signs, or abide the consequences. When a man puts his name to the above contract he is fast. A history of a county, if properly published, is of great value. Don't pay or subscribe in advance for county histories or atlases. Pay for what you get, and see that you get what you pay for. Cheap work, poorly executed maps, worthless and inaccurate biographies, cheap paper and rotten press work constitute the chief features of most of these books. These publishers are in business for money, not for their health or complexion.

On page 110 we present a fac simile of a contract made by swindlers with farmers, for the sale of various kinds of agricultural machinery. The fraud has been perpetrated on a great number of worthy people, who certainly ought to have known better than to attach their names to any document of such character. A man we will call Wm. Johnson calls upon a farmer, named Geo. Wright. Johnson introduces himself as the agent of a first-class seeding machine. He talks Farmer Wright into agreeing to act as a sub-agent for his section of the country, under the impression that he will reap a rich financial harvest from the sale of the machine. Johnson says he only wants $10 for establishing the agency, the same to be paid only after he (Wright) has sold $275 worth of the seeders. Wright feels that this is a splendid opportunity, and he signs the "contract."

This note is apparently innocent enough. A contract to pay $10 *when* machines to a certain value have been sold. Surely there is no great risk in an arrangement of that kind!

Now, this contract is nothing less than a note of hand that binds the maker to pay $275.00, with ten per cent. interest, on the order of Wm. Johnson, one year from date. This is what it is, and when Wright signed it he placed himself under obligation to pay that amount. The contract is so worded that when cut in two makes it a pure note of hand. Try the experiment. Place a sheet of paper over the right hand end, and then see if you could consent to sign such a contract were some oily-tongued fellow to present one to you.

These notes are discounted at banks on liberal margins, and collections made by bankers when the limitation expires. That will usually be the first the unsuspecting farmer knows of what he has done. But it is too late to help himself.

Every man should scrutinize carefully any paper, document or contract he is asked to sign, and when dealing with strangers it would be well to write all receipts and contracts in full themselves, according to agreement, and not trust to being swindled by some ingeniously worded and arranged contract.

SWINDLING NOTE.

RICHMOND, Ind., May 16, 1902.

One year after date I promise to pay Wm. Johnson, or bearer, ten dollars, when I sell by order Two Hundred and Seventy-five Dollars, worth of Seeding Machines, for value received at ten per cent. per annum, said ten dollars, when due, is payable at Richmond, Ind. . GEO. WRIGHT. Agent for Wm. Johnson.

Witness: John Gray.

This is the way the note appears and reads when your local banker presents it to you for collection:

RICHMOND, Ind., May 16, 1902.

One year after date I promise to pay Wm. Johnson, or order, Two Hundred and Seventy-five Dollars, for value received, at ten per cent. per annum, payable at Richmond, Ind. GEO. WRIGHT.

Witness: John Gray.

Most farmers and country people manage to keep pretty well posted in these times by reading the daily and weekly papers, but for all this thousands of them fall an easy prey to the cunning devices of sharpers. Any fraudulent or misleading letters, circulars, statements, advertisements, offers, propositions, etc., received from strangers promising something for nothing, or asking for money, should be burned and no attention paid to them. Once a person can be wheedled into correspondence they will be overburdened with propositions and schemes, frequently to their sorrow.

One of the most plausible and easily worked schemes is for a stranger to appear who wants to sell some sort of farm implement. During his conversation and walk about the farm with the farmer, he is sure to see a horse that just suits him, and offers to pay a small sum to secure the bargain. If accepted, he asks for a receipt for the money deposited, stating that he will go to the bank and return in a few days after the animal. Such receipt turns up later in the bank as a note against the farmer. These tricks are continually played, and as continually exposed, showing that the farmer who is swindled does not "read the papers," or is too dull to heed what he does read. Sign no receipt for a stranger unless you are able to write out the entire receipt yourself.

Don't sign a receipt, recommend, or anything for a stranger. By strictly observing this rule money and annoyance will be saved.

Bogus cattle buyers frequently visit a section and swindle the confiding farmer in a most thorough manner. These rascals confine themselves to sparsely settled regions, in which the news of their dealings travels but slowly, so that the chances of being caught are quite small. They usually operate as follows: A man, in dress and general appearance like a drover or cattle buyer, appears in the neighborhood, looks over the cattle on one or more farms, " dickers " awhile as to the price, and finally agrees to take the lot at a certain sum, generally a slight advance on the current price. He may be in no hurry, and perhaps is entertained by the farmer for a day or two. When he comes to settle for the cattle, he may pay a small portion in cash, and then offer a draft on some Chicago or New York bank for a good deal more than the balance. The farmer gives the drover money for the extra amount of the draft. Of course the draft proves to be worthless. The rascal is always careful to see that the cash balance thus obtained is far more than the small proportion of cash he first paid down. In some cases the drover gives no money, but only the draft in excess of the bill, so that the whole balance paid him by the farmer will be clear gain.

In one instance in Iowa a fraud bought a lot of young cattle and sheep amounting to $214.50, paid $25 in cash, and " having no other change, and not having time to go to town to get the bank to cash it," tendered a draft on the Chase National Bank of New York for $275. This, of course, was $60.50 too much, so the farmer paid him that amount in cash. The drover said he would come the next day for the stock, and went off. The farmer waited several days, went to the bank, and then, by inquiry of the Chase National Bank, found the draft to be bogus. He was thus cheated out of $60.50. In one or two cases the humbugs have gone still further, and after concluding the trade, borrowed the farmer's horse and buggy for " an hour or two " and driven off. That was the last seen of them. The horse was recovered in a jaded condition, miles away, after much difficulty.

This is a species of fraud that farmers should be specially warned against. All farmers are naturally anxious to secure a good price for what stock they have to sell, and an offer a little above the local market, especially if part of the purchase money is paid on the spot to "bind the bargain," is very likely to be taken up. Nor, if the scheme is well worked, is the farmer likely to have his suspicions aroused by the tender of an apparently good cashier's draft, even though he has to pay back in "change" a number of dollars more than the first payment received. This same idea is applied with equal ease to the purchase of other farm products. To be sure, such operations are a very serious crime, but usually the swindler is well out of the way before the fraud is discovered. The farmer's safeguard is to accept only cash from all strangers who wish to buy of him. If the stranger offers a check or draft in whole or part payment, let the farmer, like all careful business men, insist upon evidence that the draft or check is good. Ask the cashier of your nearest bank to inquire by telegraph of the bank on which the drover's check is made if he has a balance there to pay. This will only cost twenty-five cents to a dollar or so, and is the most certain way. Or tell the stranger you will take his paper if he will have it indorsed by some of the well-known solid men in neighboring towns to whom he may glibly refer. If you can't get absolute evidence that the paper is worth its face value, don't take it. If the would-be buyer is a reputable and reliable dealer, he can readily furnish such evidence. If he can't furnish it, you don't want anything to do with him, whatever price he may offer.

Another favorite mode of swindling, that is meeting with a measure of success, is for rascal No. 1 to call on a farmer and make a contract for the purchase of the farm at a stipulated price, and gives him $50 or $100, as the case may be, to bind the bargain. In due time a confederate, rascal No. 2, calls upon the farmer and offers him a third more or double the contract figures, and expresses much regret when the farmer tells him the farm is under contract already. After stewing over the matter several days, visiting the farm with other confederates, and making mysterious explorations into ravines and gullies, as if in search of coal, oil or salt springs, rascal No. 2 confidentially suggests that the farmer go quietly to the man holding the contract, who is always quartered in some neighboring village pretending to be very busy about some bank business, and buy him off so as to make a new contract at a far higher price. This the farmer usually does, giving him from $500 to $1,000 bonus to release him. Of course rascal No. 2 never calls again. It is a cleverly worked swindle, pure and simple.

Don't buy any patent rights. It is strange that men with brains enough to acquire property become idiotic in the hands of swindlers. Let strangers of all kinds severely alone.

Farmers are warned to keep an eye open for an agent who sells the "corn binder," who is swindling farmers in different parts of the country by getting postal card orders for one binder and raising them to 100. The binder is a small wooden stick about eighteen inches long, with a brass ferule on the end, on which there is fastened a string which binds the fodder.

The lightning-rod men in past years have flourished more especially in the newer and partially settled regions of the conntry. Now, however, they appear to have made a general descent upon the older settled states. In Pennsylvania, they carried a battery along with them, and by "applying shocks of electricity," pursuaded even "the best citizens" to sign bogus contracts. In Essex county, New Jersey, they induced a man to sign a contract for lightning-rods at a stipulated price, and then after they were erected a demand had been made upon him for an amount far exceeding the original sum agreed upon.

This is a favorite mode of working: A stranger calls and introduces himself as the president of the "North Western

Protection Company," which has a new lightning-rod superior to all others. He wishes the privilege of placing it on the building for nothing, inasmuch as its superior qualities would advertise itself. He, the "president," then proceeds to prepare a statement showing that 195 feet of the rod was to be put up for nothing. The farmer signs the same statement giving his consent to the rod being put up. Three days later three men representing the "North Western Protection Company" appear, and after ornamenting the building with rods present a bill for 395 feet of rod, or 200 feet more than the original agreement stipulated. But this is not all; immediately following the erection of the rods, the farmer is presented with a bill for $150.00. When he sets up a protest, that the rods were to be put up without expense to him, the paper which he had signed is produced, wherein words were adroitly arranged which holds him to terms, and finally settles by paying $125.00. If people would let strangers alone the lightning-rod men and other swindlers would find their avocation gone.

Some people, after being swindled, take a long breath, bite their lips a trifle, and forever afterwards hold their peace about the transaction. This is not right. Others should be protected, and the proper procedure is to expose a swindler whenever he is found.

A swindle that has been worked repeatedly and is liable to turn up at any time is to purchase a farmer's corn at a certain price per bushel and get the agriculturist to sign a contract for the delivery of the corn. The contract then turns up in some bank as a promissory note. There is another and still later swindle. The sharper has a double fountain pen which is so arranged that it uses two kinds of ink. One will fade and the other will remain. The sharper writes out an agreement with the farmer, using the ink that fades. The unsuspecting granger is then handed the penholder to sign his name, but by a turn of a knob the durable ink flows. By this arrangement the words of the contract soon disappear, while the signature remains. The sharper then writes out a note for whatever amount he sees fit above the signature, and has the instrument discounted at the local bank. Many farmers have been swindled in this manner.

Another contemptible swindle frequently perpetrated should be known to every one. A farmer making a purchase of an implement or something else from a stranger objects to giving his note and having it discounted for cash. The sharper says, "Oh, we'll keep the note," and writes across the face, "Not transferable." In a short time it is found in the hands of another party, with an "e" added to the "Not," which makes it read, "Note transferable."

The Bohemian oats and kindred seed swindles have been worked threadbare, but the seed wheat swindle will probably never die. A fraud appears in a community with a new variety of seed wheat which yields double that of any other kind. They refuse to sell the seed, but furnish it and take half the crop next year for their pay, and enter into a contract. As an inducement they agree to purchase the farmer's half at $3 per bushel, but leave that part out of the contract.

There is always a great outcry in rural communities against well dressed, plausible, traveling swindlers, who secure the signatures of unsuspecting farmers on a slip of paper ostensibly to secure the prompt payment, on delivery, for some horse-rake, pump, plow, or other article, offered for sale at a very low price, and on very easy term, at some future time. On these slips of paper they have the signature written in such a position that they can easily fill out a promissory note for any amount, and the victimized farmers soon afterwards find these notes in circulation with their names attached. To all of our readers we have to give the oft repeated advice, "Give such rascals a wide berth, and never sign anything for a stranger." If people would consult their nearest banker they would be saved much money. Bankers being accustomed to business, know a fraud at once.

Bogus commission men, operating from the large cities, annually swindle farmers out of hundreds of thousands of dollars. Farmers are continually hearing from commission men, from whom they receive circulars quoting prices higher than the regular market price. Care should be taken to ascertain their standing and reliability before any shipments are made, as the little trouble will pay in the long run. A great many commission men without principle start in, and through these circulars obtain produce, etc., which they dispose of at prices lower than the regular market, and then move to another point and repeat the same operation. These scoundrels usually operate in gangs and change their names and locations almost weekly. The plan by which the fish are caught is novel, and, apart from being new, has the advantage of shielding the culprit fron legal prosecution. There is a stringent law on the statute books in most states, providing a punishment for commission merchants who solicit shipments and do not pay for them after disposing of the goods. Thousands have been caught in this way, and it is but occasionally now that a country dealer will ship his goods on consignment to any house unless he has first made inquiries as to the firm's standing.

Aware of this fact, the swindlers have devised a new scheme. They offer to buy the goods outright, and generally bid above the market price. The offers are made through circulars, and sometimes one of the conspirators makes a visit to the country shipper and buys the goods. The shipper is given a New York or Chicago address, and all he receives in return for his stock is a promise of a check as soon as the goods are received, The goods are received and sold, the proceeds pocketed and the farmer defrauded.

The people who never read the papers are always contributing to the exchequer of swindlers. A bogus Indian doctor has been traveling about the country for years, and offers a bottle of medicine, a box of salve and a bottle of perfumed disinfectant for a dollar. He specially commends the disinfectant, and says that when the cork is left out of the bottle a pleasant and healthful odor is diffused. He leaves a sample bottle, from which he purposely removes the cork, and when he calls a few days later to take his property or its price, half the contents of the bottle have evaporated. Unless he gets half a dollar as the value of the goods he is troublesome. He usually gets the money, instead of which he should be treated to a good thrashing.

Look out for all specious advertisements in newspapers. If you purchase anything, have it sent on approval, with privilege of examination before purchase. No reputable and square-dealing firm will object to this. A swindler and fraud will.

An army of frauds are always traveling about the country representing themselves as agents of seed firms. They call upon a farmer and desire to sell him a superior quality of seed wheat. The price usually asked is $15 per bushel, but the agent would give a bond of the seed company, binding the company to purchase from the farmer twice as much wheat next year as the farmer bought this year, and at the same price. Besides this, the seed company agrees to purchase all the remaining crop at $5 per bushel. The agent is always very obliging, and offers to take the farmer's note for the amount of the purchase, being $120 for eight bushels. The farmer usually bites, it is such a fair proposition, and gives his note for the amount, and for a day or two is happy in the thought that he has made a good bargain. But going up to town shortly after the transaction, and hearing that the agent has been trying to sell the note, he begins to suspect that something is wrong, and hunts up the seed man and demands his note back. He is informed that the note had been sent out of town to the headquarters of the seed firm. He eventually has to pay the note. It seems strange that any sane man could be caught by such a clumsy swindle. All seed schemes can be set down as frauds and swindles.

Hundreds of farmers are annually victimized by a fraud whose plan is to interview a farmer, get a good description of his farm, and then showing the prospectus of an atlas ask the farmer to sign his name, recommending the book. He is followed later by another man who collects from the farmer $15 for the book, showing a contract signed by them to that effect. When will a gullible public learn to stop attaching their names to every paper presented them for their signature?

The most contemptible individual known to modern society is the traveling quack doctor. He abounds everywhere. His victims are confined to no class. The rich and the poor, the learned and the ignorant are alike susceptible to his promises and persuasions. He works in different ways. Sometimes he charters a column in the city papers, in which he tells of his wonderful exploits in medicine. He inserts a picture of himself, which is sufficient evidence in itself that he is a man of no ability and less character. He describes himself as the renowned and eminent Dr. Bangs from the Imperial Symposium of Medicine at London, New York and Chicago. He comes by request of his innumerable patients throughout the Northwest. Consultation free. The other specimen of of this perennial barnacle comes without blare of trumpets.

He steals into a community with his advertising material. He inquires who is sick and makes a personal canvass. Sometimes he employs some member of the community more contemptible than himself to go with him and introduce him and recommend him. He finds some individual suffering from one of the many ills that beset us all and tells of the great number of cases of this kind that have been cured by him, and that notwithstanding the case has baffled the skill of the local physicians it is a very simple case for him, and if he doesn't cure he will ask no pay. People who are afflicted with disease are ready to respond to any proposition that will relieve the weary, oppressed body. Fifty or $100 they consider a slight remuneration to a man with skill sufficient to effect a cure and they really sign a note for that amount or more. The promise of "no cure no pay" is not incorporated in the note and the eminent doctor, as soon as he secures the note, considers his work ended.

There are a thousand and one schemes for entrapping the unwary farmer, but if he is caught napping in any transaction he has only himself to blame. Let strangers alone, and only deal with reputable houses. Give all questionable transactions a wide berth, sign nothing unless you know that it is legitimate and in any deal that necessitates a money transaction consult your local banker.

CHAPTER X.

THE "NEXT OF KIN" SWINDLE.

THE PRIDE OF ANCESTRY—ONE OF THE MOST DILIGENTLY WORKED AND PROFITABLE SWINDLES IN THE COUNTRY—HUNTING UP ALLEGED HEIRS TO MYTHICAL ESTATES—ESTATES IN CHANCERY AND BANK OF ENGLAND—GENEALOGICAL HUMBUGS—HOW SHREWD LAWYERS WORK THE SCHEME—HOW HEIRS ARE PICKED OUT—A SPECIMEN LETTER—THE BUSINESS FULLY EXPOSED—CREDULITY AND WEAKNESS OF PEOPLE—FORMING SYNDICATES TO SECURE ALLEGED FABULOUS ESTATES—NEXT OF KIN ADVERTISING AGENTS—ACTION OF THE BRITISH HOUSE OF COMMONS—AMOUNT OF UNCLAIMED MONEY IN THE COURT OF CHANCERY—THE INTERNATIONAL CLAIM AGENCY—REPORT OF AN ABLE AMERICAN LAWYER—SWINDLING ENGLISH ESTATE INDUSTRY—VALUATION OF IMAGINARY ESTATES—EXPOSING A GAUZY SWINDLE—AMOUNT OF MONEY COLLECTED FROM AMERICAN DUPES—SUGGESTION TO THE BRITISH GOVERNMENT—TO CATCH THE UNWARY—LETTER USED BY FRAUDS—A PALPABLE FRAUD—WORKING GERMAN ESTATES—LEVYING ASSESSMEMTS AND MAKING FRAUDULENT REPORTS—THE ANNEKE JANS ESTATE.

Of concerns which purport to collect " claims " to estates pretendedly awaiting heirs, in foreign lands, there are many in the United States; and of them all, nine in every ten are only servers of the men inside the institutions. Not long since the New York police authorities placed the "nippers" upon one of these affairs, but yet they flourish, and send their circulars wherever the Federal mails can carry them. The " business " of these concerns is simple enough. In their offices they have books of record, which the British or other nation's chancery publishes, as a public document, and the *primary charge* is for trying to find a corresponding name, or some similar name (anything is enough to hang a hope upon), and then follows a proposition to give power of attorney, with a larger fee, upon an assurance that " investigation " will be made abroad. Half the time these " agencies " do not know the shire towns of the counties with which they assume to be so familiar, and not one time in a thousand do they arrive at even the semblance of a tangible result.

The pride of ancestry is usually great among those whose ancestors possessed any traits of character worthy to be remembered, or did deeds of which history has made emblazoned record, or who held large estates, or were in other respects distinguished,—and justly great is this pride, perhaps. However, it is not to be overlooked that, as a general thing, how great soever the pride of the progeny may justly be, that of the ancestors would probably not have been extreme, in most cases, could they have looked forward for a few generations, and seen what their successors in time were to be.

But a " pride of ancestory " has developed itself in this country, which, if it is not altogether profitable to those exercising it, is sometimes made so to others ; to lawyers who seek fortunes for others, and who, for due fees, are ready to hunt up " Estates in Chancery " in England, and find them, too, *if* they are there,—which is the only requisite for the finding, except the fees. At sundry times many families get it into their heads that there ought to be property of their ancestors preserved somewhere for them, and talking up the the matter among themselves, get feverish over it, and finally assure themselves that such property exists, and that it is their first duty to procure it. Such people become an easy prey to speculating lawyers and others, who find it an easy thing to whet their hopes, and procure money from them to make " primary investigations." A shrewd lawyer, wishing to make the tour of Europe, for example, can readily play upon the credulity of some such family, and induce them to advance him a few hundred dollars to go to England with to examine records, and so forth; and when there, can send home such a "statement of the case," so full of hope, as to evoke a few hundred, or a thousand or two more dollars, in order to retain and pay first-class counsel. It is a shame to our people that so many of them fall victims to the greed for money in this line. Whether to be vexed at the stupidity of the sufferers, or amused by the skill of the intriguing scamps who perpetrate the swindles is hard to tell.

The usual mode of procedure is to pick out people in different localities with names that indicate their ancestors were English and then write them a letter gotten up elaborately displaying flaming coats of arms, with highly colored seal representing the writers are Queen's Counsel. Following is a specimen of the letters sent out from New York and Chicago:

John William King, Esq., Jefferson City, Mo.:

DEAR SIR—Our firm, in the course of investigations which it has made during the last year among the records of the High Court of Chancery in England, discovered that there is a vast estate lying in chancery there for the descendants of John King, who came to this country in the year 1754, as near as we can learn. In behalf of the King family in this country, I have undertaken to make out a genealogical list of the direct descendants, and their branches, from said John, and have found a branch, of which I suppose you to be a member, and if so, entitled to your share in the estate. Will you have the kindness to forward me your pedigree, as fully as you understand it, or are able to obtain it? I am making out a genealogy of the King family, which will be furnished to those wanting at its cost price, one dollar. This list will be used in bringing suit in England, and it is desirable that all Kings claiming relationship to the said John should be registered therein, as this will be made a part of the pleadings in the case, and, according to a peculiarity of the English law, only such as are thus made parties to this suit will receive a share in the estate. Your name will be at once registered on receipt of the dollar and your pedigree. Please be as particular as you can about the latter. Yours, very respectfully,

JAMES K. JACKSON, *Attorney.*

These genealogical frauds also write to the postmasters of a large number of towns, inclosing to one a letter for King, to another a letter for a Perkins, to still another a letter for a Graham, asking each postmaster to have the kindness to read the accompanying letter and to pass it over to any King, Perkins, and so on, who might get mail at his office. The names used are common names and similar names can be found in any community. From a hundred letters fifty to sixty answers are usually received containing remittances of one dollar. Sometimes people will send ten dollars for a guarantee from the swindlers that especial effort will be made in their behalf to hurrry the legacy along.

But credulity in matters of this kind is a weakness alike of the poor and the rich, the educated and uneducated. The device of these swindlers prove to be more profitable than one would have, on first thought, judged possible, so much greater is human credulity than we are wont to consider it. Perhaps credulity is the only thing in the world that we are apt to overrate. But it is not strange that it should be great touching material things, when in matters of religion the most absurd fancies have, from time immemorial, down through the ages of Oriential, pagan, and other religions to the days Mohammedanism and Mormonism, had possession of the human soul, ruled nations, gathered armies, and taught millions of millions of human beings to sacrifice each other in death, willingly and proudly. And in the matter of money-getting, where hope may be whetted, in order to inspire the actor—as in reaching out for a fortune in chancery—their credulity usurps a wondrous supremacy and carries all along with it.

The following advertisement appears in a number of papers, the address of the concern being in Boston, and styling itself the "Foreign Claim Agency":

$450,000,000

and over, are now held by the Court of Chancery, London, England, besides large amounts held by the Bank of England, in the shape of deposits and interest, whose owners are not now known. The following list contains a few of the names of persons deceased, whose Heirs-at-Law and Next of Kin are wanted.

A.

Abbott, Abel, Abney, Abraham, Ackerly, Ackerman, Acton, Adams, Addison, Agnew, Alcock, Aldrich, Alexander, Allen, Allison, Angell, Anderson, Andrews, Ansell, Anthony, Appleby, Appleson, Archer, Armitage, Armstrong, Arnold, Arthur, Ashton, Atkins, Atkinson, Atwood, Austin, Ayers.

Following this is an alphabetical list of common English names reaching all through the whole alphabet. People who answer this are informed that money lies in the Bank of England awaiting a claimant and that for a small "fee" their interests will be watched and the money eventually collected.

The following article from a recent number of Chambers' *Journal*, a reliable English publication, will be found interesting:

"The funds in court in 1894 amounted to the huge total of £64,075,187 4s 1d.; but the proportion of this sum in want of owners is not stated. It is interesting to note that during the preceding year payments were made to successful claimants and others amounting to £16,324,152 3s. There is also a large sum in court under the heading 'Foreign Currencies,' made up of rupees, crowns, dollars, florins, francs, guilders, lire and marks. Reference should also be made to a long list of boxes and other miscellaneous effects remaining in the custody of the Bank of England, on behalf of the Supreme Court of Judicature. An official list of the titles of Chancery causes undealt with for fifteen years or upward is published triennially; but as the names of the testators or persons entitled to the funds are in the majority of cases not stated, the information is of little value to the general public. To give an instance: In 1823 Nathaniel Briggs, one of the next of kin of Thomas Storke, who died in 1760, was advertised for by order of the Court of Chancery. The fund was not claimed; and in the latest list of dormant funds we find the title of the Chancery suit given thus: 'Pomeroy vs. Brewer.' No mention is made that the next of kin of Thomas Storke are wanted. An idea of the large number of similar cases may be gained from the fact that the list of unclaimed funds fills 187 pages. This list is only an index to the titles of accounts, and is not in any sense either a register of next of kin wanted or of lapsed legacies, intestates' estates, unclaimed dividends, prize money, etc."

A short time ago a meeting of the "Lawrence heirs" was held in Springfield, Ohio, which resulted in the formation of a ring or syndicate, with duly elected officers, for the purpose of securing an alleged fabulous sum of money at present said to be in the custody of the British chancery court to certain "next of kin" in the United States, basing their claims upon fraudulent circulars sent them by "next of kin barristers."

The press of the country has repeatedly called attention to the deliberate systems by which, during the last quarter of a century, credulous and confiding person have been swindled out of large sums of money by "next of kin" advertising agents. The aggregate of such sums doubtless is something astounding.

These "next of kin" frauds became so importunate a few months ago that on the suggestion of the American minister in London, an inquiry was instituted in the British House of Commons by Honorable E. Robertson on the subject of unclaimed funds in chancery, the result of which ought to forever dispose of the delusions of this "next of kin" business. Mr. Robertson, speaking on the vote for the pay office of the Supreme court, said that no public office caused a larger amount of heartbreaking among the ignorant public than this; that it was believed by many that the amount of unclaimed funds in chancery reached something like £100,000,000; that there existed flourishing agencies in England and the United States, which laid themselves out to deceive the public by the most grossly exaggerated statements of the amount of money lying in the pay office; that a gentleman of the press had informed him that a particular adventurer had been spending as much as £350 a week in advertisements asking people to apply to him for information; and finally, that as a matter of fact the actual amount of unclaimed money in the court of chancery was not much more than £1,000,000.

There is in New York city an institution calling itself the International Claim Agency which purports to exist for the purpose of endowing American heirs with the four hundred and eighty million dollars awaiting them in the Bank of England, in France, Germany and other countries. Nearly a thousand surnames are given as a part of those in whose name these great fortunes are deposited. Any person who happens to possess one of the names published or any other surname, is invited to send a dollar to the "agency" for the purpose of opening correspondence. A dollar seems a very small sum to pay as an initial step toward receiving a share in all those millions. Nevertheless all schemes of this kind worked under any name or guise are frauds. One of the ablest lawyers of this country, after a long and searching investigation, reported that there were no funds or property of any kind in the Bank of England or court of chancery awaiting unknown claimants in America or elsewhere. Second, these so-called "agencies" which advertise this business are mostly myths. If one had any colorable claim to a foreign estate he would scarcely be likely to employ such an agent to pursue it. There is about about as much chance of becoming rich through an "international claim agency" or "next of kin" scheme as there is of finding a pot of gold under the end of a rainbow.

The swindling "English estate" industry flourishes in spite of official publications on the authority of the British government, of the United States minister in London and of banking authorities that there are no such estates in England as the sharks and cheats have described. The names of these fictitious estates are as numerous as the families of dupes who have been robbed by their pretending to have means within their power for the recovery of fabulous sums of money. The Hyde estate, the Chase estate, the Lawrence-Townley estate, are some of the mythical properties for which associations of claimants have been organized in the United States.

The usual story is that a century or more ago the possessors of valuable landed and other property in England died intestate without local heirs; that by some means the estates were tied up in chancery, the rents, interest and other revenues accumulating and being deposited in the Bank of England; that the true heirs are American collateral branches of the family whose descent can be traced with one or two breaks; and that with a little more money the lapses can be supplied from old chancel records, family Bible or moss-covered tombstones.

The valuation of these imaginary properties is always

large enough to stretch the most elastic credulity. None of them is less than $100,000,000, and the estimates are sometimes four or five times that amount. If a tenth of the stories are true, the Bank of England holds enough money belonging to American heirs to bankrupt the institution ten times over, if repayment should be enforced.

Not only has this gauzy swindle been exposed in the press, but there have been criminal prosecutions of bogus claim agents who have bunkoed suppositious American heirs out of funds to prosecute the "claims." Rev. George William Burgone Howard, of Tennessee, is serving a penitentiary sentence for complicity in English estate frauds. A man named James F. Jaques and another named Howell Thomas are in an English prison for swindling claimants to the Lawrence-Townley "estate." They had collected $75,000 from their American dupes.

Recent dispatches in American journals describe the Holmes estate in England waiting to be distributed to American heirs. Some of these heirs are at Macomb, Ill.; others at Decatur, Ill.; others at Madison, Wis., and a thousand other American cities and towns. A romantic story of the clandestine marriage of a daughter of Sir James Holmes, an Irish baronet of the last century, to a man named Baldridge, and of their flight to America, form the basis of the claim. There are the the usual incidents of the copy of a will, of missing records, and of attempts to complete the chain of evidence. The inevitable "law firm" in England, which is getting the proofs together with the help of American lawyers is a part of the narrative. The Holmes estate is modestly estimated at $400,000,000—enough to divide among an army of descendants and leave a nice portion to each.

Before the Holmes or Baldridge "heirs," so styled or any one else, expend any money in the pursuit of this phantom or any other mythical estate they should write a letter to the American minister in London. He will send them an official pamphlet showing that there is no such estate as is represented to them, and there is nothing more conclusive in human evidence than the fact which will be established.

In almost every town in the United States can be found three or four people who have been swindled by this " Next-of-Kin " delusion and who have spent a great deal of money in trying to get estates which have no real existence.

It has been suggested to the British government that the only perfect way to dispose of these parties who for years have made the people of the United States and Great Britain their illegal prey is to make an end of the entire fund—to confiscate the moneys for the use of the state. Possibly until that is done, and in spite of repeated warnings of the press, this " next of kin " delusion will continue to flourish.

If any one has a supposable claim to any estate in any part of the country, the only thing to do is to place same in hands of a local attorney and he will look up and protect your interests—if any exist. Advertisements for claimants for enormous sums of money which has lain idle in the English banks for long years are always written to catch the unwary and take from them the fee required to establish their right to the money, simply this and nothing more.

As a matter of fact these English estate swindles have been exposed a thousand times. American ministers to England have been bothered with letters from deluded American " heirs " until they have prepared printed circulars to inform applicants that there are no fortunes lying in the Bank of England waiting claimants and that the stories of American successions to vast English estates are almost without exception bare-faced fabrications devised to assist in the operations of swindlers.

As a further specimen of how diligently this swindle is worked we reproduce another form of letter used by this class of frauds. Should any reader of this ever receive one you will know how to act:

"DEAR SIR: A proposal of settlement has been made in the case of the Allen heirs. This suit was to recover a property left to John Allen. It is important that before making any settlement we receive the names of all the parties in interest in order to avoid any complication. There will be no liabilities incurred by entering a claim, as the expenses and my fee are to be met by the property recovered, and were entirely contingent upon the money being recovered. There has been a genealogical list prepared by which you can easily trace any connection of your branch of the family with that of John Allen's descendants. If you are in doubt as to whether you are entitled to any share in this property, for the sum of one dollar we will send you a copy of the list in question. It is important that we receive a prompt reply, if you are one of the heirs, as after the distribution is made it will be too late to consider any individual claim if proper attempts have been made to find the heirs.

Very truly yours,

H. A. ALLEN."

This is a remarkably enticing document, and many persons have been inveigled by it into sending a dollar bill to this "H. A. Allen." He sends them the list of names referred to in return for their money, under the title of the "British-American Claim Agency," or some other high sounding association.

People who remit a dollar and fail to receive the list make a complaint and then they will receive the following encouraging note:

"Mr. Allen is in England, having been called there soon after writing to certain members of the Allen family. He left directions to notify all senders of remittances that orders could not be filled until his return, and to return their fees. Nothing of importance will be done until he gets back in September."

The above does not coincide with the urgent advice given in the first letter, to remit promptly. Is it because the second letter is written only to those who show fight? It is a cold blooded swindle from start to finish, and in these days of enlightenment any one caught by such a palpable fraud deserves no pity at the hands of any one.

For many years unscrupulous lawyers and others have made a good living out of credulous people in this country who, they asserted, were heirs to large and unclaimed estates in England, which might have been more justly styled estates in the moon. Despite the fact that the American Legation in London and the Governor of the Bank of England time and again pointed out that there were no such immense sums of money in existence, and that even if there had been an act of Parliament of 1869 bestowed upon the crown all unclaimed lands that had been in chancery for over fifteen years, a rich harvest continues to be reaped by the swindlers. Contrary to all precedent, hope deferred did not make the hearts of the claimants sick, and, although some of them died paupers, they never wavered in their belief that their heirs would eventually become millionaires.

There are now indications that, in the opinion of the promoters of these confidence games, the English field is unproductive, and so they have sought " fresh fields and pastures new." A woman in Ohio has received notice that she is one of 200 heirs to an estate in Germany valued at $100,000,000, and on the same day that the good news came to her a man in Texas was informed that he was one of four heirs to a fortune of $10,000,000 left by an uncle in Brazil. The usual process will undoubtedly be carried out in these cases. There will be assessments levied and fraudulent reports submitted, and then, presto, all will vanish.

When the French Academy of Science defined a crab as a red fish that walks backward, the celebrated naturalist Cuvier was asked his opinion. " Gentlemen," said he, " the crab is not red, it is not a fish, and it does not walk backward.

With those three exceptions your definition is perfect." Outside of the fact that there are no estates as valuable as those mythical ones, and that there is no money to be distributed, the stories told about them are absolutely true. It is easy to inherit millions from relatives who have died in foreign lands, but it is not easy to collect them. This is all the more to be regretted because the heirs are generally street car conductors or bricklayers or factory hands, or washerwomen, and therefore need the money badly.

There was held in New York City recently a meeting of over a hundred persons who believe they are heirs of a Dutch woman named Anneke Jans, who died in New York nearly two centuries ago. She and her husband were owners of about sixty acres of land lying west of Broadway, toward the lower end of the island. It was farm land in 1700. It is now building property of enormous value.

These claimants think they should have a portion of this real estate. So do numerous individuals residing in other cities, who have formed associations for the purpose of taking steps to get what they say are their rights. There are lawyers, or persons calling themselves such, who tell these heirs that they have a good *prima facie* case, and that if they hand over money enough to pay legal expenses, the estate can be recovered for them.

The continued existence of this Anneke Jans delusion gives one rather a poor idea of human intelligence. It shows how desperately people will cling to a belief, no matter how transparently absurd it may be, when they think there is a pot of gold awaiting them. When Anneke Jans and her husband died the colonial authorities resumed possession of the farm they had granted them, and subsequently the governor, Lord Cornbury, gave it with some other land to Trinity church, which has held undisturbed possession ever since.

Whether the authorities took wrongful possession of that farm or not, in 1705, matters nothing now Anneke Jans may have had children and they may have been the legitimate heirs of that property, but that cuts no figure now. The corporation which has been the proprietor for nearly two hundred years can not be ousted now. Furthermore, this whole matter was gone over fifty years ago, and the utter hopeless emptiness of the claims made then in behalf of the heirs was shown conclusively. They have absolutely no standing in any court.

The pretensions of the heirs are greater now than they originally were. At first they claimed only the property given to Trinity church. Now they assert that they are entitled to acres upon acres of real estate in New York City and on the Hudson. The persons who inspired that false belief did so only to excite the greed of claimants, and make them more willing to pay fees.

It is singular that men who are well informed about most matters can not get it into their heads that there are statutes of limitation which cut up by the roots, after a certain time, claims which may have been meritorious originally. In this state no person can bring an action to recover lands unless within twenty years after the right to bring such action accrued. There are exceptions in favor of infants and insane persons. A case might be imagined in which these exceptions would extend the limit far beyond twenty years, but possession for two centuries gives an unattackable title.

Every cent which deluded heirs pay to lawyers is money thrown away. If they will consult lawyers who are not hunting for jobs they will be told they are entitled to nothing.

CHAPTER XI.

FRAUDULENT ADVERTISEMENTS.

TRICKS OF UNSCRUPULOUS ADVERTISERS—BEWARE OF PLAUSIBLE LOOKING ADVERTISEMENTS—LOOK OUT FOR BUSINESS OPPORTUNITIES—GETTING RICH QUICK—BOGUS EMPLOYMENT AGENCIES—A CASH DEPOSIT REQUIRED—SPECIMEN OF FAKE ADVERTISEMENTS—A BLIND ADVERTISEMENT—LOOKING FOR A POSITION—FLEECING APPLICANTS—HOW THE WORK IS DONE—PAYING SALARY AND EXPENSES—SETTING A TRAP FOR GUDGEONS—A RASCALLY WORDED AGREEMENT—CUT-THROAT CONTRACT—A CONTEMPTIBLE SWINDLE—WORKING YOUNG MEN WHO DESIRE HONEST EMPLOYMENT—SIGNING A CONTRACT—ADVERTISEMENTS TO AVOID—MATRIMONIAL ADVERTISEMENTS—THE WORK OF SWINDLING ADVERTISERS FULLY EXPOSED—BOGUS PIANOS AND ORGANS—HOW WE ARE SWINDLED—EXPERIENCE OF A COUNTRY JUDGE.

Some one has said that confidence is an excellent thing in any community. It has been called the ground plan of all individual transactions; the bone and sinew of all dealings between man and man. Fraud and swindling furnishes food, raiment, and, indeed, most of the luxuries of life, to a large army of enterprising and insinuating individuals. The requisites to its successful working are not many: an easy manner, cheerful disposition, plenty of nerve and "brass," a good judgment as to human nature, and a confiding, honest, simple-minded set of people on whom to act, are all that are needed. The gullibility of people has always been—and probably always will be—a matter to be wondered over. Swindling has been reduced to a fine art.

The "business opportunity" ads. in the leading daily papers of the country are full of danger to the unsophisticated, and before parting with money as the result of business opportunities brought to attention through this they should be carefully and cautiously investigated. All sorts of specious schemes for making money and getting rich quick are presented for the consideration of the gullible public. If you desire to make a business arrangement with a stranger find out if his business is legitimate and insist on references as to his character, business methods and standing and investigate same carefully. A little precaution oftentimes saves a man a vast amount of trouble and annoyance.

In every city are hundreds of institutions called "Employment Agencies." The public should understand that whenever an employer demands a cash deposit and refuses a bond he is a fraud and should be left severely alone. And those seeking work through employment agencies should remember that when a fee is required in advance the agency requiring it is a swindle and the money so paid will be lost.

We reproduce a specimen of an advertisement that fairly well illustrates the most favorite form of entrapping the unwary. It reads innocently enough, as most fraudulent ones do, and is known as what is termed a "blind ad.," as it does not give any street address, but answers are to be sent to a certain letter or number to the office of the newspaper in which the advertisement appears:

> WANTED—YOUNG MAN OF GOOD ADdress and business ability; permanent position and good salary to right party. Address B 284, care Eagle office.

In response to the above advertisement which appears in a daily paper some forty or more young men appear, each anxious to receive the promised employment. The outer room of the suite occupied by the advertisers serves as a reception room, into which the applicants are huddled until, one at a time, they are ushered into a private room for an interview. Of these private rooms there are usually three or four, in each of which during business hours may be found an individual who calls himself a "superintendent of agents." The advertisement appears regularly every day the year round in different forms—different wording—but is invariably of the class which advertisers designate as "a blind ad.," so called from the fact that it conveys absolutely no information of the nature of the business advertised. This style of advertisement is known to be "a puller," hence it pays to use it, hence fake advertisers always use it.

The young man who is looking for a position sees the advertisement, reads it carefully over and seeing no conditions in it that any ordinary young man can not fill proceeds to investigate He joins the crowd of applicants in the reception-room and in his turn is ushered into a neatly furnished private office, where he finds the exceedingly smooth individual described above as a superintendent of agents. This person is thoroughly conversant with all the frailties and weaknesses of human nature. He does not allow the applicant to make inquiries about the nature of the business, but keeps him busy answering questions. A long string of questions are asked the applicant and by answering them he enables the other to know not only his history, but his likes and dislikes in business, the amount of salary which he has earned in the past, and all other information of value that will help the advertiser to successfully work the young man.

The superintendent of agents then carefully unfolds his plans to the applicant, who has by this time become convinced that the employer is a good fellow and will treat him fairly. The position promised turns out to be an ordinary business chance or book agency, in which business about one man succeeds where a thousand do not; yet the confiding applicant, though he may have served unsuccessfully in the same capacity a score of times before, is so thoroughly under the influence of the genial fellow to whom he has applied for the position that he thinks seriously of accepting any offer that is made him. By this time the young man has developed the symptoms of a sucker, and though he has probably never before earned more than $30 per month, when he is offered the magnificent salary of $65 per month and all expenses paid he fairly springs into the trap.

Security is the next question discussed, and the employer suggests that a deposit of $100 would be about the right thing, but, learning that the applicant can not raise so large an amount, he offers to take $50, which the applicant thinks he can borrow from a friend; or perhaps he can not do this and the employer offers magnanimously to make still further concessions, sometimes accepting a cash deposit of $5 or $10, or a note for $25, or a watch—anything, in fact, that is worth taking, for whatever it may be it is just that much profit. This security is put up as "liquidated damages" for the faithful performance of the agreement entered into between employer and employed.

The agreement is an elaborately printed document, originally drawn up by a shrewd lawyer, and is so deftly worded that, while perfectly legal, it is firmly binding upon the employe, but is full of loop-holes through which the employer can escape. Not only can he cause the agreement to be canceled at his option, but he can oblige the employe to forfeit his salary as well as the security deposited.

The agreement provides that the employe shall pay his own traveling and hotel expenses, and is allowed to retain a certain proportion of his receipts, usually 40 per cent., as an offset and to apply on his salary, and that at the monthly or quarterly settlement the remainder of the amount will be paid him in cash. But as his employer is almost certain to force him to break the agreement before that day of settlement arrives, the man is virtually acting in the capacity of a book-agent on the old commission plan and does not know it, while at the same time he has paid the amount deposited as security for the privilege of doing it.

One clause in the cut-throat contract illustrates the manner in which this may be done:

"And the said party of the second part agrees to commence work on or before —— day of ——, 18—, and continue to —— day of ——, 18—, except as hereinafter provided, and prosecute said work under the direction of the party of the first part in such territory as party of the first part shall direct."

To the casual reader there is nothing unfair in that; to the man who signs the contract it appears to be perfectly square; even a sharp-witted lawyer might be caught with it. But nevertheless it is one point which enables these so-called publishing houses to get rid of their agents and cause them to forfeit the security.

For example: John Smith may be selling trees or books for the house in Ohio; the settling time is coming; commissions haven't paid the salary, for they rarely do; the company therefore wants to get rid of John, so orders him to remove to a new field in Texas; John hasn't $10 to his name, so can not go, as by agreement he is obliged to pay his own expenses; by not going as directed he breaks the contract and loses his salary, security, and the amount which he has already paid out for expenses.

The agreements drawn up by the publishing houses that are doing business in that way are full of just such irregularities and they are there for a purpose. If in reading the agreement over the applicant should find fault with such clauses a few deftly chosen words of explanation set his mind at ease, as the shrewd employer can well afford to make all sorts of oral promises, especially as the agreement contains this paragraph:

" It is expressly understood that no verbal agreement can in any way change or modify any condition named in this contract."

When an agent hired under such a contract feels that he has been swindled he very naturally objects, but it is a part of his employer's business to be prepared for such emergencies, so he takes him again into his little private office, calls his attention to a paragraph over his signature which reads: " I have carefully read the conditions of this contract and sign it with my eyes open," or words to that effect; then proceeds to show him half a dozen or so points wherein he has violated his part of the agreement, and ends not infrequently by convincing the agent that the house has been the greatest sufferer, for these shrewd fellows, having successfully "worked" their man in the first instance, have but little trouble in repeating it.

It is an actual fact that a number of concerns in New York and Chicago and other large cities calling themselves publishing houses, library associations, and similar titles are using contracts of this kind with their agents, the conditions of which no man living could carry out, and the amount of money lost by the agents in this way is not a few dollars or a few hundreds, but as a total runs up into the thousands. It is the salary feature that catches the men, while the salary is merely a blind, and young men who are willing to work will do well to work for small but honest wages rather than sign a big agreement full of vague conditions in the hope of drawing a larger salary than they are able to earn.

There are hundreds of responsible and reputable publishing houses that do business in an honest and straightforward manner, and if prospective agents will make a few inquiries as to the character and standing of people who wish to employ them much trouble will be averted. Any reputable and honorable house will treat agents fairly and honestly, and there are plenty of first-class book and publishing houses.

Of all forms of advertising that is worked for gain and with a marked degree of success is the matrimonial adventurers. Advertisements are inserted in newspapers for a husband or wife. Swindlers watch these matrimonial journals and columns and enter into correspondence. When a man advertises for a wife he will in a short time receive a letter running somewhat after this fashion:

DEAR SIR: In perusing the columns of the —— I read your ad., and becoming favorably impressed I concluded to answer, trusting my photo above may prove to be your ideal. My object is matrimony and an early marriage if you are likewise inclined. I would prefer your photo as soon as possible. I will now give you an outline of my life, accomplishments, etc. I was born and brought up in the State of Rhode Island on a farm, and am the only child of American parents. Since their death, four or five years ago, I have lived with a maiden aunt. Eight months ago she decided to come to Chicago and reside, at the earnest request of several of her friends here, I coming with her. She, being a practical dressmaker, has since engaged in that line, and I am working with her. My age is twenty-one; height, 5 feet 6 inches; weight, 130 pounds; brown hair and eyes, full regular features, fair complexion, rounded form, amiable disposition; sing soprano voice; play piano and organ; fairly well educated; good housekeeper and cook; domestically inclined; economical; strong and healthy, and my own dressmaker.

I will now close, either expecting a favorable reply or a return of my letter. I remain yours sincerely,

MAMIE B. CURRY.

The above letter is written by a man usually, and for the sole purpose of swindling. A photograph of a handsome woman is always enclosed. A correspondence would then be opened, and in a very short time the swindler will receive a sum of money from his distant admirer, sent for the purpose of defraying the railroad expenses of the young girl in her trip to her admirer's home. The girl, of course, never arrives, and the would-be husband soon discovers that he has been swindled.

Hundreds of such advertisements as the following fill the newspapers, and thousands of young men and women are swindled and duped: "A Sure Fortune for Every One;" or, "$77 a Week Guaranteed;" "If You Are in Debt and Without Work, Write to Us and Fortune Will Be Yours;" "A Good Income Without Much Work and No Canvassing;" "Telegraphic Instruction Free and Positions Guaranteed;" "Fifteen Dollars per Week for Clerks;" "Bright Young Man to Assist in Books;" "Five Dollars a Day Guaranteed;" "Wanted: Bookkeepers, Salesmen, Timekeepers and Clerks," and a thousand more catchy and deceptive advertisements to trap the unsophisticated.

Young men and women who are tempted by these advertisements should think before they act, and don't give up your good money and hope, after money which never will come and brings only disappointment. There is nothing but a "trap" in these advertisements, and the foolish persons who are caught therein only part with the money expended.

Here are a few more forms of a class of advertisements that wise people will shun:

PERSONAL--GENTLEMEN—A SPLENDID photograph of a lady who wants to correspond with a view to matrimony; also full particulars sent postpaid for 15 cents. We have 500 members, many of them beautiful and wealthy. Address, The Harris Matrimonial Association, 1416 —— street.

WANTED—YOUNG LADY CANVASSER immediately to travel South with gentleman; stylish, energetic, and good address. Call or address J. N. GRAY, 210 —— street.

A GOOD BUSINESS MAN WITH FROM $3,000 to $5,000, wishing to go into the grocery business, can learn of an opportunity seldom offered to purchase a clean stock, new fixtures, and good will of the best known, most popular grocery store in this city, situated down town; rent low; business paying; good reasons given for selling; stands investigation. Particulars. X. Y. Z., Times office.

PERSONAL—"OUR HEART," AN ORIGINAL matrimonial journal, published in connection with Read's Matrimonial Association, which has brought about 296 marriages during the past 20 months, and which now contains the names of 7,000 candidates. October number now out; do not miss sample copy. Inclose 10 cents or call on H. B. READ, 296 —— st.

PERSONAL—A LADY OF 32, WHO UNderstands housekeeping perfectly, and who always moved in the best of society, wishes to make the acquaintance of a well-to-do middle-aged gentleman, with view of matrimony. K. E. 8, Times office.

MME. LA LULA, THE GREATEST CLAIRvoyant of the age, can be consulted on all affairs of life; has the world-renowned Egyptian charms, guaranteed infallible for love, marriage, business and health; unites the separated, restores lost love, causes the absent to return, locates and cures diseases, removes evil influences, succeeds in the most obstinate cases where all others fail; asks no questions; uses no cards. Call and be convinced. 2073 Potter-av. Parlor floor. Ladies only.

MME. DE TRUAX, CLAIRVOYANT AND trance medium, astonishes all by her wonderful power, revealing every important event that has occurred in your past or will occur in your future life; has the celebrated Parisian charms, guaranteed infallible: brings the separated together, causes love, marriage, success in every undertaking. Consultation from 10 a. m. to 8 p. m. 986 White Terrace. Gentlemen only.

FIVE HUNDRED DOLLARS A MONTH—Wanted, good agents; will pay big salary; commission; railway and hotel bills. Small cash deposit required. Address X. Y. Z., Times office.

> TO BE SACRIFICED—THE —— COMPANY will sell sound, gentle road horse, with Brewster side-bar (nearly new, cost $300), new harness, whip and blankets, for $120; closing an estate. No. —— Fifteenth street.

Advertisements similar to this appear frequently in the leading city dailies:

> WANTED—SEVEN GENTLEMEN IN THE city offices of Western Telegraph Company to learn telegraphing on our lines and take situations paying from $70, $80, $90, $100, $120, $125 to $150 monthly; steady employment. Apply immediately Telegraph Superintendent.

The variations from day to day are in the number of gentlemen or ladies wanted, and the monthly compensation named. Many young people who desire to engage in telegraphy as a business, read these advertisements so cursorily that they fail to observe that the advertiser is not the Western Union Telegraph Company, and that no employment is actually promised. Those who answer the advertisement find, if they pay the tuition fee, that they are only wanted to "learn telegraphing on our lines," which begin and end in "the city offices," and then they are to take situations on Western Union or other lines, provided they can get them. The managers of the Western Union have been much annoyed by this sort of thing. As the Western Telegraph Company is merely a school of telegraphy, those who desire to enter as students have only to go in with their eyes open to the real facts.

Look out for swindling advertisements which desire to make you rich in a few days and as a "guarantee of good faith," request you to remit a dollar or two at once. Here is a favorite form of advertisement used by swindlers, with the wording and form changed to fit different enterprises:

> IF YOU WANT TO MAKE A COMFORTABLE income at home, varying from $15 to $50 a week, write to the International Artograph Company, post office box—, New York. No previous knowledge of the business required.

Here is a specimen of the average answer:

DEAR SIR—The business we advertise and in which we need the services of many ladies and gentlemen is the making of a beautiful picture which we call the artograph. We send you a certain kind of picture on a delicate, specially prepared Gaina paper. We require you to put it on cardboard and apply the colors as directed. You can do it after a very few days' practice.

We send you, when you decide to undertake the work, a book of instructions, for which we charge you nothing, being desirous to have you in our employ, and a box of paints and brushes for which you pay less than cost price—namely $1.50. No natural taste or artistic training is needed for this work; bear in mind that any one can do it. For every picture you send to us satisfactorily finished, we pay you 45 cents.

We send you at first five, which, when finished, will net you $2.25, and after a little practice you can easily finish the five in one day's work. We sell these pictures to canvassers and have never been able to get enough of them to supply the demand.

As a matter of form before sending you the first five pictures we require you to make a deposit of $1 as a guarantee of good faith, and we cannot undertake to start any one in the business who is not willing to make this deposit.

We feel sure that you will be able to do this work well and that the money earned will surprise you. State how you prefer to be paid—by the week or by the month, or whenever you send us the finished pictures.

Very truly yours,

Dictated B. G. L. JAMES T. HOWARD.

Together with this typewritten circular comes a paper supposed to be a contract, in which the victim states his willingness to do the work required, and agrees to devote so many hours a day to it and do his best. He is supposed to sign this and enclose it with $2.50 to the Artograph Company. In return will come five little pictures on tissue paper, and some cardboard upon which to mount the pictures, and a little box of cheap paints and brushes, the whole outfit worth perhaps half a dollar at retail figures. This is the comedy part of the performance. The tragedy part begins when the unfortunate victim attempts to do the simple work which requires "no artistic skill or previous knowledge of the business."

As a matter of fact the work is made purposely impossible; when an attempt is made to paste or mount the tissue paper picture upon the cardboard it seems to dissolve, and the victim regards it with mingled astonishment and indignation. No matter how much care is given or how delicately it is done—and even experts have tried their hand at it—the result is an awful botch, which the Artograph Company will be perfectly justified in refusing as not up to the high standard required by their patrons. Of course the upshot of the business is that the victim loses his faith in human nature, his $2.50 and a good many hours' work.

It will be noted that in the letter sent by the swindlers they say "the money earned will surprise you." The victim earns nothing and it does surprise him.

> BEING ABOUT TO MAKE AN EXTENSIVE tour, a lady will sell magnificent rosewood cabinet Upright Piano, seven and a quarter octaves, overstrung, iron plate, used five months, warranted five years by maker, cost $800, for $200, including Stool and Cover. Call at private residence, No. ——— street.

The above is a specimen of advertisements continually appearing in metropolitan papers. Inquiry at the given number, which was a furniture salesroom in spite of its outward appearance of being a private house in response to a recent advertisement in a Chicago paper brought to view a piano, not second-hand but new, brightly polished, and with fair but uneven tone, with poor quality of wire, uneven quality of felt in the hammers, bad spots in the sounding board, and cheap lumber throughout, being a fair sample of a legion of pianos made for sale and not for use. The term "secondhand" was evidently used as an excuse for the apparent cheapness of a supposed valuable piano. Ignorance of the location of the factory was claimed by the salesman. The factory was, however, discovered by proper inquiry. No sign graced the door, but upstairs two work rooms were found, and one workman putting together a duplicate of the instrument already seen. The proprietor was conveniently away. A little questioning, however, elicited from the workman that the instruments were sold only to the trade, and for $125; that the component parts were mostly bought in various places, ready made; the action in one place, the iron castings in another, the pegs, wire, etc., in another, and the frame in still another. The reader may form his own impression of the value of the maker's guarantee under such circumstances. Such instruments are specially deceptive, as they are seen and heard at their best when new, and may hold out in fair condition for six months or a year, but will afterwards rapidly deteriorate. These fraudulent pianos are pushed everywhere, but in the country they are the most successful, as they cannot be so readily compared with better.

In cabinet organs also the amount of fraud and trickery is surprising. The proportion of poor instruments is greater than in pianos, for the cash outlay being smaller, less care and scrutiny are usually employed in the selection. In the country, and to some extent in the city, the instrument swindle often takes the form of an oily-tongued canvasser who begs the privilege of leaving a piano or organ on approbation a few weeks or months. This looks plausible, and where an instrument is desired, the offer is frequently accepted. The instrument once within the door, the agent finds ways and means to make its stay permanent. The true inwardness of the instrument does not usually develop under six months, possibly one year. If otherwise, the agent argues away the dissatisfaction or juggles the refractory note. If these do not suffice, he charges the family with abuse of the instrument, and in extreme cases threatens a suit for damages. Under the most favorable circumstances, the customer finds that the payments already made will be lost if the instrument is taken away. Once fairly domiciled, the work of decay goes merrily forward. The piano tone becomes uneven, some notes thick and "tubby," other sharp and wiry, the action fails to repeat, and the piano will not stand in tune. In time the sounding board warps, or the iron plate cracks. The organ becomes wheezy; the keys persistently stick; the action warps, letting the wind into the wrong set of reeds; some reeds crack; and in both piano and organ the varnish cracks, letting out the moisture from the unseasoned wood. The guarantee of the maker when most needed proves to be worthless. It is a queer element of human nature on which the salesman largely depends, viz., the disposition to praise one's own property, and never to acknowledge one's self the victim of a swindle. Prevention is better than cure. Where the services of a disinterested expert are not available, a wide berth should be given to all instruments new or old that do not come from houses of established repute.

A well-known judge in an Iowa city saw the following harmless little advertisement in an eastern publication, and answered it. He describes his experience in his own way, and it will be found not only instructive but really interesting reading:

WANTED—AUTHORS IN EVERY TOWNship—No experience required. Write to ——— for information.

"I wrote, and in reply received a circular to the effect that a company was compiling material for a most gigantic history of the United States. Each state was to be done in one volume at the uniform price of $5. The company wished a correspondent in each township, and as remuneration would send the writer a copy of the history of his own state—as soon as it was published. If they needed his services after he had written up his own township they would let him know and pay him in cash or with more books. In conclusion, the circular demanded a quarter of a dollar as a guarantee of good faith and to pay for a list of questions which they desired answered. I sent the quarter."

"And never heard from it again?"

"No. I did hear from it, for by return mail I received a second circular containing about thirty questions concerning the topography and history of the township in which I lived."

"Did you answer them?"

"Yes. It amuses me yet when I think of the serious way in which I worked them up. In fact, if I should meet the 'publisher' I would be willing to give him another quarter as an acknowledgmeut of the trick he played on me and of my own gullibility. And still I am afraid that he did not make very much out of his game. There were two letters to each victim, with a postage of six cents, two envelopes, and two printed circulars. His profit could not have been more than 15 cents. Of course, I never heard of the history again."

Whether or not I had ever been duped, even to the small amount of a quarter, I did not propose to confess, but just to keep the conversation up and to see if my companion had any more reminiscences I asked if he had ever stumbled up against the "portrait copying" swindle. He confessed that he never had and asked me what it was.

"If you ever read the personal columns of the daily papers you must have come across the 'ads.' I read them every day. Not for information, but for amusement. There are some queer things to be found in those columns."

"I know it," he replied, sententiously.

"Within the last year or so several enterprising Eastern gentlemen have advertised for "artists;" the work, copying portraits; the advantages, work at home and no canvassing;

the pay, princely. I spotted the scheme as a swindle, and thought no more about it; but one of my friends was taken in."

"His name, please?"

"Never mind his name. In reply to a letter of inquiry he received a circular asking for $2 for apparatus. The $2 was sent and the material for copying received. My friend was something of an artist, but to save him he could not make a decent picture with the material sent to him. He even called in the assistance of a professional artist. The latter told him that it was impossible to turn out anything but "blotches." So he gave it up. He had the curiosity, however, to send his carricatures to the Eastern gentlemen, who promptly replied that they showed talent, but were not quite up to the required standard, and urged the artist to persevere."

"It's queer how people are taken in," said my companion, meaningly, but I passed over his remark in silence.

"Do you know," he said after a few minutes, "that the literary dodge is almost taking the place of the counterfeit swindle? Of course there is plenty of the latter going on, but not so openly as formerly. It seems almost as though the 'sharpers' were taking advantage of the literary craze which has captured the feeble-minded of the country. Did you ever have any experience with the cheap book game?"

"What do you mean? ——and——?"

"No, no. They are legitimate publishers. I see you never have and will give you a pointer. It is a neat swindle, and one which rarely gets its perpetrator into trouble. A book is hastily compiled from other works—generally consists of some very valuable, practical hints for farmers, mechanics, and others of the working class. Of course it ought to have some good in it, for all the author has to do is to steal his copy from some standard works. Then a catchy title is secured, such as 'The Farmers' Handbook,' 'Knowledge for the

Masses,' or 'How to Keep Well.' Then the services of a cheap printing office are secured and a cheap edition printed on poor paper and with broken type. The expense is very light. A few copies are gotten up in good shape for canvassing. The 'agent' visits a small village and seeks out the leading man of the place, generally a retired politician or 'Squire who thinks much of his title. A few notices are artfully inserted in the local paper, and the public is soon well acquainted with the gentlemanly canvasser. You know very little is needed to interest a quiet country place, where sensations are few and far between. At length the judge is induced to take the agency for the work. 'His name and influence,' you know, will be worth so much that special terms can be given him. The books are to be sent him; he is to secure agents and superintend the sales, and on each book he is to have a commission of, say, 25 per cent. Before the agent leaves he secures the signature of the ''Squire' to some such an agreement as this:

" '$——. I agree to take 2— dozen copies of "The Farmers' Handbook," paying all charges, and to act as agent for the same in Kokomo County, at $2 per copy.

" 'J. L. SMITH, J. P.

" 'Witness—Richard Roe.'

"The agreement is afterward raised from two dozen to twenty by inserting a cipher after the figure two, and the dollar blank is filled up. Sometimes, almost always, the victim tries to make trouble, but there is his signature, with the agent as witness. He knows that he has been swindled, but it would be difficult to prove it."

CHAPTER XII.

PITFALLS OF A GREAT CITY.

City Perils for Young Men—Disguise for Meanness, Moral Cowardice and Misery—Evil Resorts and Improper Amusements—Pernicious Places in a Great City—Curiosity and Conscience—Ingenious Schemes to Fleece the Unwary—Laying for Country People—Entrapped by Designing Rogues—Well-Dressed and Plausible Gentlemen—Some Sound Advice—What Police Officials Say—The Card Shark and His Methods—Paying Dearly to Learn the Ropes—Various Swindling Tricks—The Stripper Game—Three-Card Monte Men and Thimble Riggers—The Work of Confederates and Cappers—Changing Money—Mock Auction Sales—Methods of Shell Workers—Swindling Without Reserve—Avoid Questionable Resorts and Strangers—Keep Your Money and Your Wits About You.

What are the particular temptations and perils of the city for young men? One of these is the excessive business activity. In the country there is often a stagnation which promotes dullness. There is not enough of activity, energy, and ambition to stimulate the powers to full exertion. But the other extreme has also its deeply injurious effects. In our modern cities business is overdone, and consequently young men can think of nothing else but business, and how to make money quickly and easily.

Again, the passion for wealth is a peril of the modern city. It is in the cities that great fortunes are made. It is here, too, that wealth has an opportunity for display on a large scale. Its palatial residences; its brilliant social gatherings; names that otherwise would be execrated, on account of their millions are held as illustrious and honorable. Business methods and practices unscrupulous, dishonest and villainous are quite overlooked, merely because attended with success.

And what a pernicious tendency must this have upon young men who are growing up. The danger is that they will be blinded by this gilded glare. They will not see how thin a disguise it is for meanness, moral cowardice and misery. If there is one thing in the world that a sensible, manly youth should not envy, it is this ill-gotten wealth which we so often see around us, united with littleness, coarseness, dishonesty, fraud and knavery. Yet how many are so deluded by it as to think it the supreme end of life, and to be willing to gain it by the same execrable ends, and at the same sacrifice of honesty by which others have secured it.

Another peril of the city for young men is found in evil resorts and improper amusements. Our nature demands recreation, and, especially, overtaxed as many of our young people are. But the taste of the multitude is proverbially low. Improper amusements, coarse in taste, sacrilegious toward sacred things, and dissolute in morals, too often draw the largest crowds and the most responsive applause. As a consequence, these pernicious places in a great city spring up on every side.

In the thronged thoroughfares they spread out their emblazoned signs, and, perhaps led by curiosity, or induced by companions, young men will sometimes enter. One step leads to another, and conscience is dulled. A refined taste is at first shocked, then loses its sensibility. Late hours and dissipated habits follow.

Yet another peril of the city for young men is the facility for secrecy. In a small town it is not so easy to lead two lives. There one's character and actions come out largely to view, and the fear of discovery and loss of reputation exercise a wholesome check. But in a large city one can easily hide under the ambush of a large crowd. Your neighbors do not know you; youı acquaintances do not observe your every step. There is ready facility for concealment of any reprehensible part of life. And how often this is encouragement to wrong-doing! A young man is tempted to say: " I can do this or that and no one will ever know it. It will not injure my reputation; it will not hurt my prospects; it will not tarnish my good name."

And how are our young men resisting these iniquitous influences? Are they wisely seeing through their guile and delusiveness? In the midst of all these seductions and enticements are our American young men holding by their principles, keeping their balance and common sense? It is a common remark, a most painful and alarming one, that pious, conscientious, manly young men are constantly becoming fewer. This is more especially the case with the sons of the wealthy, but it is largely true of all classes. And if this evil be not corrected society will take a downward course; there will be fewer Christian homes, and there will be fewer upright and useful citizens.

The rascal who depends upon his process of persuasion and his capacity for inventing ingenious schemes to fleece the unwary, is more to be feared than the man who robs by rougher methods, because, as a rule, he is well educated and so plausible that he can deceive even those who are above the average intelligence. Thousands of people come from the country each year to the city to make fame and fortune and are easily entrapped by designing rogues. To them every smooth talking and well dressed man is a gentleman. But this nonsense is soon removed from their mind. A man may be warned and warned, but he usually thinks he is proof against the schemes of anyone until a slick gentleman ropes him in with some specious and plausible swindle.

There is only one word to be said to those who intend to stake their money against the skill and adroitness of men who make a living by deceiving their fellow men, and that is—Don't! The advice is not given with any idea that it will be heeded, because there is scarcely one man out of a dozen who reads this book, who will not believe that he has seen so much of the world that he can see through the devices of all the sharpers in it. Let him try half a dozen times to beat a man at his own game, and then he will begin to realize that he doesn't know so much after all.

Police officials often wonder how it is that a man from the country is invariably allured into card playing when he strikes the city.

The card sharper is an individual against whom it is almost useless to speak a warning word. Nine men out of every ten who play cards believe they are fully competent to detect any trick or turn in whatever game they may undertake. These are the very men for whom the "short card" player lies in wait, although he may be perfectly "square" the victim must necessarily be the loser, for a number of reasons. The first thing to be taken into consideration by the man who "knows it all" is the fact that a professional gambler plays to win. He never sits down to play for amusement. His bread and butter depends upon his winnings at the gambling table, and as a consequence he is ever on the alert to gain an advantage—by fair means if he can—by foul means if he must. Poker being the favorite American game, the professional card player makes that his specialty. In every large city, no matter how strictly the laws against gambling may be enforced, there can always be found poker-rooms, conducted for the purpose of money-making. In the majority of cases these rooms are run honestly, but that does not alter the fact that the room-keeper derives an extraordinarily large profit. Scarcely one player in a hundred takes into consideration what he pays for the privilege of playing a game. It is very easily reckoned if he stops to consider for a moment. Let five men with five dollars each sit down and play for five hours. At the end of that time, no matter if the game is honest as they run, the room-keeper will have every cent of that.

How? Any poker player who stops to think will readily figure it out. The "kitty" eats up everything. To those who do not understand the game it can be quickly explained. In a game of poker, certain "hands" are compelled to pay tribute to the room-keeper, to remunerate him for his rent, gas, attendance, and the cards which he furnishes players.

To explain all the swindling tricks with cards would take a formidable book. The favorite method is to "stack" the deck—that is, to arrange the cards in such a manner by a quick movement in shuffling, so that the dealer shall receive a better hand than his opponent. "Strippers," or a pack with certain cards just a trifle wider at the ends than the others is another method. After the victim has shuffled the cards the professional strips the deck—that is he pulls his thumb and finger longitudinally along the pack, and draws out the wide end cards, which he puts on top. He sees how many he pulls out and consequently knows where they go, giving him an unfair advantage.

These methods, however, are mere bagatelles compared with the trickery of the "three card monte" men, the "guessers" and the "thimble rigger." The monte man has a number of ingenious schemes to entice the unwary into betting on his game. Sometimes he pretends to be drunk, sometimes to be clumsy, but the regulation method is to have a confederate in the crowd who pretends to be a spectator. Three ordinary playing cards are used—say queen, ten spot and ace. The manipulator throws them face down on a board in front of him, and offers to bet anybody in the crowd that the queen cannot be picked out. Then he turns his head to expectorate, and at that moment the confederate, who has been standing close to the board, quickly picks up the queen, and turns down one corner so that every one can see it. The operator apparently does not discover this when he picks up the cards. and when he throws them again there is always some greeny who is willing to bet that he can pick out the lucky card. Mr. Sharper sees that the money is put up, and then greeny picks up the card with the turned corner, and finds it isn t the queen at all. Long practice has enabled the operator to turn up the corner of one card, and turn down the corner of another while throwing the cards.

The "thimble rigger" or "cup and ball man," is familiar to every one who has attended country fairs or who has seen a circus in a rural town, but those who have seen it at home will be inveigled into the game in the city—and of course lose everything. "Three little cups and three little balls—no deception, gentleman—step up and see if you can tell under which cup I have placed the little ball," is the cry of these fakirs, who do a wonderfully large business year in and year out, despite the frequent warnings given by the newspapers as well as by the victims. The deception is an extremely simple one and is aided by a confederate, or "capper" in the audience who points out exactly where the ball is when the operator's head is turned. Of course Mister Greeny bites, and puts up his money and that is the last he sees of it, because he loses his bet.

A contemptible set of rascals hang around depots in the principal seaport cities and waylay passengers who they know are about to sail to some foreign country. These sharps ask the victim if he wishes gold of the country he is to sail to for his American money. If he replies in the affirmative he is taken to a small broker's office where the money is fairly counted out in front of his face. Then he is made a present of a money belt which he is told to buckle around his waist. The money is put in the belt and the sharper assists in putting it on. The victim is then caused to turn his head and at that moment the belt is exchanged for another, similar in appearance, but filled with copper coins. This is strapped around the victim's waist and he is told not to open the same until the ship sets sail, as he may be robbed. As he has his ticket and a little spending money he does as told. When a few days out he opens his belt to examine his wealth and is horror stricken to learn he has been so thoroughly robbed and swindled.

Mock and fraudulent auction sales of gold watches and jewelry at forty or fifty per cent. less than the value of the gold are quite common, with the usual gaping crowd of innocents in attendance. The periodical bankrupt, and the nameless "assignee" of the unknown estate, are generally rank swindlers, and no matter what one buys or what price is paid they are sure to be swindled.

The shell workers of a city are considered petty thieves, and any one who is caught by the flimsy trick deserves all he gets. The way it is worked is easily told: The operator puts a pea between his finger and thumb, and while pretending to convey it under the half shell of an English walnut, he dexterously uses his thumb, and places the pea between the second and third fingers, where it is clipped or held tight; at the same moment he lifts one of the shells and perhaps, if very clever, may allow the pea to roll out of his fingers, and in a feigned condition of surprise and hurry instantly covers it, seemingly with another shell. The victim now fixes his eyes upon the latter, and is greatly surprised when it is raised to see the pea under it. The person deceived supposes, of course, that all the parade of placing the hand under the shell he is looking at is only a blind to draw his attention off from one of the others. The operator may so arrange matters that the pea is always concealed between his fingers, and if the three shells were knocked over simultaneously, the fraud would be at once discovered. If the pea is kept in the hand, the unfortunate person who is induced to bet upon the game must of course lose every time; but a clever trickster can always manage to deceive the eyes and leave the pea under one of the shells; and the victim is sure to select the wrong one.

The unwary visitor will come upon one of these bands in a city who are evidently playing the shell-game for their own amusement. They talk loud and become excited in their betting. The sight is a big treat to the stranger. He feels that he sees an example of city life, something he can go home and tell the folks about. He studies the faces of the men. He knows they are gamblers; he fancies that at night they inhabit the vilest resorts in the city, and the fact that he has come face to face with these characters, which he has so often read about, is a fascination. He even goes so far as to ask a few questions, because he desires to hear them talk. Their slang talk, full of oaths and expressions which he never heard before, fills him with wonder. All this time the gamblers take little notice of the visitors, or pretend to. Presently another (presumably) stranger comes along, and he, too, is interested in what the men are doing. He tells the real stranger he can " beat that game." The men keep on playing among themselves until the second stranger interrupts and wants to bet just for the fun of it.

" Of course; free game! " exclaims the worker.

Stranger No. 2 bets and wins.

Before he is aware of it stranger No. 1 also bets. He

may win also at first, but soon he loses. Strangers have been known to drop hundreds of dollars in an hour. Business men of no little repute from country towns have been "roped in" as well as green-horns. When they find their money gone they usually report the loss to the police. Perhaps the swindlers are caught, and perhaps not, usually not.

A man from the country is usually lured by ingeniously worded advertisements and makes an application for a position. He may be required to pay a sum of money for an outfit, put up a cash bond; invest a few hundreds in the business, "as a guaranty of good faith," it being hinted that an interest in the business will be given him if his work is satisfactory. The scheme is to extort money; give impossible work to perform and then declare contract unfulfilled and money forfeited. Don't pay any one for securing you work; don't put up a cash deposit; don't patronize intelligence offices; don't go in the employ of any concern without a good reputation before making inquiries about them.

A volume might be written on the traps set for the unsuspecting in a great city. The best advice that can be given is to attend strictly to your own business; deal only with reputable people; keep out of questionable resorts; keep your money and your wits about you and all will be well.

CHAPTER XIII.

BUNCO AND CONFIDENCE MEN.

How They Fleece the Unsuspecting Public—Requisites of a Confidence Man—Gullibility of the Public to be Wondered At—Swindling Reduced to a Fine Art—How They Work Their Games—Oily Tongued Rascals With Spurious Schemes—"Meeting a Friend From Home"—Fleeced by His "Friends"—How to Avoid the Bunco and Confidence Man—Working Country Fairs—How Weak Points of a Man are Discovered—Swindling Storekeepers—People Who Are Anxious to Get Rich Quick—Partnership Schemes—The Flim-Flam Trick Described—The Stranger Who Wants to Purchase a Farm—Working a Card Game—Honesty the Best Policy—Drawing Money From the Bank to Please Swindlers—Schemes to Extort Money by Force—Persuading People to do Idiotic Things—Let Strangers with Money Making Opportunities Alone.

The confidence operators are about the only class of talented criminals who flourish. The reason they flourish is because their victims seldom make complaint, preferring to suffer their loss rather than let the public know what fools they have been.

"Bunco" is a word familiar to all Americans, and the way these sharpers work should be carefully noted.

The "bunco gang" consists of three, sometimes four neatly dressed men. Number One is called the hand-shaker, or "first joint," who grasps by the hand a man whose appearance indicates that he would make a good subject for fleecing. The hand-shaker calls the stranger by the name of Mr. James Lawson, and finds out from him that his name is really Mr. John Link, of Bordentown, Iowa. The hand-shaker at once begs to be excused, as the gentleman so much resembled Mr. James Lawson, of Hammond, Ind. Mr. John Link, while explaining what his name really is, will naturally tell the hand-shaker that he is in town collecting some money due him for oats sold to Brown Brothers, which he intends to bank " to hum." The hand-shaker leaves him, and immediately joins the steerer, or " second joint," who receives all the information thus obtained. Then the steerer pulls out of his pocket a bank note reporter, which contains the names of all banks, names of presidents, vice-presidents, cashiers, etc. Looking for Bordentown, Iowa, he notices that Jacob Smith is president of the First National Bank there. He then jumps on the other side of the street, walks rapidly until he gets ahead of Mr. Link, then recrossing, comes toward Mr. Link, whom he meets. He looks at him for a moment, and exclaims, while grasping his hand: " Why, Mr. Link, who expected to see you here; how is my father, and how is all folks at Lamberton?"

It is unnecessary to state that Mr. Link is delighted to meet some one from Lamberton, but just now he can't remember his friend's name from home, but recognizes the face. The bunco man's reply is: " Why, Mr. Link,—well, I declare, that is a good joke,—not remember me! Why, I am Charlie, son of Jacob Smith, president of the First National Bank. I have been away from home for some time; I am with a wholesale house, and I am doing very well."

Then he goes on glibly to relate his success, treats his old friend nicely, and asks him if he will not just come around to a house where there is a very valuable oil painting which he has just won in a lottery—and he displays the ticket. Good-natured Mr. Link goes around with his friend, President Smith's son, and is induced to join Charlie in winning all the money which is displayed behind the screen in the bunco room, and of course if good Mr. Link puts up, he is fleeced by Charlie Smith's friends. If the money they obtain is a fair amount they vacate the rooms and engage another room, generally on the first floor of a furnished room house, and on a quiet side street.

In a number of cases where the man fleeced gives his check for the amount of money lost, he is apt to think it over after he leaves the game, and will conclude that he has been swindled, and is apt to have the payment of the check stopped on the ground of it having been obtained from him by fraud.

To prevent the stopping of payment of any check the bunco men so obtain, the steerer has a neat device. After his friend, Mr. Link, has lost his money and check, the steerer, having concealed in his hand a piece of paper about the size of a check, will quickly reach over, snatch up the check of Mr. Link, and exclaim, "You swindlers! you have cheated my friend out of this check, and you shan't have it," and while making a great bluster, will substitute the paper for the check, and commence to destroy the former by tearing and chewing it, causing Mr. Link to think that his check has been destroyed, and make him think Charlie Smith is a "right smart fellow." There is only one way to avoid the bunco man, and that is to make no chance acquaintances on the street. If you do, and are asked to take part in any speculation where to win it is necessary for you to put up a sum of money, you may depend you are in the hands of sharpers, unless you have previously informed yourself as to the standing of your new-found friends.

The confidence game which is closely identified with "bunco," is generally practiced in large cities, and upon verdant looking strangers, whose manners and attire evince the easy-going and susceptible victim. Of course, the most common, and, strange to say,. one of the most successful schemes, is that of watching either at railroad depots or hotels, for the genial and unsuspecting farmer or country merchant, whose well filled purse and general air of rusticity warrants a belief in his innocence and gullibility. The first move, therefore, is for one of the confidence men to approach the stranger, and with a frank and hearty salutation, to claim an acquaintance, as described in the bunco game.

Confidence men operate in gangs of two, three, or four, never more than four. They are, as a rule, good-looking, educated men, and are very careful in their dress. They are helped much if their whiskers are partly gray and their heads bald. Another method of the confidence man is this: He loiters about a hotel and bows right and left to guests. Finally he selects his victim and shakes hands with him. A conversation ensues, during which, at a prearranged signal, a confederate steps up and asks the operator to loan him some money or cash a check. The operator is unable to do so and turns to his new-found friend, who is glad to accommodate the gentleman. Before it can be found that the check is bad both the swindlers have disappeared.

Notwithstanding the warnings in the public press and the police officials of the country the bunco and confidence men swarm the country and find plenty of gullible people to operate on. Country fairs are usually regarded as a good operating field, as it brings together a large class not well versed in the ways and wiles of dishonest men.

To these places flock three-card monte men, chuck-a-luck and wheel-of-fortune sharps to pluck the uninitiated, and the guileless farmer will again find himself reposing in the confidence of the confidence man, unless he keeps his wits about him. A stranger will accost him—at country fairs there are lots of strangers—he will be very glad to see Mr. Jones. Your name not Jones? Smith? Oh, excuse me, Mr. Smith, a case of mistaken identity, I assure you, and after a suitable apology and a thousand and one excuses the stranger takes his departure. But Mr. Smith is not to escape. In the course of half an hour or an hour another gentleman greets Mr. Smith. Of course he knows Mr. Smith and all his family connections. Has known him for years. His father and Smith's father were great chums. Of course Mr. Smith does not know him, but if he is not aware he will know him to his financial cost before they are many hours older. This class of crooks are generally very smooth talkers, and have the knack of drawing their victims out to their utmost capacity. It does not take them long to discover the weak points of a man they are working and it is not long before they have him interested in making a fortune.

No matter what business a stranger accosts one about at a fair it can be set down as risky, questionable and generally a fraud and swindle. It would be well for the managers of fairs to caution their patrons against such people. They are generally dressed in the height of fashion and carry an expression of business capacity and importance, which serves their purpose to a great advantage.

To give a fair idea of the many ways to which confidence men resort in order to "rope" in the innocent, we call attention to the manner in which people are preyed upon by gentlemen of "fine address and sandy complexion," who reap an immense income from the storekeepers throughout the smaller towns in the country. The impostor in question goes to the storekeeper and represents he is authorized by Lord & Taylor, of New York, to place a small stock of notions with them, to be sold on commission. If they are not sold, at any time afterward the firm will take the goods back. The firm will bear all losses due to accident, and only exacts a small advance payment as a guarantee of good faith.

The alluring proposition of entering into commercial partnership with the powerful and prosperous New York firm proves irresistible. The cash payment is handed to the swindler in an envelope, which to all appearances he encloses in another large express envelope, seals, directs and returns to the storekeeper to be forwarded to Lord & Taylor. By artful manipulation, however, the envelope that holds the money is secreted up his coat sleeve or in his pocket, and an envelope containing worthless scraps of paper slipped into the express envelope and forwarded by post to Lord & Taylor. An "agreement" drawn up with high-sounding legal precision is handed the innocent victim, and the adroit thief pursues his way, seeking other trusting merchants.

The smaller dealers usually jump at the chance to take goods worth $500 to sell on commission, and pay $10 "guarantee" to the "agent." Payments were to be made by these fortunate storekeepers monthly, less 40 per cent. commission. A man foolish enough to take a long chance with strangers usually deserves all he gets.

Nine hundred and ninety-nine men out of a thousand are always ready and anxious to get exceedingly rich, and are ever anxious to grasp almost any opportunity to make a fortune where it requires but little outlay and less manual labor. It does not take the average confidence man long to discover just what kind of a scheme they would readily take hold of, and as a result, the unsuspecting victim is soon deeply pondering over papers and partnership propositions, etc., that contain highly colored pictures of the fortunes that are sure to be the outcome. All it requires is a few hundred dollars to get the thing in shape; won't the gentleman stand in with them; won't he put his name to that paper? Alas, he is too often too willing, and before he is aware of it someboby has a judgment note or some other kind of paper against him, of which he is not aware. He must either pay it or carry it to court, where nine times out of ten he will have double the amount to pay. His signature is no forgery; it is there in black and white, and no matter what excuse he may offer, he is compelled to pay up, which he often does to prevent his actions from being made public.

There are many forms of confidencing and buncoing that the public should be warned against. Flim-flamming is a quiet and easy manner of fleecing the unwary storekeeper. Keep your wits about you when making change. It is a simple matter to be flim-flammed out of a good sum, and any merchant is liable to be a vlctim, either of the unconscious or intentional flim-flammer. They operate in this manner: A customer owes a bill of $1.95 and tenders a $20 gold piece in payment. The merchant pulls a couple of $10 bills out of his pocket, lays them on the counter and then opens the cash drawer to get some small change.

"Hold on," says the customer, "I don't want to rob you of all your change. Come to think of it, I've got a couple of silver dollars here; just give me a nickel and we will be square."

And, handing the merchant the $2, the customer picks up the $20 gold piece and drops it into his pocket. Then he picks up the two $10 bills and the nickel and lays them away with the gold piece and walks out. The merchant studies the situation a few moments and then realizes that he is out $20. The customer who secured the money was an eminently respectable person, however, and the act of flim-flamming was undoubtedly a piece of absent-mindedness. All flim-flammers are not of this class, unfortunately, and a close eye should be kept on the change.

Frauds and swindlers representing newspapers and magazines fleece the public regularly. No reputable paper solicits business without giving their agents proper credentials which the public should always insist upon seeing.

Look out for the stranger that wants to buy your farm. They make you a price which you accept—say $5,000—and then produce a box said to contain that amount. Stranger No. 2 then appears and tells the farmer that there is no money in the box and offers to bet $4,000 on it, and will let the farmer in the scheme. No. 2 wins and tells the farmer that he can have half the money if he can produce a like amount to show that he meant business and that if he lost he would have been able to pay. The farmer usually goes to the bank and draws the money. It is all put in a tin box for safe keeping until they go to the barn to count it. The rascals are satisfied the farmer is honest, put his share in a box before his eyes, seal it and tell him not to open it until he gets to the bank. When his back is turned, the box is changed for one similarly arranged. They take leave of each other, the farmer chuckling over his good luck, and the rascals chuckling over their good luck too.

The card game is often worked to gull the farmer. It is a trick and a losing one every time. Don't play cards with strangers; don't get your money out of bank for any one; don't be fooled by any chance games on unbusiness like methods. You can not get something for nothing. Before you give any money to strangers consult your local banker. Be careful, be cautious, be honest, and above all don't think you can beat some other fellow's game.

Of course, not everybody can be operated upon, but the bunco-steerer is an almost infallible judge of human nature and rarely makes a mistake in selecting his subject. Take the hard-fisted farmer, who has fought the battle of life for sixty years and has been a winner all through. He has his hundreds of acres, his well appointed home, a comfortable balance in the bank, and some outside investments. He has mingled with the world, kept abreast of the times in reading and general information, has an unclouded brain and a keen mind for business. Along comes a stranger who, perhaps, seeks his advice regarding the purchase of some neighboring property. The conversation runs on the value of the land, quality of soil, yield of crops and kindred topics. It is said that an essential step in the process of swindling is to fix the attention of the subject on some bright object. A mental picture will serve as well as a material one—perhaps better under some circumstances. At all events, the farmer finds himself interested, even fascinated, and soon becomes apparently incapable of resisting any suggestion that his captor may make. Soon another stranger comes along who is a confederate of the first one. He says he is merely on a journey from one place to another, but he is companionable and in no particular hurry. The three have a jolly time together. Perhaps an innocent game of cards is played; perhaps a lottery scheme is displayed; perhaps investments are discussed. These are mere matters of detail.

The usual climax of the game is to induce the farmer on some pretext to withdraw his money from the bank where it is on deposit either to "demonstrate his responsibility" or for the purpose of placing it in some other bank in a neighboring town. The victim, strange to say, sees nothing out of the way in the proposition, though if in his right mind he would spurn the idea that a total stranger could induce him to do anything of the kind. But he does it and rides across the country with his new acquaintances. The sharpers now have no more time to waste. Force takes the place of *finesse*. When a suitable spot is reached they rob their victim by the simple process of knocking him over the head or holding a pistol to his face and helping themselves to his cash. They then drive rapidly away and somebody subsequently finds the farmer in a dazed condition by the roadside. This is one of many schemes used to fleece the unsuspecting. It is strange that a man usually safe and careful in all business matters; a money maker and saver; good judgment and well balanced, will under the influence of some smooth talking rascal virtually throw his savings away.

A writer has said that the bunco man and the confidence c erator are hypnotists. It is said that the secret of their success is solely due to hypnotic power. He persuades his victim to do the most idiotic things. He has, to be sure, an insinuating way, a glib tongue and a plausible style of putting things, but these are not enough. He also has a personality of the most positive characteristics and a will that projects itself with dominating force. After a certain point in reached the victim is helpless. He violates every known rule of prudence, buys lottery tickets, plunges into gambling games, pays his losses cheerfully, and even after his pockets have been emptied thinks his robbers are very good fellows, who under no circumstances would do a dishonorable act. It generally takes the buncoed man from twelve to thirty-six hours to gather his scattered wits together and come to the conclusion that he has made a fool of himself. Then he wonders how it was done, and is amazed at the temporary paralysis of volition that afflicted him. He probably has been hypnotized, but will never realize the fact.

It is curious how all sorts of people will invest their money on a wheel of fortune. There never was one made which don't give the operator 75 per cent. advantage to begin with, and by trickery this advantage is increased fifteen or twenty per cent. You must know that the operator has things so fixed that he can stop the wheel at will. If there is any raffling or dice shaking, it is all fixed, of course. In the prize drawings you may find gold and silver watches and sums of money displayed, but these cannot by any possibility be drawn. Let shell games, thimble rigging, and all games of chance severely alone. Mind your own business; keep your money in your own possession; be chary of making the acquaintance of strangers, and you will avoid trouble, loss and annoyance.

There is something so marvelous in the human heart in the way of its disposition to adventure in order to make money easily; such a wonderful credulity in the minds of large numbers of people, and a willingness to fasten in trust upon the merest shadow of success, that confidence men will never lack victims.

CHAPTER XIV.

PANEL THIEVES AND BLACKMAILERS.

How Blackmailers Ply Their Profession—The Panel Thief—Artful Women Who Tempt Men and Then Rob Them—How the Scheme is Worked—Catching a Man—The Spider and the Fly—The Attractive Woman—Part Played by the Husband—Robbing the Victim—How Easily the Work is Accomplished—How the Room is Arranged—New Panel and Blackmail Game—The Handsome Woman—The Photographic Blackmailing Scheme—Paying Tribute to Avoid Exposure—How a Photograph is Doctored—Blackmailing Respectable Women—A Nervy Procedure that Works—Ensnaring Innocent People—Alleged Detectives Who are Blackmailers—Cowardly Methods Adopted to Extort Money—Bogus Newspaper Men Who Levy Tribute to Suppress News—Blackmailing Business Men—Weak People Easy Victims of Blackmailers.

Among the many dangerous and curious characters who live by their wits in a great city none is more interesting to the "outsider" than the blackmailer. To the reader of sensational literature the ideal blackmailer is a person who holds some great family secret which he turns into money at rapidly narrowing intervals. Although this character is generally overdrawn, no one familiar with city life pretends to doubt his existence. The blackmailer is a well-known character in all large cities and certainly the arch swindler of the day.

Blackmailers are ever on the alert to learn anything detrimental to a person's character, and let them once obtain this and they fatten on it. Men's passions are taken advantage of by that particular class of thieves known as "badgers," and their operations are very rarely followed by exposure or punishment. A pretty woman is the bait used by these thoughtful rascals, who know full well that where a hundred men will resist a burglar, scarcely one will resist a robbery where disgraceful publicity must surely follow.

Briefly the mode of procedure is as follows:—A house is rented in a quiet side street, not far from the principal thoroughfare. One man, occasionally two men, run the house —that is, they do the actual stealing, while they have from three and often as high as a dozen women out on the street picking up the victims.

The qualifications necessary for the woman to have is to be pretty, plump, wear good clothes, and understand the art of making herself attractive. It is an understood thing that she shares one-third the proceeds of the robbery. The house is arranged especially for the purpose. The rooms on each floor are fixed so that the door separating them has the panels cut out and put in again on hinges, and fastened with a small button not noticeable. The hinges are well oiled, and a small hole is bored through the door, so that the thief can see into the room, or hear any slight signal given by the woman. The house rented has a front and rear entrance, the latter for the thief or thieves, who always station themselves on a corner of a street near the house, by which the woman will always bring the victim, so her pal can see him.

The woman goes out in the evening past the principal hotels and through the principal streets, never speaking to a man, but if she notices one who looks like a stranger and well-to-do, she will give him a coquettish glance and pass on, looking sideways to see if she is followed. If so, she will continue slowly, turning the first quiet street, until the man who follows her has a chance to overtake her. The chances are ten to one that he will address her. She will appear shy at first and not inclined to speak, but after a short time she will talk, and after some conversation she will convey the idea to the man that she is a married woman ; that her husband is out of town and no one is at home. If he will be discreet he may accompany her to her home, she says, and have a talk. The pair then walk to the house, passing the corner where the male accomplice is lying in wait, and the woman, pulling out her latch-key, will open the door; and the fly is in the parlor of the spider.

The male thief waits a few moments and then makes his way into the house through the rear. As soon as he enters he takes off his shoes and in his stocking feet stations himself in the adjoining room, and there bides his time. The woman is all smiles and affection. She betrays an affected nervousness, which makes her all the more attractive. She talks about the sudden fancy she took to the gentleman who was weak enough to be inveigled, and in a thousand and one ways manages to give the idea that he is, above all others, the very man she could have. All this time she is gradually disrobing, and at the expiration of about ten minutes she is ready to do her part of the robbery.

Meantime her male accomplice has put on his shoes. He goes around to the front of the house, opens the front door noisily, and, walking heavily, he knocks loudly at the room door, and calls out, "Mary!" or any name that may suggest itself. The woman will at once exclaim, "Oh! that is my husband! Dress yourself quickly, and be ready to go out as soon as I get him away from the room door."

The victim will hastily put on his clothes, and as soon as the woman slips out and gives him the signal he escapes, only too glad not to be caught. Before he goes, however, and while he is talking to the woman, her pal has opened the panel, put his hand in all of the victim's pockets—(his clothes having been put in front of the door), and nearly all his money is taken. A portion is left, so that he may not immediately discover his loss. Jewelry is never disturbed, as it would be missed at once. The favorite method is to take out the middle of a roll of notes, if in a roll, or if in a pocket-book, the bottom notes are removed, so that when the victim examines his purse hurriedly he will not discover that he has been robbed. If the amount stolen is large the house is vacated, and the woman skips the town for a time.

The women who work for these badger houses work in one city for a time, then go to the next large city with a note to the thief who runs the house there. The women generally wear wigs, so in case the man reports his loss to the police he will perhaps describe a fair-haired women when perhaps her hair is black. A blonde wig is discarded, the case is fixed.

A female badger and her lover may be poor and unable to rent a house. In this event they will rent a furnished room in a furnished-room house, the bolt on the door is fixed by simply taking out the screws from the nose of the bolt, and the screw holes are enlarged. The screws are well greased and then put back, the key taken out of the lock, so when the time comes for the thief to go in as previously described, he pushes in the door easily and quietly, as the hinges are well oiled, and the victim is robbed while he is making violent love to the supposed "married woman."

Only a downright fool or egotist can become the victim of this scheme. He deserves to lose whatever he has if he is foolish enough to be taken in. The only way to protect yourselves against the work of these thieves is to mind your own business.

The new panel and blackmail swindle called the "Photographic Catch" is one that dupes are frightened into paying hush-money, and otherwise putting themselves in the hands of unscrupulous and designing people.

The old panel game has been brought up to date and is being worked vigorously. This new swindle is one of the coolest " bluffs " ever attempted to be worked upon an unsuspecting person.

The victim selected by the coterie of choice spirits who work this fraud is always a married man. The blackmailers learn about his habits and if his wife and family have removed to the country they immediately set about landing him in their net. If the family remains in town the swindlers spot their man and wait until his wife and children go to the country or seashore, leaving him to " work himself to death " in the bad, wicked city.

The bait used is a handsome young woman. She soon finds an opportunity to attract the attention of the victim, who is always a business man, generally of middle age and wealthy, for upon handsome but penniless clerks they do not waste a moment of their time.

As soon as the intended victim has taken the bait he is enticed to some luxuriously furnished apartment. It makes not the slightest difference how long he may stay there, and it is not even important what he may do there.

In the course of a day or two the victim is called upon at his place of business by a tall, well-dressed young man of gentlemanly manners, but with much firmness. This is one of the conspirators. He secures a private interview with his unsuspecting victim, and as soon as the door is closed he proceeds to outline his little game.

He pulls from his pocket an alleged instantaneous photograph showing the victim in a compromising position, and for the sake of appearances, makes some broad hints about his outraged feelings as a husband. It very soon develops that these outraged feelings can be assuaged by the payment of money, and the sum mentioned is always a large one.

The victim is thrown into a state of fright by threats of exposure liberally made by the conspirators, and freely "gives up" in order to put a stop to the matter. He gets a considerable reduction upon the original sum demanded by paying down the cash.

Now, while this game is nearly always successful, it requires but a moment's reflection on the part of any intelligent man to see that it is a swindle pure and simple, the exposure of which would put a stop to it. The payment of the money is compelled by displaying a photograph with threats of sending it to the victim's wife.

Anybody who knows anything about photography will see at once that such a photograph must be fraudulent. It is impossible to take an instantaneous photograph in a room without a flashlight. It is likewise impossible to photograph the interior of a room lighted by gas without a very long exposure, generally extending over hours. No court of law would place any reliance upon an alleged instantaneous photograph of the inside of a house professing to show people who were unconscious that they were being photographed. If any such picture were to be used as a means of establishing evidence in court it is not unlikely that the person so producing it would get into prison as an impudent impostor.

The photograph which is used by the gang working this new panel game is, of course, a fraud made up by the conspirators. It is an easy enough thing for them to secure a picture of the interior of the room, showing another person. But in order to get the victim into the picture it is necessary that a photograph be taken of him elsewhere; probably in the street. Then his features are pasted on the photograph of the room, which is again placed before the camera and reproduced complete. No matter how skillfully such piecing together is done, it always shows to the practiced eye, and any professional photographer can detect the fraud.

With the guilty knowledge of such swindling in their mind, the conspirators who impudently produce such pictures can easily be "turned down" by a brief explanation of their criminal proceedings and a threat to turn them over to the police. They confine their operations to gentlemen who have been indiscreet and who can be easily frightened into paying money to prevent a scandal.

Blackmailing the wives of business men is carried on to quite an extent, and it is astonishing how many of them will pay blackmailers to hush up something that really amounts to nothing if the same were exposed. If you refuse to pay blackmail, that usually ends it They want money, and when they fail to get that, the matter drops.

The blackmailer operates on women in this manner: A man has an accomplice, a woman who passes as, and probably is, his wife. She is well educated, of refined appearance, and dresses fashionably and well. The two work together. As the summer season comes on and the wives of business men, who cannot leave business themselves, start for Eastern resorts and watering places, the woman blackmailer joins the exodus. She knows the people who are wealthy, and these she spots. She watches their every movement, and if the slightest indiscretion is committed it does not escape her eye. She knows the names, business, and homes of all the gentlemen they meet, and when and where they meet them.

The season ended, the facts she has obtained are in the hands of the male partner and he studies them. Selecting his victim, he arranges to meet her, as if by chance, usually is one of the leading retail establishments of the city where she resides. He approaches and addresses her with the greatest cordiality, expressing surprise at the unexpected meeting. She is generally surprised, and of course fails to recognize him. Then he uses the name of one of the gentlemen she has met in the East, recalls who introduced them, where the meeting occurred, and, in fact, all about it. Then she recalls it, or thinks she does, and it ends in her inviting him to call at her home. Here is the web quite complete.

He calls, and, of course, when her husband is out, and may repeat the call several times. Then he springs the trap. During one of his visits a note arrives for the lady threatening disclosures unless paid, say $100. Even if innocent of any wrong, the woman is alarmed and shows the blackmailer the note. He appears greatly alarmed also, declares that he is a married man, and that to have his visits known would ruin him. He argues that the money would better be paid. He has only $40 about him, but if the hostess will advance the balance of course she shall lose nothing. She does it, and is thereafter in the power of the blackmailer.

A fraud claiming to be a detective often visits a reputable business man, having gained knowledge of indiscretion early in life. To hush it up they will demand from time to time money under threats of exposure, thus causing the person to commit crime after crime to satisfy the heartless leach who never stops until his victim is ruined.

In a similar manner does the alleged detective blackmail a man who has committed a crime and who has been imprisoned for it. Upon his release the man may feel like reforming and becoming a good citizen if given the chance, but this the detective will not permit, for as soon as he notices the ex-convict he will say, " Look here, young fellow, you know my name and address, and when I am in of an evening I want you to come and see me or I'll have you run in." The fear of being " run in" forces the man who has a desire to do right to steal to satisfy the blackmailing demands of this corrupt class of people. If the ex-convict obtains employment he is worked in a similar manner, under threats of exposure to his employer, and so forced to steal, and then the smart detective will exclaim, "There is no reformation in that fellow; I knew he would steal. He will never stop."

One of the most contemptible of creatures is the store-keeper who has caught some one (who has the appearance of having money), stealing some trifling article, and will exclaim, "Here, here! I have had stolen three hundred dollars' worth of goods by some one, and if you will settle for all I have had stolen, I will let up on you, and not prosecute."

These cowardly methods are simply mentioned to show to what depths of meanness some men will descend, and are not to be classed with the professional thief, with whom stealing is a trade. As to how the female blackmailer can be foiled, the remedy is obvious, and no man who possesses proper self-respect will ever become a victim.

One of the most dangerous blackmailers in large cities is the man who pretends to be a journalist and who threatens his victim with exposure unless a certain amount of money is forthcoming. This is worked by a very simple method. The blackmailer first obtains some information about the early life of the person he intends to approach, and there are very few men who have not in their youthful days committed some indiscretion which might be brought against them after reaching maturer years. An escapade with a woman, or a mischievous boyish prank which proved more serious than was intended, are the usual indiscretions selected, and there can always be found plenty of gossips who are only too willing to relate full particulars. The information thus obtained is written up in a sensational style, and is taken to a cheap printing office, where it is put in type for a trifling cost. A slip, or what is known in a printing office as a "proof," is then printed, and armed with this the blackmailer pays a visit to the person he intends to fleece. He represents himself as being connected with a reputable newspaper, and says that he has been sent to get the "other side of the story," at the same time producing the slip on which is printed the startling tale, which, if made public, would in all probability seriously affect the social standing and the commercial integrity of the intended victim. In the majority of cases the person approached will at once inquire how much the newspaper would pay for such an article, and the reply usually is, "From twenty to twenty-five dollars." "Suppose I pay for the article instead of the newspaper?" says the victim, "and I give you fifty dollars, wouldn't that repay you for trouble in writing the article?" This is just what the blackmailer has been waiting for. He hems and haws for awhile, so as not to appear too anxious, or for the purpose of getting a higher bid, but the interview usually winds up in his securing a sum of money to suppress the information. As he is leaving the house it may occur to the victim that as long as the story is known to the editor of the paper there may be a publication anyhow, and on this point he makes inquiry. "Oh," says the blackmailer, "there will be no danger of that. I will report that I have fully investigated the story, and that there is not a word of truth in it, and of course they will not dare run the risk of being sued for heavy damages for printing it."

There is no necessity for any man being victimized by the "newspaper beat." In the first place no reputable newspaper ever puts a damaging story in type before every side of it has been thoroughly investigated. The very fact of a man exhibiting a "proof" is evidence that he is a fraud and has no newspaper connection. It can be said with truth that the reportorial profession of America has fewer "beats" in it than any other profession or business that can be mentioned. The majority of reporters are ambitious to gain higher positions, and it is a rare thing to find a man regularly connected with a newspaper descending to such trickery. If he is a genuine reporter he will exhibit his credentials, and should he be assigned to investigate a story that affects the standing of a respectable citizen, and be offered a bribe, he would undoubtedly publish that fact as an additional proof of the truth of what he has written. The treatment for this kind of a blackmailer is to kick him out of the house, and bid him do his worst. Depend upon it, the "scandal" will never become public.

A New York City police official who is thoroughly conversant with the blackmailer's art and method says the scheme they work nowadays is this:

They watch some disreputable resort of the higher order until they see some respectable looking man or woman coming out of it. Suppose it is a woman who may or may not have gone there for an improper purpose. The blackmailer follows her home, thus ascertaining her place of residence. The next day he calls upon her. He puts on an air of deep solemnity.

"I am an agent," says he, "employed by a society to ascertain the character of certain suspected houses. I saw you enter one of them yesterday and know that you remained there more than an hour. You know its character, and I shall therefore subpœna you as a witness." Then he puts his hand in his inside pocket as if to get the subpœna.

Of course he hasn't any, but the woman usually faints about this time, and on her recovering is usually willing to take the jewels off her wrists and fingers, if she has no money, to buy her immunity from the subpœna. Once she makes a payment she is lost and has to continue it month after month and year after year, till some kind of a scandal breaks out and she finds, with shame and sorrow, that her previous payments have only put off the evil day.

CHAPTER XV.

JEWELRY AND DIAMOND THIEVES.

The Work of a Shrewd, Versatile and Ingenious Class—Articles of Great Value Always Objects of Temptation—A "Pennyweighter" and His Work—How They Dress and Operate—Stealing Diamond Jewelry—The Duplicate Envelope Game—Substituting a Paste Diamond for a Good One—How to Detect a Jewelry Thief—Breaking Store Windows—How Plate Glass Windows are Split—Fastening the Door—The Umbrella Trick—Stealing Loose Diamonds—Licking up Stones—Attracting a Clerk's Attention—The Watch Thief—Constant Fear of Jewelers and Diamond Merchants—The Diamond Thief and His Methods—The Ingenuity of Jewelry Thieves—Despoiling Jewelry Establishments—The Handkerchief and Hat Trick—When Jewelry Thieves Work—Trick of Diamond Thieves—How Diamonds are Secreted—How to Select Diamonds—Tricks of the Trade—Bogus Diamonds—To Test a Genuine Diamond—Artificial Diamonds—Counterfeiting Gems—Precious Stones Imitated—Painting Gems—Loaning Money on Diamonds—Work of the Jewelers Protective Association—Watching Traveling Salesmen—How to Thwart Jewelry and Diamond Thieves.

It is natural that articles of great value are objects of temptation. There is no class of business men that stand more in constant fear of thieves than the jewelry and diamond merchants. With these people eternal vigilance is the price of security. All sorts of dodges and schemes are worked and if the exposures and suggestions given in this work are heeded, the work of this class of marauders will be reduced to a minimum.

Jewelry thieves are known by the slang term of "pennyweighters," and their pursuit is termed "pennyweighting."

Gold chains are especial objects of their search. They are more easily stolen than any other article, and a market can always be found for them. A "pennyweighter" is necessarily well dressed. One hand is generally gloved, and the other glove is carried loosely. When the chains are on a tray, and are not hung on separate hooks, he will lay down the glove beside one he wants to steal, and pick it up with the glove. If there is not such an opportunity he will lay the glove on the glass case, and examine several chains, when it is an easy matter for him to drop a chain into the palm of his hand. Then handing back one of the others which seems to strike his fancy, he will inquire the price. While the salesman is looking at the tag the thief seizes the opportunity to dispose of the palmed chain by picking up his glove with the hand that contains the chain, and dropping the chain into his pocket while seeming to put away the glove. Chains are generally stolen by palming, and there are several ways of disposing of the pilfered articles. It is a natural thing for a purchaser to draw a chain across his breast to see how it looks. This action is a favorite one with the "pennyweighter," for in doing so he has no difficulty in dropping the palmed chain into his vest pocket.

Another way is to take out a pocket-handkerchief to wipe the mouth, and thrust back the chain with it. The manner of stealing jewelry on cards is similar. A number of cards are examined, and when several are in the hand it is an easy matter matter to palm one, which may be disposed of in the same manner as a chain. Two "pennyweighers" generally work together, only one of whom steals. The other serves to divert the salesman's attention when necessary. There is no particular locality affected by this class of thieves. They work equally well in large cities as in country villages—better, in fact, because in the rural districts they would be known to be strangers, and would be regarded with that suspicion which is usually accorded to all visitors.

At times "pennywrighters" purchase gold settings, in which they have set paste stones of different sizes and styles. They then stop in a jewelry store, look at diamond rings, and with the assistance of a partner, the clerk's attention is taken for a moment from the tray of diamond rings. Then the thief, with the paste stone ring of his own already in the palm of one hand, lifts up his hand, and with his other hand picks out a diamond ring as near in appearance to his paste as possible. He skillfully substitutes one for the other in the tray, an operation that requires only a second, and as the tray is generally full, a bare space where the ring had been would at once be noticed—hence the substitute.

Diamond jewelry displayed on the cardboard has been stolen in the following manner:—The jewelry is picked out, and the purchaser (the thief) will say, "I want to place this jewelry in an envelope; be kind enough to put it aside for me; I will leave a deposit of ten dollars on it for an hour or so." If he can avoid it he will not leave the deposit. If the clerk assents, the thief produces an envelope from his pocket, places the jewelry therein, and seals it. Then he asks for a pencil to write his name and address. The clerk's attention is called off for a second, and in on instant a duplicate envelope is quickly produced, filled like the one in which the jewelry had been placed, and is substituted. The jeweler lays it aside to be called for.

Of course that is the last seen of the customer. Loose diamonds are a field for neat and well-dressed thieves. They purloin a paper of the diamonds as skillfully as a prestidigitateur.

There is no difficulty in detecting a jewelry thief if the proper method is pursued. His eyes, and not his hands, are to be watched. His eyes will invariably indicate the actions of his hands, for he never steals until he looks to see if the coast is clear. The " pennyweighter," as a rule, is an adept and does not attempt to ply his dishonest calling until after many months of practice and observation.

Nothing should induce a man behind a jewelry counter to remove his eyes for an instant from the eyes of his supposed customer.

Breaking store windows for purpose of robbery has been brought to a system of which few persons are aware of. It is a bold piece of work and requires a man of some nerve to attempt it.

The old method was to smear molasses on a pane of glass and then stick a sheet of paper thereon. After that the glass was forced in and the sticking paper prevented the pieces from falling and making a noise, that was for the robbery of store windows after closing hours. The style of having large plate glass windows suggested another mode of breaking glass which was by inserting the sharp end of a three cornered file under the glass and between the wood work and the lower edge, and then giving the file a quick turn splitting the glass. The piece broken is pried out without a loud noise.

Smashing windows for jewelry is first done by fastening the store door, if it is a double door, by a flat piece of boiler iron fourteen inches long and twelve wide, with a two inch wide slit cut in it. This is hung on the handle of the door so that it cannot be opened from the inside. As soon as the iron is put on, a stone in the toe of a stocking is held in one hand and smashed against the window, which is broken. Then the jewelry is jerked out. Before the astonished inmates can realize what has happened or come out, the thieves are away. Later on an iron plate similar to a shield with handle in the back and a sharp iron rod projecting out about five inches, which was pushed with force against the window, was adopted. This carried the window in and left an opening fully large enough to clean out the contents.

Advice :—Use a revolver and with your best ability. There is no prevention.

A frequent ruse of jewelry thieves is to visit a store on a rainy day and while examining jewelry drop a few pieces in an umbrella. This game is repeatedly worked on unsuspecting jewelers and usually with marked success. Jewelers should be on their guard against this.

But perhaps the cleverest of all tricks is the "pennyweighter" game. It is known but to a few and practiced by a still smaller number, for it is a difficult one. It has been most successfully worked in many parts of the country. The mode of working is for a thief to go to a jewelry store and ask to be shown loose diamonds on a tray. He pretends to be very shortsighted and bends over and very close to the tray, examining the diamond through an eyeglass. He exposes his left hand so as not to be suspected, and at a propitious moment drops a one carat diamond into the tray and with his tongue, on the point of which he has pulverized alum, he licks up a two carat diamond. He cannot find the exact counterpart of the one he wants to match (which he has not with him) and goes to another store, where he exchanges his two carat diamond in a similar manner for a three carat, and so on *ad infinitum*.

Nearly all jewelry stores are fitted up with tall show-cases, which are arranged against the wall, behind the cases on the counters. In these cases the silverware and large articles are kept for display. The counters are generally short, arranged in rows with passage ways between them, and on these the cases containing watches and the smaller articles of jewelry are tastefully exhibited on small trays. The thieves enter the store and one of them, securing the attention of the clerk, walks deliberately behind the counter, and pointing to some article of silverware in the case against the wall, engages the clerk in bargaining for its sale. While thus engaged he stands between the counter and the clerk, who is obliged to turn his back to the counter in order to face his supposed customer. While this is going on his attention is entirely diverted from the other thief, who seizes the first favorable opportunity to transfer some of the most valuable articles on the counter case to his own pockets and to pass quickly out of the store unsuspected.

An easily worked swindle on jewelers is for a man to send a firm a watch for repair either by mail or express. Later a man will call and demand the watch, representing himself as the one who sent it. Of course the jeweler is satisfied he is the rightful owner, as no one knows anything about the transaction. In about a week a stranger, claiming to be the original consignor, lays claim to the watch, and it not being forthcoming demands damages. The jeweler will compromise. It has been discovered that a gang of swindlers are playing this game on jewelers throughout the country, and that they are in collusion with employes of express companies. Look out for this fraud.

All jewelers have to be continually on the lookout for diamond thieves. A diamond thief is the slickest of all thieves. The thief may be a man, or perhaps a woman, but in either case their tricks are numerous and hard to keep track of. They are indefatigable in their labors, and when one scheme fails they try another. There is no way to guard against them, and eternal vigilance alone is the price of safety, or, rather, the safety of a jeweler's goods. The diamond thief employs many original schemes and is versatile and ingenious to a high degree. Men in the trade have learned to distrust everybody, be it man or woman, and when inspecting goods a sharp watch is kept on them.

There are tricks suited for every emergency, and the thieves are a smart class of rogues. They think of everything. A Buffalo jeweler was recently robbed of a number of watches, and although the scheme tried was by no means a new one, it worked successfully. It was this: An old man came into the store at the proper time, leaning on a cane. He waited his opportunity, until the watch-repairer left his place, and then, reaching over his cane, which was supplied with a hook on the bottom, he quietly helped himself to a number of the best watches and departed.

The diamond thief is abroad in the land wherever a jewelry store is to be found, and his operations generally leave a lasting impression on the memory of those he visits. A thief will enter a jewelry store, and while examining a number of diamond rings substitute a paste one in place of the real. The theft is generally not discovered until too late. This is a very common trick, and it needs the closest watch on the part of the clerks to prevent a clever thief from changing rings. Another feature of the case is that it is a difficult matter to trace a stolen diamond after a brief time has elapsed.

The fact is, stones of a given weight resemble each other too closely to admit of detection when the setting has been changed. Unless there is some flaw or peculiarity about a stone it is an almost impossible thing to identify it.

There seems to be no limit to the ingenuity of jewelry thieves. Every appliance that can thwart them has been purchased by the tradesmen regardless of expense; organized bands of the shrewdest detectives are constantly on the alert and keep a sharp eye on all suspicious characters, and every large jewelry establishment employs a lynx-eyed detective to look after its own particular interests. Despite these barriers the jewelry thief occasionally makes a big haul right under the noses of the detectives. Often there is no trace of the goods or thieves ever discovered.

Recently two thieves walked into one of the largest jewelry stores in Philadelphia and asked to be shown some gold chains. As the system against robbery was supposed to be perfect in the establishment, the salesman spread chains to the value of $5,000 on the counter in the white flannel rolls. They selected half a dozen chains, and handed the salesman a roll of bills in payment. As he left his customers to go to the cashier's desk the thieves picked up the three rolls containing 150 chains and leisurely walked out of the store. The robbery was executed in a masterly manner, and no trace of the goods, which were worth nearly $5,000, or the thieves has ever been discovered.

The system of espionage in the larger establishments, however, is daily growing more effective, and the ingenuity of the jewelry thief will have to make big strides in order to keep pace with the safety systems. Despite these precautions an occasional robbery of large proportions startles the trade and causes consternation for a time until the newest trick is met by an equally ingenious preventative on the part of the jewelers.

If the artistic thieves exhaust their cunning in the robbery of big jewelry establishments, their less accomplished brethren are almost equally as ingenious in their methods of despoiling the smaller stores. About two years ago they descended upon Philadelphia in droves, and the jewelers became panic-stricken at the bold robberies that were of almost daily occurrence. Their favorite method was to visit the stores in pairs, engage the jeweler's attention, and snatching a tray of rings or watches, dash out and lock the man in his own store by inserting a thick stick in the door-latch. These robberies were repeated with such startling success that the jewelers became thoroughly alarmed, and, with but few exceptions every door-latch that permitted the operation of this trick was changed.

As a magician some jewelry thieves' skill is equal to Herrmann's. They will walk into a store, and, looking the clerk firmly in the eye, as a sleight-of-hand man does when he is about to deceive you, will ask to see some chains or whatever he prefers that day. Then he will take off his hat lay it on the counter, pull out his handkerchief, and after mopping off his forehead lay the handkerchief also on the counter before him. The clerk will show him three or four chains from a tray. He will examine them, and, taking one from the rest, he will fling it back at the clerk, saying: "Lay this aside for me; I will be back in an hour." But with his other hand, while the clerk's attention is diverted, he will slide the other chains into the handkerchief and quietly put the whole business in his pocket. He is also so deft with his fingers that he could catch hold of one end of a chain and flip the whole chain up his coat sleeve without detection from the clerk.

Thieves often run a circle on a show window or show case and pushing same in by pressing or hitting same with a pin of iron incased in woolen cloth, to avoid noise, abstract everything in sight and decamp.

Many jewelers in an eastern city have been duped by thieves who kept watch on the windows of the chief stores and made paste gems to imitate those displayed. Then on a given day members of the gang visited the different stores, made small purchases, looked at the jewelry displayed in the windows, but declined to buy on account of the high price. They succeeded in nearly every instance, however, in substituting the imitation jewelry for the real, and got away with a great deal of property without detection. Some jewelers have adopted a new system, and now display imitations only in their windows, keeping the real gems inside.

Asking a jeweler to display a tray of diamonds then throw cayenne pepper in his eyes, is an old game. No jewelry store should be left with only one man in charge.

A favorite time for thieves to work in jewelry stores is when a large parade is attracting the attention of the people and most everybody is upon the street. Look out for bogus drummers. Their plan is to enter the store at a time when it is empty of customers and nearly so of clerks, bringing in big trunks to convey the impression that they are drummers, and getting the proprietor off his guard, while the other men make away with diamonds and anything else of value in sight.

A very ingenious and clever trick of diamond thieves is to call upon a firm and ask to see some diamonds, and after examining them for some time, he returns the paper saying he would call again in reference to buying them. It is at once noticed that a large stone is missing. A hasty search is made, but no trace of the diamond being discovered the customer without more ado is accused of having taken the brilliant. He indignantly denies the charge and submits without hesitation to being searched.

The stone is not found and profuse apologies are offered for the false accusation The following day the customer appears again, this time with a paper of diamonds to sell, but also with another object in view, which he takes good care not to disclose. A careful observer might have noticed that while the stones were being examined at the light the customer runs his fingers along the under surface of the portion of the counter near which he sat and picked off something that stuck to the wood. It was nothing more nor less than the diamond which had so mysteriously disappeared the day before. He had fastened it to the counter by means of a piece of wax with which he had provided himself, and on the occasion of his second visit secured his booty.

[A chapter in another portion of this work on "How Safes are Broken" should be carefully read by every jeweler in the country. The method of safe breaking is fully explained and other methods there explained is applicable to all kinds of safes.]

When purchasing diamonds do not go to a pawn broker and expect a bargain, but patronize a reputable firm and you will never have cause for regret. When people are choosing diamonds they should ask themselves the following questions: Is their trasparency conspicuous? How much do they resemble a dewdrop hanging from a white rose; that is, are they of pure water and do they possess the power of refraction to a high degree? Have they a full play of color? Are the facets sharply cut and perfectly defined? Is the stone of good proportions—not shallow, proportionate to face? Lastly, has it perceptible imperfections? The latter point is in itself sufficient reason why diamonds should be purchased from responsible retailers whose guarantees are not of wind and who would be willing to rectify any accidental error. Two diamonds may appear of perfectly equal worth to the uninitiated but a flaw in one of them might cut its value in two, and nobody but a good judge could even see the fault.

The three main flaws are termed "feathers," "clouds," and "sand." "Feathers" are little rents or fissures in the interior of the stone. At times there may be a half-dozen of these flaws that cannot be detected without the aid of a glass, and then only by those who know how to look for them. "Clouds" are gray, brown, or white spots, also in the interior of the stone, and are much easier to find than "feathers." "Sand" is seed—like little bodies, usually of white, brown or neutral tints. When unusually fine and in large numbers this flaw is termed "dust." A few stones are also "chipped"—that is, there are fissures on the exterior edges of the facets. A bad chip or two largely reduces the value of a fairly good stone.

In an article where not one in a thousand has any knowledge and not one in ten thousand is a connoisseur there is necessarily a great deal of imposition. The tricks of the trade may be divided into three general sections. The first and most common is when flawed, imperfect, or off-colored stones are sold for first-water gems. There is no such thing as an absolutely perfect, flawless diamond any more than there is a perfect specimen of humanity in the world. What are called perfect stones are gems as flawless as any found, but if a glass of high power is used imperfections can be found in the best of them. The selling of poor stones as perfect ones takes place every day and almost every minute. The principal sufferers are would-be smart people who snatch at a "bargain" and get the worst of the deal. If people would recollect that fine diamonds are the easiest things in the world to sell; that any jeweler who deals in gems is always willing to purchase at a small reduction from prevailing rates, they would not be imposed upon so often.

The other two methods are simply robbery. Many imitation stones are still sold as genuine brilliants. In Europe, especially in Paris, the art of making fine imitations of diamonds has been brought to perfection. Many of these, of course, are sold for what they are, many are made up to order for wealthy people who in temporary difficulties wish to raise money on the real goods, and have these stones set in the same style to wear while the genuine articles are lying at their "uncle's." A fine imitation stone is often put into "cluster" or "half-hoop" rings by an unscrupulous jeweler. Some have even been set as solitaires (rings or earrings) and sold as genuine. Small fine paste has been used in combination with colored gems, such as rubies, emeralds, sapphires and others, and when so mounted they can victimize good judges and dealers.

The third method is another bare-faced swindle. There are several precious stones which are of an entirely different composition from the diamond, but resemble that gem so closely that none but experts can distinguish them, and even they have often to subject them to severe tests before they can discover the imposition. The basis of the diamond, as almost everybody knows, is carbon. The stones referred to have as their base alumina, and they are known in the trade under the general term "carodums." The principal varieties sold and substituted for diamonds are the white sapphire, white topaz, and the jargon or zircon. All these imitate, when properly cut, the second-class diamonds with the most perfect fidelity, and when mounted an expert can seldom positively determine their genuineness.

A white sapphire or topaz is worth from $2 to $6 a carat, jargon much less, and the poorest quality of diamonds cannot be bought for several times the maximum. Bushels of the stuff have been and are still sold for diamonds. When experts have an opportunity to test them properly they can discover the fraud on account of their inferior hardness and the difference in specific gravity. The specific gravity of the diamond—flawless or flawed, Indian, Brazilian or African—is always 3.9, that of white topaz and sapphire is 3.5; of jargon, 4.4. But for all that dealers have been stuck with this stuff by mixture with the right goods, and even our firm has not altogether escaped.

A simple test to tell whether a diamond is genuine or not is to make a small dot on a piece of paper with a lead pencil, then look at the dot through the diamond. If you can see but one dot the stone is genuine, but if the mark is scattered, or shows more than one, you will be perfectly safe in refusing to pay ten cents for a stone that may be offered you at five hundred dollars.

Electricity is now used to detect paste diamonds from the genuine. A small disk of aluminum is attached to the spindle of a small motor. A clamp, with a small flat spring, provided with an adjustable screw, holds the article to be tested. It is then moistened and placed in contact with the rapidly revolving aluminum disk. If the stone is a genuine one it will be left intact; if it is bogus it will show brilliant metallic marks.

The practical production of the diamond by artificial means has been the theme of a great deal of thought and a good many experiments, but up to this time it has eluded all the efforts of the experimenters, though carbon crystals closely approaching the gem have more than once been secured, while many persons still think it is merely a matter of time and not a long one at that, when this secret will have been wrenched from nature.

The finest imitation diamonds are made out of rock crystal. The basis of the most successful counterfeits of all kinds of the gem is a pure, very dense and highly transparent sort of glass, which is termed "paste" by the trade. For false diamonds this glass is simply cut and polished in facets, while for imitating other stones, such as rubies, emeralds, sapphires, etc., metallic oxides are mixed with it.

Attempts have been made, but not without success, to form minerals. Artificial ultramarine has long been an article of commerce. The formation of the diamond is said to have been actually effected, but the process is so difficult and so dangerous that the diamond miner and the diamond merchant need not feel uneasy. The ruby and the sapphire have lately been reproduced in Paris, and, curiously enough, the coloring matter in both is found to be due to one and the same metal —chromium—in different states of combination. Red and blue stone, or an intermediate violet form which might be likened to the rare and beautiful oriental amethyst, have been obtained in one and the same operation from the same lot of material. The jewels thus produced have so far all been small—large enough to form the pivots of superior watch-works, but not large enough to rank as rare and costly ornamental objects.

Artificial pearls and rubies are now made with such skill as to deceive experts and introduce confusing conditions into the commerce of these costly and precious ornaments.

One would suppose that the expert knowledge of diamonds had extended so that no rogue would think for a moment of endeavoring to deceive the eye by any trick not positively the work of genius, and which depended largely for success upon its complete novelty of method. The old scheme of painting these gems so as to make yellow stones resemble the most beautiful blue white, is again being practiced to some extent, Even a connoisseur may be deceived in a careless moment or a poor light, and the inexpert is always a sure victim. The simplicity of the trick is remarkable. The swindler takes a very yellow diamond in one hand and an ordinary indelible blue pencil in the other. Then he wets the stone and pencil all round the surface, both upper and lower sides. When this is done he equalizes the color by rubbing it with a piece of linen, and presto! the yellow stone is transformed into one with tint of perfect blue. The fraud can be detected by placing the diamond in alcohol for a few minutes, and afterward scrubbing with a toothbrush, as in the regular process of cleaning. The bogus blue diamond will at once reassume the yellow tinge which belongs to it.

Don't loan money on diamonds, especially to strangers. Rascals will visit a local jeweler and ask for a loan on diamonds and promise to redeem the same in a few days. They will put diamonds in an envelope and place them in the vault of a local bank to be held in escrow for a few days. During the operation the envelope containing the diamonds is changed and one substituted containing worthless imitations. As the package is not called for the local merchant claims the diamonds forfeited, and is horrified to learn that he has been so easily swindled.

The Jewelers' Protective Association was formed some years ago for the purpose of recovering jewelry stolen from its members. It has successfully captured the thieves and recovered most of the stolen property in almost all of the cases that have come into its hands since it was established.

To watch the home stores is but a part of the jewelry detective business. Every wholesale house has traveling salesmen who carry with them samples in trunks and gripsacks that contain from $10,000 to $50,000 worth of jewelry. The lynx-eyed robber is always on the track of these salesmen, closely watching their every movement and seeking an opportunity to pounce upon them in an unsuspecting moment. These dangers make the services of a reliable salesman doubly valuable while on the road. An intemperate salesman who is intrusted with fortunes in diamonds, watches or jewelry is at the mercy of these thieves, and to guard against such misfortunes the services of the detective corps are again called into requisition. The traveling salesmen for every large jewelry establishment is known to them. About a year ago the traveler for a well-known New York firm was robbed of $40,000 worth of gold jewelry in broad daylight in Cincinnati. The detectives of the Jewelers' Protective Association had tracked the robbers so closely that within forty-eight hours after the robbery the jewelry had been recovered and the thieves safely lodged in prison.

To guard against the ingenuity of the jewelry and diamond thief, who of all others is the most dangerous man in the criminal classes, a constant, unceasing vigilance must be maintained. No stranger, no matter how respectable his appearance, should be permitted to handle jewelry without a constant eye being on him, nor come within five feet of any desk or any drawer where money or valuables are deposited. Many errors will be made in enforcing this rule, and many enmities will be formed, but it is safe to err on the safe side. No honest man will be offended after the matter is properly explained to him. Strangers have no right to expect that any jewelry house, bank, or any mercantile house will permit them to place themselves in a position where large amounts of cash or valuables are within easy reach, and no sensible man will object when told that such proximity cannot be permitted. As to the mechanical means for preventing robberies, one of the very best preventatives is plenty of light, roof, front and side. With the methods of the sneak and thief so thoroughly explained, there need be no hesitancy in taking summary measures should any of the actions herein described be discovered.

CHAPTER XVI.

SHOPLIFTERS AND STORE THIEVES.

METHODS USED BY THIEVES TO ROB STORES—HOW SHOPLIFTERS PURLOIN GOODS FROM DRY GOODS STORES—"KLEPTOMANIA" AND ITS USES—HOW SHOPLIFTERS DRESS AND OPERATE—THE SATCHEL, "HOISTING KICK," "BAND BOX," AND OTHER SCHEMES FULLY DESCRIBED—SALESMEN MUST BE ON THE LOOKOUT—ENGAGING THE ATTENTION OF A CLERK—THE WELL-DRESSED CUSTOMER—ROBBING CUSTOMERS—SHOPLIFTERS' FACES AND DRESS—HOW CONFEDERATES ASSIST—HOW THEY STEAL AND SECRETE GOODS—EXPERIENCES OF STOREKEEPERS—SMART AND INGENIOUS SHOPLIFTERS—HOW THEY WORK A RETAIL DRY GOODS STORE—CAPACIOUS OVERSKIRT POCKET —DESCRIPTION OF SHOPLIFTERS' "KICK"—THE FALSE SATCHEL—PUZZLING CLERKS—ANOTHER CLEVER DEVICE—INVISIBLE POCKETS—THE SHOPPING BAG TRICK—THE CLOAK SCHEME—THE CANVAS "POCKET"—USING AN UMBRELLA TO PILFER—THE "BABY" SWINDLE USED BY SHOPLIFTERS—STOWING AWAY STOLEN GOODS—HOW SHOPLIFTERS DRESS—HOW STOLEN GOODS ARE DISPOSED OF—EXPERIENCES OF A CLERK—HOW PROFESSIONALS ACT WHEN APPREHENDED—PRECAUTIONS AGAINST SHOPLIFTERS.

A thief is a thief the world over. A kleptomaniac is a thief. A man or woman occupying a prominent business or social position in their respective localities is found stealing from a merchant and all their friends are quick to apologize for their action and intimate that insanity caused it and put them down as a "kleptomaniac." Not an ordinary thief by any means.

Kleptomania has been defined as an irresistible impulse to steal. Is it a disease in itself? Here medical authorities differ, some regarding it as a disease *per se*, others as a symptom of insanity in one form or another. One of the first writers on insanity, Esquirol, was inclined to believe that there is such a disease, but his observed cases have been relegated to other forms of mental disease, especially general paralysis, which in his day was not well understood. So from every point of view opinion as to the cause, responsibility, etc., might be multiplied. What is kleptomania? We all know what "mania" means, and a knowledge of the Greek alphabet will enable us to find that "klepto" means "to steal, spirit away, cheat, beguile, to conceal," etc.

A propensity to steal is often a symptom in advanced insanity and imbecility. A poor demented creature will be found gathering hoards of gold in the shape of yellow, glittering stones or jewels in the guise of bits of broken glass. Yet it is related that persons who otherwise exhibit no signs of mental failure may be afflicted with this form of impulsive monomania, as a French author has called it. For instance, this case is on record: A young lady sound in body and mind was possessed with an irresistible desire to take any small object coming in her way. Her room contained a collection of her stealings in the shape of handkerchiefs, gloves, stockings, and lace which she had stolen from her mates at boarding-school. She was at length discovered. She made no denials, her profuse weeping gave token of her sincere sorrow, and with shame she promised in the future to avoid her evil tendency, but repeated offenses of a like character at length obliged the principal of the school to send her home to her parents.

One of the best evidences of the disease is the brightness or color of the things stolen. A kleptomaniac seldom if ever steals money. Nothing excites the cupidity of a diseased mind so much as color, and, as a rule, it will be found that the goods taken by a kleptomaniac are bright or colored to a high degree. Another peculiar thing about the thefts of kleptomaniacs is that they are committed ostentatiously or without any adequate precautions to conceal the act. Then, again, in the majority of cases the articles stolen are of no value in themselves, or, at best, quite useless to the thief.

The act is apparently without motive. It is solitary and independent. As a rule the articles acquired by the kleptomaniac are disregarded almost immediately. They can be returned to the place from which they were taken and the diseased person be unmindful of the fact—so unmindful, indeed, that they will steal again and again the same articles as many times as it is returned to its original place. Though common to both sexes, kleptomania is most manifested in females. It depends upon nervous disorders altogether, develops from deep-hidden and unknown causes, and its cure depends upon the character of the disorder. It is a disease or affection that is on the increase, and one that calls for prompt and immediate action.

A celebrated French writer on insanity says: " Such examples establish sufficiently the existence of a diseased propensity to theft. The trifling value of the articles stolen, the the ridiculous selection, the use to which the articles are or are not put, the social position of the patients, their character for morality, the voluntary restoration on detection, and acknowledgement of guilt, all seem to point to the existence of this form of impulsive monomania. In the cases of theft by connoisseurs of books, antique and precious objects, it is difficult to fix the bounds which divide the irresistible impulse of insanity from the dominating desire of one whose soul and mind are wrapped up in certain studies or pursuits."

Of course a dissertation from a medical point of view would not greatly interest general readers. It is probable that the weight of medical opinion inclines to the belief that to call kleptomania a disease when the impulse to steal is not associated with other indications of insanity is to put all vice into the catalogue of disease.

Kleptomania is an evil familiar to all, and it is regarded variously by different shopkeepers. Those who profess to have confidence in medical science, or who possess charitable natures, frankly avow their belief in the theory that kleptomania is a disease of the mind which its victims can not resist or throw off. To such kindly disposed merchants kleptomaniacs are objects of pity and tender consideration; but to another class of merchants they are simply provocative of wrath. It is generally conceded that kleptomania is a standing complaint, which is constantly manifesting itself in a moderate degree. It does not appear to increase or decrease, but remains about the same from year to year.

Much depends on the social standing of person in calling the criminal a kleptomaniac or a thief. A poor person is rarely called a kleptomaniac.

Medical men say that kleptomania is not so rare a disorder of the nervous system as is naturally supposed. It is common enough. The large establishments in most cities employ private detectives to protect them from loss at the hands of irresponsible persons, but it is said the kleptomaniacs are by far more numerous than the shoplifters. Marked cases in relation to the character of the person must be considered, the interest and previous deportment of the individual must be looked to, the nature and use of the articles taken, and to the motives which seemed to have determined the action. For instance, a young boy was arrested in Chicago for stealing a Bible. He could not read, nor did he try to sell the book. He merely took it. He was punished for the theft, and had no sooner been released than he immediately stole another Bible.

Shoplifting has become such a nuisance in St. Louis that well known firms have adopted the plan of keeping a gallery containing the photographs of offenders. To this collection trusted employes have access, and they are expected to keep a sharp lookout for the originals of the pictures, and see that they are arrested if an attempt is made to carry off goods. The gallery also contains likenesses of women of society who are politely known as "kleptomaniacs," and who have to be dealt with tactfully. The number of women afflicted with this unfortunate malady in that city reaches well up into the hundreds. Scarcely a day passes without an attempt on the part of kleptomaniacs to purloin articles of value from some of the large dry goods or millinery houses in that city. They usually seize upon lace handkerchiefs, bits of ribbon, lace patterns, fancy articles, ornaments, and the like, and seldom purloin anything that cannot easily be secreted in the folds of their dresses, tucked away in their corsage, or concealed in the hand. Frequently the stolen articles are of little or no value, but as a general rule the costliest bits of lace or fabrics are the things that happen to strike their fancy.

All large stores now employ a regular detective to look after shoplifters and thieves. The most skillful shoplifters invariably travel in pairs, or, in detective parlance, one "stalls" for the other. That is, one of the thieves will undertake to engage the attention of the clerk, while the other deftly abstracts a piece of silk, a package of gloves, or a card of lace from the counter. It is frequently the case that the confederates will not enter a store together or exchange any perceptible signs of recognition while plying their vocation. A well-dressed woman, of respectable appearance, will step up to the lace counter, for instance, and ask to be shown some fine lace embroideries. The clerk, mentally noting her well-to-do appearance, thinks he sees a chance of making a good sale, and is, consequently, very obliging. He finds his customer hard to suit, and places box upon box of choice goods before her. Soon a second woman comes up, and calmly ignoring the first customer—as women have a way of doing—she demands to see a peculiar kind of goods which belongs to that particular department.

The clerk pulls down something for her. It turns out to be the wrong article, and leaving the first customer to contemplate the extensive assortment of embroideries before her, he endeavors to please the second customer. Immediately he finds himself the victim of two exacting and unreasonable females, and, after showing them a large share of the goods in his department, he is mortified to see them walk away, each one in a different direction, without having bought a dime's worth, and he is subsequently mortified to find that two or three cards of the most costly lace have been stolen.

The shoplifter sometimes works with a confederate. She first espies a woman with a pocket-book in her hand—and they are legion. She will follow that woman in the generally gratified expectation that she will ere long deposit it on the counter where she stops to examine goods. The thief will crowd near and snatch the pocket-book in a twinkling at the first opportunity and pass it to the confederate, who disappears and has not been noticed near. The real thief can remain beside the victim with safety, as, should she be arrested, nothing can be found on her.

On a recent visit to the "Rogues' Gallery" in a large city the faces of shoplifters were carefully studied. They were mostly women. As a rule they affect shawls or loose sacks and jaunty hats. Some of the women were not over twenty or thereabouts, but the majority were middle-aged, and, from their appearance, had grown hardened in crime. Some of the men had been decidedly averse to having their photographs taken, and in some cases had drawn their faces into all sorts of contortions. Where a man had absolutely refused to look the camera squarely in the face a policeman had obligingly held up his head for him; but with the women it was different. Their pride in having their photographs look as well as possible had overruled their desire for disguising their countenances. In one or two cases, however, the less hardened of the wretches held their heads bent over as far as they could, and their eyes were closed. This was possibly the first time they had been asked to contribute mementoes of themselves to the Rogues' Gallery.

There is a regular system of education in vogue among shoplifters. There are numerous instances where young girls and boys have been caught in company with well known professional shoplifters, and some of these juveniles have confessed that they have been taught how to steal. To become successful in the business, it is necessary not only to acquire dexterity in taking articles out of boxes or from counters, but also to learn to pass the goods quickly and secretly to a confederate. The first lesson taught beginners is how to receive stolen goods from the hands of the more experienced thieves. Then, step by step, the young shoplifters are advanced in the art until they are permitted to do the fine work of stealing laces, silks or jewelry directly under the noses of the salesmen. If a young and inexperienced thief is caught she is usually terrified, while an old hand at the business makes very little outcry, and takes it all as a matter of course.

If a thief is one of a gang, she has no difficulty in obtaing bail; in some cases the person arrested and bailed out has paid the sum, perhaps five hundred dollars, rather than appear in court. Two thousand dollars was the bail fixed for a woman who recently stole several rolls of silk. Nothing is too valuable, naturally, for these people to steal, and at the same time nothing is too small or trifling. Whenever their homes have been searched, articles of every conceivable description have been found. All is fish that comes to their nets.

Fully nineteen-twentieths of the shoplifters are women. It is seldom that a male shoplifter attempts to "work" a retail store alone, and the instances where women are assisted by men are not frequent.

Male shoplifters operate mostly in wholesale stores. They go in couples and generally drop into a store soon after the porter has opened the doors, and while one of them engages the attention of the porter the other makes off with a package of goods. The usual pretext given by this class of thieves is that they have "just come to town and thought they would stop on their way to their hotel." One of the men carries a hand-satchel, into which the stolen property, of course, finds it way.

Professional shoplifters were formerly in the habit of affecting the "kleptomania dodge" when detected, but since the storekeepers have become so exacting in their demands for proofs of good character in such cases the thieves have abandoned that subterfuge and now depend upon their skill and luck to escape detection.

The increasing experiences of the storekeepers and the improved facilities for thief-catching have driven the bunglers out of this branch of the rogues' profession, and it is now an even match between sharp and experienced detectives and smart and ingenious thieves. There are plenty of evidences that "the smart and ingenious" thieves are numerous and that they operate in all the large retail stores with a fair average of success.

The amount of dry goods, millinery and toilet articles filched from under the watchful eyes of saleswomen in retail stores is something enormous, says one of the oldest floor walkers in New York City, and those not acquainted with regular shoplifting practices conducted by scores of light-fingered females would be greatly surprised at the tales the proprietors and floorwalkers could tell and at the names they could furnish. A pretty lace handkerchief or some other article of feminine use, which can be conveniently secreted in a muff or flipped into a convenient fold of a dress, seems to offer a temptation too great to resist, even to respectable ladies, who would grow hysterically indignant if an accusation of theft was brought against them. The practice of shoplifting has developed enormously in the past five years, and many firms have adopted a new and novel method of abating the practice of petty pilfering.

From the counters of these concerns are daily stolen articles which are never missed by the saleswomen until a customer calls for that particular thing, when its absence becomes conspicuous. Gradually the shoplifters become known, and when one enters the door of a retail house a signal from the floorwalker puts a clerk on guard, and the suspected woman is carefully watched. If the clerk has reason to believe that the woman has stolen from the counters, she is taken into a private room and searched. These little rooms have witnessed many astounding disclosures, but what it will see in the future will be something very unique. Every shoplifter will be photographed by a kodak, which has been purchased for the purpose, the use of which has been taught to one or more of the clerks. The moment a shoplifter is caught and a theft is proved against her, her picture will be taken and placed in a private rogues' gallery, and under promise of secrecy the clerks will have access to it.

By becoming familiar with the picture the saleswomen can easily recognize the woman whose pilfering proclivities are so well developed and their thefts prevented.

One would be greatly surprised, said a veteran floor-walker, to know the names of some of the woman we have to watch, and they themselves would be greatly chagrined if they were aware of the espionage over them. Fashionable and wealthy ladies, who have no use for the articles they steal, daily take articles from counters, and do not seem to have the mental or moral strength to withstand the temptation. It seems to be a species of mania, and it is only developed and fostered by constantly allowing the desire to steal to get the ascendency of will power. Their confusion on being detected is something pitiful, and were it not a matter of dollars and cents and a matter of self-protection storekeepers would often be tempted to overlook the thefts entirely. Then there are the professional shoplifters, who buy little and steal much, and whose very dresses are so made as to conceal even whole bolts of cloth. As a class they are a smooth, stylish class, critical buyers, and apparently fashionable women. When they become known in one city they migrate to another.

The shoplifter's " kick " is the technical name of a capacious bag or pocket she wears in working a retail dry goods store. It is concealed under her cloak, or rather sewed to it on the left side, pretty much as we have under the left coat-tail. This is the old " kick." Store detectives say that the methods used in " working " it had become so well known to them and to the salesgirls that shoplifters saw the necessity of moving with the times. A more convenient contrivance was gotten up.

The " hoisting kick " consists of a regular dress-skirt, so far as appearance goes, covered by an apron overskirt, which is short and can be raised easily. In the front of the underskirt is a wide vertical slit, which is the opening to the immense bag the underskirt consists of, the same going around the entire body and down to the heels. This was found more convenient than the side "kick," from the fact that it necessitated less movement and a motion that aroused little suspicion. The thief stands close to a counter where small articles are exposed, generally lace or silk handkerchiefs or stockings. She takes one in her hands, examines it, holds it in front of her, calls for something else, and while the salesgirl has her back turned slips it into the slit. The stolen article goes down easily, as the "kick" is made of paper muslin. Should she by any chance miss the aperture the article falls to the floor and the thief picks it up and replaces it on the counter. A pure accident. This worked well until several of the fraternity were arrested and searched.

A simple device and one used for a long time with considerable success because it creates no suspicion is the satchel game. It is in full blast now, and will be extensively used until all storekeepers are acquainted with it. The satchels are, in appearance, like ordinary hand satchels, but they open and close by means of a spring. The thief's right hand presses a button and the left, which is ungloved, does the rest. It is by this means that pocket-books are so often stolen in crowded dry-goods stores, and so deftly does it work that salesgirls are puzzled and sometimes get into trouble over the missing articles.

Another clever device gotten up almost contemporaneously with the "kick" is the elastic band-box. It is made like a gentleman's hat box, of card board, the cover being held close to the box by two elastic bands in the interior of the box. The shoplifter will place the band-box on a counter containing articles that has captured her fancy, especially where there are few salesgirls. She will call for a certain cheap article which will cause the salesgirl to turn her back to the purchaser. The shoplifter will then lift the cover of her box with one hand, throw in as many articles as she can take hold of, and by means of the elastic bands the cover will be instantly and automatically closed, leaving no trace of the robbery. This contrivance is so deceptive by reason of its innocent appearance and *raison d'etre*, so to speak, and worked so admirably that it was a long time before the detectives "caught on," and many thousand dollars' worth of articles were stolen by this means before an arrest was made.

Another device is a beautifully flounced dress, covered with a short apron overskirt, draped and caught up here and there in such a way as to form natural looking puffs. This goes around the entire body, and a little to the right is a pocket rendered absolutely invisible by the drapery. Into this capacious pocket can be stored an incredible amount of goods.

The ordinary shopping bag is sometimes turned to account. This bag is carried in the left hand and filled with whatever goods the shoplifter can secure. Then she will go into the toilet room or some side street or alley, take out the goods, paper and twine, wrap them up in a neat parcel and try again to replenish the bag.

Another simple trick: The shoplifter lays her handkerchief carelessly on some small article she wants to steal, feigns a desire to buy something else, is not suited, and while the salesgirl replaces the goods on the shelf, the thief jerks up her booty with her handkerchief. If she should happen to be caught she naturally claims that she did not know she had taken the article in her possession.

There is the Connemara cloak trick. The long, loose cloak covers the hands. It enables the thief not only to steal with safety, but also to conceal her pickings. All she has to do is to get near a crowded counter, throw the edge of her cloak partly over the thing she covets, slip her hand underneath the cloak, take the article, step back and hold it in her hand. Unless caught in the act she can not be arrested.

Store detectives say that once a professional shoplifter is caught she usually disappears as soon as the law allows. He or she never tries the same game in the city. There is another class that really gives more trouble, so-called respectable women. It requires much more skill to handle them. Accusation of an innocent person may be ground for a criminal suit, and possibly cost the storekeeper thousands of dollars. The kleptomania excuse is on top every day, but the theory of " volitional insanity " is scoffed at by the detectives. They maintain that not one woman in a thousand steals inadvertently; that where wealthy men's wives are found among the culprits, a little investigation usually reveals the fact that an insufficient allowance for clothes is the true cause. Not all that are captured are prosecuted, but the examining room reveals side lights of domestic life that are at times astounding.

The rainy weather fills the hearts of the shoplifters with joy, for umbrellas and voluminous cloaks increase the difficulties experienced in detecting the act. It is very easy to lean an umbrella against a counter which is covered with small articles such as handkerchiefs, gloves, jewelry and so on, and then quietly push one of those articles into the partially opened rain-shedder. It is astonishing how much one umbrella can hold if judiciously handled. The full-skirted gossamer cloaks or caped mackintoshes are utilized by experts in concealing not only the plunder but the manipulation.

Another dangerous device is the " pocket " scheme, and the " pocket " is indeed something of a curiosity. It is made of strong lightweight canvas and looks like a petticoat. It consists of two pieces of the material sewed together around the edges, gathered full at the top and a strong cord puckering string run through. In the front of this great bag is a slit two feet long opening from the top to within a few inches of the bottom. This petticoat is worn under the dress skirt. On each side of the outside skirt is a long slit concealed by the folds. In operating, the shoplifter seizes through the front of her dress the cloth on one side of the slit in the canvas petticoat, pulling it slightly forward. With her other hand she slips the stolen article through the slit in the side of her dress and into the petticoat bag through the opening in front. The capacity of that bag is enormous This is really the most dangerous contrivance worn by shoplifters, as nothing is shown that would indicate that goods are being carried, and is the most successful mode of shoplifting in vogue.

Another successful mode of shoplifting, and one that usually disarms suspicion, is for a young woman to enter a store carrying a baby. The baby wears the conventional long-skirted baby dress, and the shrewd thief will place that innocent bundle of dimples and smiles upon a counter and proceed to stuff those long skirts full of silks, satins and gloves, which she carries away in her matronly arms.

A decidedly assuring manner of shoplifting is for a woman to go into a store and lift and conceal an article, then to leave the building and enter another store, purchase something, and ask to have the article which is stolen in the first store wrapped up with the purchase, and the bundle kept until sent for. The next day she will send for her plunder.

Stowing away the stolen goods is at all times a difficult matter. The present fashion of gowns fitting close to the hips does away to a great extent with the " kick," or shoplifter's pocket, extending to the bottom of the skirt. One young woman recently caught had a unique contrivance fastened around the leg just below the knee. It was a strong band of heavy cloth, which fitted like a garter, and to it was attached a number of small hooks. The instant she stole anything she would stoop down as if to tie her shoe and slip the article on one of the hooks. She could only steal small things, but when she was caught a tiny watch and several pieces of costly lace were found in the unique hiding-place.

The very best of the professional shoplifters do not visit any one store oftener than probably a dozen times a year. They know almost as soon as one is trying to spot them that they are watched. The most successful racket they work to conceal their identity is the wearing of a heavy black mourning veil. A few years ago they generally carried a basket and were more easily caught. Customers in general soon became aware of the fact that anyone carrying a basket through a store was closely shadowed, and they dropped the habit, until to-day it is a hard matter to find a woman with one.

There is a certain class of male shoplifters called early morning "hoisters." They generally go in threes. They watch wholesale houses, and when the porter opens in the morning, and goes to open the back part of the store, the shoplifter gets his work in by stealing the most valuable goods in the front part of the store. Should there be a clerk there at the same time, one of the gang engages him in conversation. Number Two talks to the porter, and Number Three does the stealing. This is done daily, and thousands of dollars' worth of goods are stolen yearly.

Professional shoplifters have regular places to sell what they steal. Pawnbrokers get most of the stuff taken by that class. Non-professionals steal only what they want to wear, and many women get enough in that way to dress themselves handsomely. They will take anything from a pair of shoes to trimmings for a hat or dress. "We make it a rule to prosecute every person detected in stealing," says the manager of Chicago's largest dry goods store, "no matter who it is.

Neither tears nor money will shield anybody caught shoplifting in this house. We are first careful to make no arrests without conclusive evidence of guilt, and with that at hand, prosecution invariably follows. It is the only way we can protect ourselves against this class of criminals."

A saleslady in the leading department store in New York City gives her experience in regard to shoplifters as follows:

"We have to resort to all sorts of disguises to get even with the shoplifters. They get so that they know us and are careful to be on their good behavior when we're around, so we change our dresses, hats and coats and the way we fix our hair in order to fool them. Often we stand right close to them in the crowd and they don't recognize us. We are always dressed as if we had just come in from the street, and no one ever takes us to be connected with the store at all. I fixed myself up as an old woman once, with spectacles, grizzly hair, a scoop bonnet and an old shawl and hobbled along for several squares behind two women whom we suspected of taking things, but whom we had no real evidence against. Sure enough, they took the things to a certain fence in Ludlow street, which some time after the police raided. Several articles belonging to the stock were found among the stolen goods that they hadn't been able to sell.

"We're instructed to be very particular about making arrests. The superintendent says he would rather have a hundred guilty people go unpunished than have one innocent person accused; besides, if falsely accused, the parties could sue the house for heavy damages. We never accuse any one, no matter how much we may suspect, until we actually see something stolen. I've been detective in this store nearly ten years and I've got so that I can tell a shoplifter almost at first glance. I judge from the uneasy way they roll their eyes around, from the motion of their fingers and the way they move their hands. They assume various disguises. Nearly all the professionals that we arrest have pawn tickets somewhere about them and they try to get rid of these in all sorts of ways so that we won't get hold of them. One girl chewed up a pawn ticket and swallowed it and was chewing up another when we found out what she was up to. Another girl had two rings in her mouth which she had taken from the jewelry counter.

" There are lots of people who take things without a good excuse—women and men who want to dress up to the mark and haven't got the money to reach it. Two girls were caught here not long ago just loaded up with ribbons and lace, fancy pins, buckles, gloves and such things. The way in which they had stowed away stuff in their stockings and various other hiding places was a caution. Among the odd articles found in the stocking of one girl was a bottle of whisky. It was crammed in and then tied tight to keep it from slipping. A bottle of cologne was fixed in the same way. These girls said they had stolen ribbon before, and promised that if we would let them off they would tell us of companions of theirs who they knew did the same thing. They said that they belonged to respectable people. I went to the address they gave a few days later and found that the family was respectable."

While the operations of shoplifters are very similar, their conduct when caught differs in almost every case. Some of them indulge in mock hysterics and create a scene that gives their arrest a great deal of publicity. These are generally professionals. Others fall in a faint and are carried to the searching-room. Quite a number pretend that they are under the influence of morphine or some other opiate, and say that they did not know what they were doing. Occasionally one assumes an air of dignity that would do credit to a queen, and fairly boils with indignation when told of the charges against her.

Notwithstanding all precautions the depredations of shop-lifters continue. It is a delicate matter to arrest a lady in a public store. It is still more painful to accuse and disgrace an innocent person—a mistake which overzealous watchers occasionally make. The proprietor of a large Chicago store, who claims to have lost quite heavily in this manner during every holiday season for some years past, says:

"I think we have found a means at last of checking this great leak. The shop-lifter who habitually steals is suppressed by this method, and those just beginning in their career are frightened by it into reform. All the merchants are adopting it. It was my idea, but I am glad to publish it for the benefit of others, and now we circulate amongst ourselves a black list of habitual offenders so that the professionals are finding this a pretty hard season."

This merchant, when a clear case has been established against a shop-lifter, summons her to his office, and proposes to her the only alternative of immediate arrest or of signing a document confessing her thefts and agreeing not to enter into that shop again. The culprit usually prefers to sign the document, thus hushing the matter up, and at the same time supplying the proprietor with an effective instrument of protection. It is asserted that some establishments have collections of these tell-tale autographs which would shock the world if they were revealed.

CHAPTER XVII.

HOTEL THIEVES AND SWINDLERS.

WHERE HOTEL SWINDLERS COME FROM—EDUCATED FRAUDS—SHARP HOTEL CLERKS—HOTEL THIEVES AND TRAVELING MEN—HOW THE PROFESSIONAL HOTEL THIEF WORKS—HOW ROOMS ARE ENTERED AND ROBBED—FIXING A LOCK—TOOLS USED—WORK OF CONFEDERATES—STUDYING THE HABITS OF GUESTS—THE HANDY "BAR-KEY"—REMOVING A LOCK AND "FIXING" A DOOR—USE OF THE "SECTIONAL STEM"—THE NIPPER GAME—HOW ARTICLES ARE REMOVED FROM UNDER MATTRESSES OR PILLOWS WITHOUT WAKING SLEEPERS—RESPONSIBLE HOTELS—DAY HOTEL THIEVES—HOTEL SNEAKS—SWINDLING HOTELS WITH BOGUS DRAFTS—THE TELEPHONE SWINDLE—HOW TO DISCOVER HOTEL BEATS—THE LETTER SNEAK—THE MONEY ORDER FRAUD—BOGUS VALUABLES IN HOTEL SAFES—HOTEL SAFE THIEVES—THEATRICAL DEAD BEATS—TRUNK CHECK THIEVES—VALUABLES AT HOTELS—WORKING HOTELS FOR DAMAGES—HOTEL CONFIDENCE OPERATORS—FEMALE HOTEL THIEVES—THE ADVANCE AGENT FRAUD—FOILING HOTEL SAFE THIEVES.

Young men who have been reared in semi-luxury, indolent, and without any knowledge of honest business and with no inclination to work for an honest living, are the source from which nine-tenths of the hotel and mercantile beats of to-day are recruited. Thousands of these men, from eighteen years of age to fifty, are to be found in all the large cities in this country. They by no means confine their operations to cities or to hotel beating alone. They combine a system of petty thieving and swindling with their beating qualities which accounts for their appearance in small towns.

This class is always without work, generally well dressed, and always insinuating. Thousands of this class are college graduates. To he an accomplished and successful villain requires education and superior intelligence. Launched from the threshold of a college life upon a world, they have nourished the idea that they are always to swim on the surface or become great lawyers and doctors. They look upon labor with disdain, and not being fitted for any useful occupation, they join the army of loafers and gamblers, and prey upon their fellow man. That our present system of education is grossly imperfect and even vicious is shown daily in all our large cities and towns.

American hotel keepers and hotel clerks are generally a bright class, and it takes a bright man to get the best of them. In former years many hotels were the favorite working ground for counterfeiters and sharpers of every grade and degree, but now the landlords have actually become detectives, and can scent a thief as far as they can see. There is no place where the study of human nature, both good and evil, can be conducted as well as in a hotel. By constant contact with all sorts of people, an ordinary clerk can tell at a glance whether he is dealing with an honest or a slippery customer. Occasional mistakes may be made, but in a grear majority of cases the sharp hotel man hits the mark. Sharpers who got the best of them on an old scheme may now retire, for those who 'bit won't bite again, and those who didn't will want some new bait now before they nibble.

The hotel thief is the bane of the traveling man. The commercial traveler is always on the lookout for him, and long experience teaches him how to thwart the best laid plans of the midnight marauder, who begins work long after everybody is in bed and asleep. As a rule, the average " drummer " is keen witted, and knows how to take care of himself and his property. An expert hotel thief knows this and does not waste much time in trying to get ahead of a man who knows more than he does. A thief who possesses any degree of judgment at all usually confines his operations to transient guests, if he can by any means pick out his intended victim. Horse races, fairs, conventions, and the like, generally cause an influx of strangers to the city or town in which they are held, and the hotels are, in consequence, filled to overflowing. All of the visitors at times like these are amply supplied with ready money and fall easy victims to the softly shod robber who enters their sleeping rooms. The thieves do not, however, restrict their operations to the times of excitement and overcrowding of hotels, but upon ordinary occasions, when the public houses are occupied by the general class of the traveling public, their depredations are carried on with a degree of boldness that is absolutely startling.

As a general thing, in all first-class hotels, in addition to the maintenance of a corps of alert watchmen upon the outside of the chambers, have also placed safeguards within the rooms. Every door is provided with a double lock—that is, a lock which can only be locked from the inside of the room, and cannot be reached from the outside, as the keyhole does not extend through the door. The ordinary lock upon the outside admits the guest to the apartment assigned to him, and when once in he locks his door from the inside with a lock that only operates upon the inner side of the door. These appliances form within themselves two distinct locks, one of which may be locked upon both sides, and the other only from the inside. Chain bolts, another ingenious contrivance, have also been put on many of the doors. And yet, with all these provisions against the entrance of the thief, the occupants of these rooms awake in the morning to find that they have been robbed during the night, and to the ordinary observer their doors show no evidence of having been tampered with in any particular. To those unacquainted with the ingenious workings of the professional hotel thief, this discovery is startling and inexplicable, but to those who have studied the modes and operations of the hotel thief, the manner in which an entrance has been effected is as plain as the sun at noon-day.

In fully describing just how entrance is obtained to apartments in hotels, the author feels safe in asserting that he can point out how to foil the most expert thief in America—not only foil him, but possibly capture him. Taken altogether the hotel thieves in this country are a rather intelligent lot of rascals, and hence all the more dangerous. They are experienced in the use of tools and will handle a brace and bit with all the dexterity of the educated artisan. They are seldom caught napping, and are far better posted as to the whereabouts of the watchman, than that worthy is of their proximity. From external appearances no one would think of suspecting the well-dressed, gentlemanly looking individual, who registers himself with a quiet and unassuming air, and whose tone and conversation bespeak both travel and education. In the reading room and at the dining table he is the dignified, yet affable gentleman of business, and his deportment is at all times unobtrusive and polite. He never dresses in gaudy colors, and his apparel is usually chosen with the utmost good taste, and a quiet style that stamps him as a gentleman of refined tastes.

His tools, which are generally of the finest tempered steel, consist of a "bar-key," a set of six bits of various sizes, and arranged for either stem or tumbler locks; a small drill; a file; a "sectional stem," or what is called the "widow;" several pieces of wire, and a pair of nippers. These are all the articles he needs, and frequently but a few of these are required, and their particular uses will be fully explained in their proper order. These implements do not occupy much room in the traveling satchel of the nomadic thief, and are frequently carried about his person.

Qualified by a long system of training, the hotel thief is then fully prepared for work with his pal, as hotel thieves almost invariably travel in pairs. They manage to secure their rooms on the same floor, and if possible, without attracting attention, close to each other. Once established in their quarters, the work of preparation begins. The habits of the guests upon the floor they occupy are carefully studied, and it is soon ascertained which of the chambers are unoccupied. These preparatory steps are always taken during the day. Having discovered the number of vacant rooms, they make a thorough examination of the locks upon their own doors, as it is reasonably certain that every other door upon the same floor will be similarly secured. One of the men is set to see that the coast is clear, while the other quickly effects an entrance into one of the empty rooms. His tools are taken in with him. If there is only a single lock to contend with, the work is soon done—the "bar-key" with its appropriate bit opens the door readily from the outside, and no further arrangements are necessary for that room.

Where there is a bolt on the inside of the door, a hole is bored through the door from the inside, immediately over the handle, or knob, for the introduction of the "sectional stem," and then this hole is carefully puttied up and the small spot in the door is colored with a quick-drying material of the same color. Ascertaining that the halls are empty, by a system of signals with his partner who is on the watch, the thief comes cautiously out, and covers up the hole on the outside in the same manner. In this way, provided they are not interrupted, all the vacant rooms on that particular floor are "fixed" for the arrival of guests in the evening.

Five minutes is frequently all the time an expert occupies

in "working" a single room. Armed with his "bar-key" his nippers, and the "sectional stem," he sallies forth, while his companion unobservedly maintains a close watch upon all the surroundings, and stands prepared to give prompt warning in case of danger.

If the guest to be operated upon has left the key in the outer lock, the nippers are used, and in a twinkling that part of the difficulty is over, and the key is turned so quickly and noiselessly that no one would be aware of what was going on. If, however, there is an inner or double lock, and a bolt on the door, the putty from the drilled hole is quickly removed, the nippers are inserted, and in case the inside key has been prepared by filing, a sharp awl is used, and fitting into the slot in the end of the key, turns it readily. Then the "sectional stem," the "fiddle," or the bent wire is inserted through the hole over the bolt, the string is pulled, and with an easy turn of the wrist, the bolt is thrown back, and every obstacle to the entrance of the thief is removed. Once inside he assumes a stooping posture, and begins to search whatever clothing is within reach.

Just how a thief can remove articles from under a mattress or pillow without awaking a sleeper, has been a continual mystery to most people, but it is very simple. The thief bares the right arm to the shoulder, and then holding either mattress or pillow with the left hand, lifts it gently and with a steady motion, and then gently inserting the bare arm underneath pulls forth whatever may be concealed there.

The hotel thief is somewhat difficult to balk, but there should be no difficulty with a person of ordinary intelligence. In the first place, it is a wise and proper thing to leave your valuables with the hotel clerk. If the hotel safe is robbed the proprietor is responsible. If, however, the traveler feels willing to take the risk and guard his property himself, let him carefully examine the door of his apartment. He can, after the description given above, readily detect whether it has been " fixed " or not. If he finds it has been tampered with, let him inform the clerk, who will (if the right kind of a man) institute an immediate investigation. If other rooms are found to be " fixed," then it is self evident that there are a pair of thieves in the house. Let everybody be aroused—no matter how inconvenient—and depend upon it, there will be no stealing done that night. The thieves will believe themselves detected and take the first opportunity to escape. If the hotel proprietor is shrewd enough he may effect their capture. One observant, quick-witted man in a hotel may save thousands of dollars' worth of loss by acting at the right moment.

The " day " hotel thieves belong in the same class with the " night workers," and are equally dangerous. They do not use nippers, or any tools in fact, except what is termed a T screw, double ender, one T shorter than the other end, sometimes called skeleton keys by locksmiths.

A small jimmy is a necessary accompaniment. The thieves look out for bridal couples or wealthy women who flash considerable jewelry. At breakfast, women as a general thing do not wear their diamonds; then the chance of the day worker is taken. The chambermaid being busy fixing the beds, the thief unlocks with his key the room door, steps inside, bolts the door and gets to work at once, breaking open the bureau drawers and trunks and securing all the jewelry and money he can find, makes his escape. If he has a pal the thief in the room will slip out a piece of paper from underneath the door, which his pal notices, and watches to see that the chambermaid is away. Then he gives the signal for his partner to come out. If the chambermaid is in the way, the thief may unlock a door on some other part of the floor, call the girl and give her a half dollar or so to fix up the bed at once, which is mussed. Foreigners have been a source of gain to the day thieves, as they invariably carry their money or jewelry in their trunks, and their rooms can be entered at any time during the day when opportunity presents itself.

Of all classes of hotel crooks the man who does the "sneak act" is the most dangerous. He is dressed fashionably and has an air of business and importance which disarms suspicion. If he concludes to work a certain hotel systematically he registers and is assigned a room. Between the hours of 10 o'clock P. M. and 2 o'clock A. M. he prepares the doors of the rooms he intends to enter. These rooms are selected according to the standing and wealth of the occupants and the amount of jewelry they display in the hotel corridor, where the thief spends days in sizing them up as desirable "marks." The preparation of the room doors, as before explained, requires considerable dexterity as well as coolness.

After getting everything ready the thief selects a favorable night and starts to work. He ascertains if the room is occupied by a sleeping occupant, easily detected by his heavy breathing. Quietly the putty is removed and a "widow" inserted to draw the bolt. A "widow" is a small piece of wire bent at one end with a piece of string attached to the bent end. By means of this instrument the bolt is easily drawn, and unlocking the door with a skeleton key the thief enters cautiously. If the sleeper does not wake all his valuables are taken from his clothes, and the thief retires, again locking the door and plugging the hole. A guest retires, and, after bolting and locking his door, sleeps soundly in fancied security which is no security at all. Should the thief disturb the occupant he backs out politely saying he has made a mistake and entered the wrong room. If the room is unoccupied the thief quietly goes through the trunk and picks up anything that suits his fancy.

Hotel swindlers will always be numerous and on the alert. Here is an ingenious scheme worked on eastern hotels by a young man who represented himself as a drummer for a wholesale silk house: After putting up at a hotel he would make use of the good name of his employers and pay his bill with a worthless draft or check, receiving the liberal balance in cash. The hotel keeper, when the paper was protested, was pretty certain to write the ex-patron. In his reply the drummer would express sorrow for the "mistake," enclose $10 on account and promise to pay the balance in the near future, which, of course, he never does.

When the hotel keeper accepted the $10 he made the swindle one for civil action instead of a criminal proceeding. Hotel keepers, when taken in by drafts and bogus checks, should not accept a small repayment "on account" when they have the swindler located. A criminal prosecution carries more terrors than a civil one does. It is a very bad plan for hotels to cash checks for anyone. They may be all right, but the number of hotel men that get caught goes to prove that they often are not. The safest plan is to cash checks for no one, no matter who they may be.

A clever swindle is often perpetrated on hotels in this manner: Telephone messages, ostensibly from regular boarders at the hotels, are received, directing the clerk to pay for packages addressed to some of the boarders, which, it was said would be sent to the hotels. The swindlers bob up in due time with their packages and collect any sums they are mind to charge and depart in peace.

The chances for beating the large hotels in New York, Chicago, Boston, Philadelphia, St. Louis, Washington and others of the larger cities is pretty slim. The opportunities for stealing even a dinner are not promising. The arrangements have been so thoroughly perfected that it would be pleasanter for a man to suffer the pangs of incipient starvation than risk the mental wear and tear and physical harm incident to the theft.

For some years hotel beats in New York had things their own way. They lounged about the corridors of their favorite hostelries, often had their letters addressed to the offices, and were so much on hand that the employes of the house supposed they were regular patrons. Then the hotels began a regular crusade against them, and they have been relegated to the free lunch counters of the more prosperous saloons.

The head waiter is the sentry of the dining-room. Five minutes before the dinner hour a list of the guests of the hotel is sent upstairs by the clerk. On the list is the number of every room in the house with the name of the occupant (if any) opposite. The head waiter stands by the door and when a guest comes in he is asked quietly the number of his room. He gives it, and the waiter instantly sends him to a table. The man, if he thinks of it at all, supposes that the number of his room has something to do with his seat, and passes on. The instant his back is turned the head waiter consults his list, and if the room of the number given is vacant, or if it is occupied by some one known to the waiter he goes at once to the man, and, while deftly re-arranging the napkin or placing the knives and forks in neat rows, asks him seductively his name. If the name fails to clear away the doubt the clerk is sent for. He may recognize the man. If he does not an investigation is made at once, and if the man is proved a fraud, he is taken out and handed over to the police. The same system is now in vogue at all large hotels.

The head waiters of the hotels are usually men of great discrimination, and accurate judges of character. They seldom make mistakes, but when they do slip up their errors are clothed in such suavity and gentleness that even the professional beats can not get angry with them. This is a good plan for all hotels to adopt, especially those who enjoy a large transient trade.

The "Letter Sneak" is one of the latest inventions of crooks that make hotels headquarters for swindling purposes. He hangs around the reading-room and notes who gentlemen writing letters address them to, and from the hotel register easily learns the writer's name. Now comes in the fine work. If the writer is in correspondence with the house he is traveling for the "Letter Sneak" telegraphs them at once for $50 or $100, signing their representative's name to the telegram. He has it sent in care of hotel, of course, but goes to telegraph office and requests that it be delivered him to some private house, where the "sneak" has a room, telling the telegraph officials that he is spending a few hours with friends, and that to send him direct would be a great accommodation. If the remittance is by telegraph he gets the cash at once, but if by draft to the hotel he watches the mail and sends a messenger-boy, saying "Mr. M—— would like his mail, he's busy and won't be in until evening." If the traveler has left the hotel he will get a ficticious telegram to give his mail to John Smith, which name the "sneak" will assume, and get it. This has been played many times, but with the best success on country merchants who are in the city, and the "sneak" sizes them up and telegraphs home for $100 at once.

Several hotels have been taken in by the raised money-order "racket." The scheme is one that is calculated to deceive even the sharpest hotel-keeper. A man registers at a hotel, calls for his mail, opens a letter and takes out a post-office money-order for $25 or $50. As that department of the postoffice is closed on account of the lateness of the hour, the hotel clerk kindly cashes the order, or advances some money to the sharper, keeping the money order as collateral. When the clerk sends to the postoffice the following day he finds the money order is worth one or two dollars, the swindler having raised the amount on the face of it while in another city and mailed the letter containing it to himself. Of course by the time the fraud is exposed the perpetrator is far away, browsing in green fields and pastures new. The hotels which have been swindled in this way should post up the sign, " No P. O. money-orders cashed here."

An often played and somewhat successful swindle is the " valuables racket." A well dressed stranger registers in an important way, and after being assigned to a room requests that his overcoat be sent to his room. The clerk summons a porter and the good natured guest gives the porter twenty-five cents. In order to get the quarter from his pocket he takes from his pocket a large roll of bills that appears to be $500 or $1,000 and counts them over hastily in front of the clerk. He excuses his apparent neglect of the porter and tosses him a half dollar. Then he places his money in an envelope and the clerk places it in the safe for security. In the morning the swindler reminds the clerk that his bills were all of a large denomination, very difficult to change until bank opens, and would the clerk let him have $25 or $100 in small bills until bank opens, retaining the package in the safe for security. The clerk generally bites, the money is readily and smilingly given, and the swindler departs for green fields. Upon examining the package, a lot of counterfeits are found, and the clerk pays dearly for his experience. Once a landlord was swindled three times in succession, and then concluded to hang up a sign announcing that no money would be loaned even upon gold, and that is about the only way for safety.

The hotel safe theft is worked by two. They put up at a hotel, pay a week's board in advance, and generally sell some patent medicine nostrum. They familiarize themselves with the hotel and learn of the safe and where the cash is kept. At an opportune time the clerk is called to one side by one of the thieves, while the other ransacks the safe. Knowing where everythlng is it takes but a minute. The clerk returns and the conversation continues, the thief with the stolen money in his pocket taking an active part. They get a couple of cigars—of course the good-natured clerk has one—and go for a walk. They never return.

One of the worst classes hotel keepers have to contend with is theatrical beats and members of traveling troupes. When they get stranded, owing to poor business or the "flight" of the treasurer or business manager, the hotel keeper has to suffer. Poor companies generally have poor baggage, and their traps used in their business is, nine times in ten, protected from seizure for hotel bills by fraudulent and crooked bills of sale. The only way to protect one's self against migratory players is to demand pay in advance, or ample security. There is not a hotel in the country but has suffered by this class of beats.

Lounging around hotels and depots, especially in the larger cities, are gangs of thieves who make a specialty of working what is known as the "Trunk Check" act. By some crooked means they have become possessed of checks leading out on the principal roads. When a trunk is seen standing in depot or hotel with check, it is quietly removed and one placed on by them, a duplicate of which they have in their possession. A confederate follows the trunk, and when it is put off claims it, rifles it, and departs for new trunks to conquer. The trick is played quite extensively on hotel baggage and coat rooms. The trick is a very old one, and at various times it has been employed at most of the leading hotels in the country. And at many of the hotels it is very easy of accomplishment. No one appears to be watching the baggage, and a shrewd or even an ordinarily clever crook would have no difficulty in changing the checks.

A guest of a hotel is entitled to the reasonable care of his baggage and other valuables so long as he is a guest or patron of a hotel and is paying a consideration for his board and lodging. The moment he ceases to be a guest, responsibility for his baggage ceases, unless a special contract is made for its care and keeping, whether a "check" is held for such property or not. The opinion that some people hold that they can get a coat checked at any hotel and with the check hold the hotel responsible, is not law. The hotel keeper takes enough responsibility in caring for the property of his guests, without becoming a free safe depository for outsiders' goods. To avoid trouble and law-suits, and ill-reports about their hotels, hotel men often pay for lost articles which they should not pay for, and this willingness to settle leads many travelers to be careless with their property in a hotel and to assess a double value when it disappears, to say nothing of the beat who puts up "jobs" to make the hotel pay for articles either not lost at all or which are worthless.

A scheme to work hotel proprietors for damages, claiming that rooms have been entered and clothes and jewelry stolen, is an old dodge. Some hotel keepers are foolish enough to submit to blackmailing rather than have reports made public that might prove injurious to them. If valuables are not left in the hotel safe no proprietor can be held responsible for loss—and no one but a coward will submit to blackmailing.

One of the most dangerous class of swindlers who resort to hotels to carry out their plans are the adventurers, both men and women, who establish themselves in hotels because of the prestige which such a place gives them, and the facilities it affords them for carrying on various kinds of shady schemes. This class get a generous supply of the hotel cards at which they are stopping and then start out to ply their swindling vocation. They generally have large desires in the direction of good clothes, books, jewelry, etc., and tailors, jewelers, hatters and furnishing houses are swindled several times a week. The process is very simple. The goods are ordered and requested to be sent to " my hotel," with bill. The goods are sent. The messenger waits in the hall while the porter takes the package and bill up to the swindler's room. The swindler receives the bundle and tells the porter that he will be down at once. And he does get down at once and leaves the house by way of a different door from that one where the messenger boy is awaiting his appearance. He has no trunk, valise or anything else to hamper his movements, and all he carries off with him is the suit of clothes or the dozen new shirts or the watch which the confiding shopkeeper has just sent him. There is a moral in this that hotel keepers should note that the reputation of their house may not suffer. Guests without baggage should pay when registering. Suspicious characters should not be entertained at any price.

A female thief and swindler has a slight advantage over a male rascal owing to the fact that a hotel clerk is reluctant to accuse a woman when suspected. A well dressed woman enters a hotel with an ease aud grace that disarms any suspicion, and making for the ladies' parlor summons a bell boy. " Key to my room, 115, please." The boy goes to the clerk and gets the key to 115, returns with it to the woman, who goes to room 115 and despoils it of all clothing, valuables, etc., that she can carry away without attracting undue attention. She has learned of the occupants of certain rooms and knew their habit was in leaving the hotel for business or shopping was to leave the key with the clerk and upon returning summon the bell boy from the parlor and have key brought her. This swindle is sometimes operated by men, but nearly always by women. They go into the ladies parlor, ring for the bell boy, and send him in a matter of fact way for the key of some room. He asks the clerk for it, and if he is busy and thinking of something else, he hands it out without question. Then the female sharper goes through the room in a hurry, trusting to thieves' luck that the occupant will not return before she gets away. Then the hotel is responsible for the loss.

What is known as the "Advance" trick is only worked in cities of from fifty to seventy-five thousand inhabitants and upwards. A hotel proprietor is notified by mail or telegraph to prepare apartments for a gentleman, wife and two children, who will arrive in about ten days. The hotel keeper is also requested to receive and receipt for any packages that may come for the guest. The swindler is, of course, in the city all the time, the telegraphing and writing having been done by a confederate. Worthless packages, with an outward look of solidity, are carried to the hotel by messenger boys, to be kept for Mr. ———— until he arrives. Charges from $10 to $50 are paid by the landlord, who always stands ready to accommodate a good guest. The packet racket is kept up until the landlord grows weary and awakes to the fact that he has been grossly swindled.

Rascals who observe guests place valuables in a hotel safe, and then call for them on forged receipt or check for same, are quite numerous. A good plan to adopt in caring for valuables is the following: Take a sheet of paper—the hotel's letter head—place on same amount, date and character of valuables deposited, and then tear in two, handing one-half to the owner, placing the other half in the safe. It is impossible for any one to counterfeit the slip of paper, as none can be torn to minutely correspond with the ragged edges of the paper retained in the safe.

CHAPTER XVIII.

TRICKS OF PICKPOCKETS.

How the Light Fingered Gentry Work—People Who Flatter Themselves on their Cleverness Easily Robbed—How to Act in Crowds and Large Assemblages—How Pocket Books Are Abstracted—How Watches are Easily Removed—How to Carry Money and Valuables—How Pickpockets Operate on Street Cars—Picking Out a Party to be Robbed—How the Work is Accomplished—Stealing a Diamond Shirt Stud or Scarf Pin—Dexterity of Pickpockets—Peculiar Make-Up of the Light Fingered Craft—The Use of a Hat—Colliding and Apologizing—The Female Pickpocket—Twisting a Watch Chain—Working on Railroad Trains—Harvest of the Holiday Season—Some Dont's for the Public to Observe—Pickpocket and Sneak Thief Impossible to Reform—Number of Professional Criminals in America—Cuteness of Thieves—Spotting a Man Who Exhibits Money in Purchasing a Railroad Ticket—Operating on Street Cars—Watching People from the Country—How Diamond Jewelry is Removed—How to Avoid Pickpockets and Sneak Thieves.

Persons who have never been robbed by a pickpocket believe that they enjoy a certain immunity from such depredations, and flatter themselves that it is owing to their own superior cleverness and watchfulness that they have hitherto escaped. But experience shows that even those most on their guard suffer at times from the operations of pickpockets. It is never safe to get in a great crowd or jam with valuable jewelry or money on your person, as this is the pickpocket's opportunity. Thieves in this particular calling work in parties of from three to five. One of the rascals will tip a man's hat as if by accident, while another one of his confederates will jostle him. The man jostled is naturally afraid his hat will fall off, raises his hands to secure it. A third confederate pushes him, and the fourth rascal, called the "wire," takes the man's watch or pocketbook. Prior to this the man selected to be robbed has been carefully looked over, and the way his watch is secured or the location of his pocketbook has been discovered. If the pocketbook is in a deep pocket in his trousers two hands may be used by the pickpocket, one to lift or press the pocket back upwards, and the fingers of the other hand to extract the treasure. A pocketbook carried in a hip pocket is easily and readily lifted in a crowd. When a watch is to be taken, the thief, with his thumb and forefinger, forces the ring of the watch open, which disconnects the chain, and as this springs readily the time piece is easily removed. The old fashioned way of keeping the watch in the fob or watch pocket is the safest, for then nothing is exposed.

The best place to carry money, except what little change one needs for current use, is in a pocket inside the vest, which should be secured by a button, for when the vest is buttoned up it is difficult for a pickpocket to get at the money. There is but one rule to observe when one ventures into a crowd of strangers and that is to leave money, watch and all valuables at home, and never to carry only enough small change to pay for the day's needs.

Crowded street cars are a favorite and profitable working ground for pickpockets, and the light-fingered gentry pick up thousands of dollars this way annually. No street railway line in the country is free from this class of thieving, and a crowded car is just arranged for a pickpocket's work. The passenger to be robbed is standing up and hanging on to a strap, and before and behind him is a thief, the one who is to do the work being generally provided with an overcoat in the winter or light coat or duster in the summer, which he carries thrown carelessly over his arm. The coat is to hide the operation of his hands. In the jostling of the crowd and the swaying of the car an opportunity is found to rob right and left. Nothing is easier than for a pickpocket to fetch a diamond stud or watch under such circumstances. If the diamond be a valuable one the wearer of it will have been followed many times, and at all hours, patiently waiting for a favorable opportunity to steal same. People who wear valuable diamonds at all times and in all places are only inviting an attack from thieves. A half dozen futile attempts may have been made to secure a certain article of value before successful, without even attracting the attention of the owner and wearer of same.

There is no class of artists who in their calling are as dexterous as pickpockets. This is due to a double incentive. Not only does the pickpocket find a bait for effort and exertion in success, but has the added spur of a fear of failure. Success means as much to a pickpocket as to any man, and failure means a great deal more. A vocation in which the slightest slip means loss of liberty and perhaps of life will ever be apt to have a degree of expertness in its followers not present in more reputable and safer avenues of trade.

Pickpockets, like poets, are born, not made. Their nerves must be iron and yet as sensitive as instinct. Their hands must be as complete in make-up and accomplishment as Hermann's, and strong as steel while light as down. Out of the vast army of humanity who are soldiers of the shadows only one-fourth of 1 per cent. can or do become pickpockets. These form the nobility of thieves, and are reverenced by the burglar, the footpad, the sneak, and the "con" man as of a higher class than they. The practice of a pickpocket while not really at work is as constant as that of some famed professor of the viol or harp. He keeps pace with the procession.

No sooner does some jeweler invent a new fastening for diamond pins or studs than these men of finest touch devise the motion which evades its purpose.

The chief object of a pickpocket after certainty is speed. He cannot dally with his victim by the hour. What he does is to be over in a flash. Speaking of pins and studs, there has never been a fastening so complex but the expert thieves could defeat it in a motion. They do in their business as fine work as any Houdin, and the thief himself could not analyze or explain its detail. His powers of execution have gone far beyond his powers of perception or relation.

A pickpocket consults his own nervous condition constantly. No fine lady ever has such a time with her nerves as this aristocrat of the outlaws. If he does not feel right he won't "work." When he does, they have been known on the impulse to take a car on some well dressed and wealthy street, and seating himself side to the window, survey the shirt-front of every would-be passenger as the car came up. The moment one showed a diamond in his linen or cravat the thief would hurry to the platform to get off. He would time his manæuvers so as to meet his man on the step of the car. They would collide. The thief's hat—a stiff silk or Derby—is in his left hand, and covers his dexterous right, which is put forward to protect its owner in the collision. It touches the newcomer right where the diamond sparkles, and is still covered by the hat in the other hand. With an apology the thief steps out of the way. The whole affair is the tenth part of a second, but as he bows his regrets he has the diamond in that mysterious hand of his, and he could not detail the moves by which he attained it, even if he should try.

Women are the most successful pickpockets. The female professional pickpockets always seek victims among their own sex, as the women of to-day are given to carrying their pocket-books and watches in exposed places. Then, too, the thieves are less apt to be suspected because of their sex, and, most important of all, for the reason that in the wide range of style of women's wraps nowadays they find plenty of opportunity to hide their hands while at work. A shawl or wrap of any sort, which seems to be carelessly carried on the left arm, hides the right hand while it feels for the location of a pocket and then makes its way to the pocket opening, where the top of the lining is seized by the fingers. It is then but a moment's work to draw the lining up until the pocket is practically turned inside out and the contents drop into the pickpocket's hand. The fingers which do this work are never inserted deep into the pocket. They just catch the lining at the upper edge. This trick is done in a crowd where everybody's attention is riveted on a special object and where a touch of a stranger's hand or even a rough jostling itself is not especially heeded.

Generally a pickpocket has a confederate. Then if, as sometimes happens, the loss of a pocketbook is immediately discovered, the real thief, having passed the purse to the confederate, can be as sympathetic as anybody, and, if suspicion makes it absolutely necessary, can submit to an examination with the same confidence in the result that might be felt by the most innocent person present. It is the wrap, however, that gives the female pickpockets the great advantage over the light-fingered thieves of the other sex, and the latter try to overcome this by using an overcoat—if the weather is not so cold that an overcoat carried on the arm will attract attention—or a linen duster in summer. Sometimes the men make a newspaper answer the purpose. If the male pickpockets are not the more successful they are at least the more adroit and audacious. They have to be so, for they don't confine themselves to women's pockets. They seldom try to take money from men's pockets, as close-fitting clothes make the risk of detection too great; but they find it an easy matter to steal, or, as it is termed, "ring" watches from men. This is done while the victim, with unbuttoned coat and expanded watch chain, stands in a street crowd. The thief slyly gets the watch from the pocket with one hand, while with the other he grasps the chain at the lower end. A short, quick jerk with both hands in opposite directions, and the ring which is the connecting link between the chain and the watch becomes separated from the watch stem. The watch is then in the hands of the thief, while the chain and ring are dangling down the front of the victim's waistcoat.

A person has but to try this trick with his own watch to see how easily it may be done. Pickpockets do these things in crowds; but they cannot always find a crowd, and sometimes have to resort to making one themselves. They do this generally on railroad trains, where the general hustle and bustle give them opportunity to get a well dressed man in their clutches. As the victim is about to enter the car he is brought face to face with a man who is in a hurry to get out. The two squeeze together in the doorway, and two other men, both in a hurry, ascend the platform and also try to get into the same car. Three of the men are pickpockets, and the stranger is between them by a prearranged plan. He is quickly robbed of his watch, and perhaps a diamond pin and his pocketbook This trick is well known to the police, but policemen do not travel on every train.

It is for the reason that crowds are constantly congregating before the windows of large stores, that if there is a crowd there is surely standing in some doorway from which he can view the face of almost everybody in the crowd a police officer. He does not watch hands; he watches faces. Not that he recognizes the face of every pickpocket, but he knows that if a man or woman in that crowd is paying no attention to the window scene or other attraction, but is occupied in viewing the clothing of his or her neighbors, he or she is, nine times out of ten, a pickpocket. The suspicion may be strengthened by the nervous or cautious way in which the thief occasionally turns his head, presumably to ascertain if he is watched. The officer still pays no attention to the hands. He waits patiently till the suspected person leaves the crowd. If the latter is really a pickpocket he will walk quickly along, turn into a side street, where, in a doorway, he will wait for his confederate; or, if there be no confederate, will take out the stolen pocketbooks and examine their contents. While he is thus engaged the officer interferes.

During the holiday season while the streets, cars and stores are crowded, and in fact where a great crowd is congregated, people should be on the lookout for the light-fingered. Here are a few "don'ts" that the public should studiously observe:

Don't carry a pocketbook in your hand.

Don't carry a pocketbook in a loose pocket which hangs away from the person.

Don't lay your hand-bag containing your pocketbook on the counter of a store while you walk across the room to examine goods.

Don't wear a watch in a pocket on outside of dress.

Don't wear chatelaine watches.

Don't judge strangers by their dress.

Don't stand long in the same spot in a crowd.

Don't go into a crowd with your outer coat unbuttoned.

Don't carry valuables in your outer coat.

Don't make too great a display of your jewelry.

Don't carry money in the pocket on the right-hand side of your trousers; pickpockets expect to find money there.

Don't forget that you are just as likely as anybody else to be a victim of pickpockets.

Don't forget it if you wear a diamond, scarf pin, shirt stud or earrings.

The holiday week is the harvest-time for pickpockets in all the large cities and towns. What makes it particularly aggravating to the police, is that this class of criminal is the most difficult to deal with. Cowardly and shrewd and gifted with a perverted intelligence which is constantly employed to create new schemes by which it can safely follow the trade and prosper.

Men versed in the different types of criminals agree that the pickpocket and sneak-thief are hopeless from a standpoint of possible reformation. They represent the lowest strata in criminology, because their vocation is carried on without personal danger. Their natures in time become honeycombed with evil and there is nothing substantial enough left on which to build a structure of honesty. On the other hand, the burglar or highway robber must possess some kind of courage, and where there is courage there is a chance of reformation.

Estimates recently made place the number of professional criminals in this country at 100,000 and the bulk of the whole number in the five largest cities. Crooks from all over flock to the great centers during the holiday season, even some of the finest cracksmen being unable to resist the temptation to do a piece of work among the women shoppers burdened with Christmas cash.

It is very hard to obtain sufficient evidence against any of these light-fingered gentry to secure their conviction for theft, owing to the adroitness they display in getting rid of incriminating articles. Time and time again detectives have pounced upon a man the very second he has been seen to steal a purse or bit of jewelry, but nothing could be found when he was searched immediately after. The reason of this is that the cleverest pickpockets always work in small squads. Three is the usual number. The instant one commits a theft he passes the stolen article like a flash of lightning to the second, who with the same speed hands it to the third.

Even when a pickpocket works single handed, it is a difficult matter to catch him with the fruits of the theft in his possession or to see him dispose of them. A policeman detailed for work in the shopping district in citizen's clothes in Chicago, stationed himself near a window where a crowd of women always lingered. He knew that sooner or later he would have a chance to make an arrest. In the early afternoon he saw a man deftly remove a gold skirt pin from the back of a reckless woman who probably knew little about the danger of shopping in the holiday season. The policeman grabbed him and the thief seemingly lost his footing and slipped to the ground, but was on his feet again in a second loudly protesting his innocence. He declared it was an outrage to accuse an honest man of such a crime, but, confident of what he had seen, the policeman then and there searched his prisoner for the stolen pin. It wasn't found, and then the sidewalk was searched with the same result. There was no doubt that the pin had been stolen, for the policeman had seen the theft and the victim stood weeping while the sympathetic crowd tried to find the pin. The man was locked up, but none of the police could identify him in court as a regular crook and the woman refused to appear against him, fearing the publicity. The man was held for a short time and then discharged. Later the woman advertised for the missing pin and subsequently it was returned to her by a young lady, who said that she found it stuck in the folds of her dress on her return home one day from a shopping tour. Further conversation disclosed the fact that the young lady was looking in the window at the time of the theft and had seen the whole affair. She did not know who the owner of the pin was or it would have been returned sooner. It seems that the instant the thief felt a hand on his shoulder he dropped to the ground, sticking the pin into the dress nearest him. He knew it would be dangerous to drop it on the sidewalk as it would have been easily found and might have helped toward his conviction. An inexperienced crook would have fallen into this error, but the quick wit of the adept did not fail him.

In working a railroad train, pickpockets generally select their victims in advance, by watching at the ticket office and spotting the man who exhibits a large amount of money. If no favorable opportunity offers to rob him while he is getting on the car, the thieves will wait until he is seated. One of them will approach him brusquely, and assuming an air of authority, say:

"Let me see your ticket, please? Where are you going?"

In nearly every case the passenger will be deceived into thinking the questioner to be a railroad official and will inform him. Then the pickpocket will answer:

"You must take the next car," indicating either the car in the front or in the rear, at the same time picking up the passenger's valise, with a view of assisting him in effecting the change, and calling out:

"Hurry along, sir!" The man follows obediently, and the mob is waiting for him on the platform. The moment he appears he is at once jammed in, and robbed. Their previous knowledge of the location of his money renders their task an easy and rapid one.

Pickpockets mount a street car and always take their positions on the rear platform—always being careful to select a car which is already crowded. For the purpose of illustration let it be assumed that there is a man on the platform, who looks as though he might have some money in his pocket-book. The first thing to be done is to learn in which pocket the money is carried, and to do this the thief lightly runs his hand across the front of both pockets of the " mark." This is called " fanning." Should the pocket-book be found in the left pocket, the " tool " will say to his companions " left kick," and they all understand where the money is located. The " stalls " then surround the " mark," and the " tool " begins his work. With his hand concealed by a coat over his arm, he inserts the two first fingers of his right hand (just beyond the first joint) into the victim's pocket, with the inside of the fingers against the pocket lining farthest from the body. Bending first one finger and then the other, he draws the pocket up little by little, which is known as " reefing," until the pocket-book is within reach. The moment he is able to take hold of the pocket-book—called " tapping," he quietly calls out " rouse! " the victim receives a rough push from the stalls. Out comes the pocket-book, and it is immediately passed to one of them. This is done to guard against accidental discovery, for should the victim miss his money and accuse the " tool " of the theft, he will not find the book in his possession, and he usually gets off. The " stall " waits to be informed when the pocket-book is taken, and when the " tool " chirps like a bird, he knows he is to receive the money, and that the robbery has been successful.

In many cases, particularly among persons from the country, the rustics have heard remarkable stories about the picking of pockets, and make up their minds that no such fate shall befall them, so they always travel about with their hands in their pockets and on top of their purses. When one of these careful gentlemen gets on a street car, the pickpockets at once select him as their " mark." The innocent is immediately pressed and hemmed in by the gang, and the hand that is not guarding the treasure in his pocket is kept back by the shoulder of one of the "stalls." A quiet command "tile him!" is given, and the countryman's hat is shoved over his eyes from behind. The victim not being able to use his other arm, pulls his hand out of his pocket to push back his hat. Simultaneously with this action one of the "stalls" gets into position, places his shoulder under the countryman's arm, thus preventing him just for a moment from again placing his hand in his pocket. In a second the "tool" is at work, and in another moment the gentleman from the country finds plenty of room on the platform, for the thieves have left and with them has gone his carefully guarded purse.

Sometimes when all the seats in a street car are occupied, a pickpocket will enter and take up a standing position in front of a gentleman who has his coat open, then hanging by one hand to the strap suspended from the roof of the car, and with a coat thrown over his other arm, he will sway about with the motion of the car, and manage to have his coat come directly under the chin of the seated passenger, and under cover of that, he will extract a pocket-book from the inside pocket of the victim, who has no suspicion of what is going on. Suppose the thief wants to get a diamond stud, fastened in the shirt bosom with a screw. He simply covers the stud with his coat or newspaper, and gently takes hold of the screw with his thumb and forefinger, then he carefully draws the bosom of the shirt away from the body of the victim, the thumb nail is inserted directly back of the head of the screw. With a firm twist of the wrist the screw will come out. No matter how difficult this operation appears under ordinary circumstances, it will invariably be successful when the thumb is put under the setting of the stone. In case the diamond is set with a flat back instead of screw, it is impossible to detach it from the bosom unless the thief takes time to wet the shirt at the button-hole by fingers previously moistened with the tongue. A diamond pin is unfastened in the natural way and then raised up straight.

The pickpocket or sneak thief of whatever degree, can never be successful, when the intended victim is forewarned and consequently forearmed by the exposure of the several methods in vogue. Knowing just how the thieves work—and they are not so ingenious that they invent new tricks every day—he is effectually guarded when he knows how to deceive them from the moment they select him as their victim.

CHAPTER XIX.

ALL ABOUT COUNTERFEIT MONEY.

Valuable Points on the Detection of Bogus Currency—Vigilance of Government Officials—The Cleverest Imitations Known—How a Counterfeiter Makes His Plate—How Good Money is Made—Greatest Safeguard Against Counterfeiting—Geometrical Lathe Work—The Ruling Engines—Lettering on a Genuine Bill—The Transfer Press—Two Methods of Printing Bills—How the Black and Green are Printed—Difference Between Genuine and Counterfeit Ink—Genuine and Countrfeit Bank Note Paper—Reliability of Check Letters—Different Methods of Counterfeiting Coin—Noticeable Defects in Counterfeiting Coin—Various Metals Used by Counterfeiters—The Most Dangerous Silver Coin—Tampering With Genuine Coin—How Sweating is Done—Short-Weight Gold Coin—The Art of Plugging—Dangerous Coins—Filing a Genuine Coin With Cheap Metal—Easy Way for Detecting Spurious Coin—Engravers and Counterfeiters—Watching Suspicious Men—Living Beyond One's Means—Punching Silver Coin—Drilling Gold Coin—Impossible for Counterfeiters to Escape Detection—Work of the Secret Service Agency.

Notwithstanding the unceasing vigilance of government officials, there is some counterfeit money being manufactured at all times in this country. Without doubt, the easiest way to make money is to have a manufactory of one's own. So evident is this fact that, although government officials, bank tellers and cashiers, and business men generally, have developed almost marvelous skill in the detection of counterfeits, and although the discovery of the fraud often leads to the incarceration of the perpetrator of it, there are persons who carry on a regular business of counterfeiting money.

Counterfeiting paper money is the highest branch of the business, as it calls for the greatest amount of skill and admits of being done on a large scale. The cleverest imitations known are of the $500 and $1,000 bills; in fact, so clever that the issues have been almost entirely retired by the treasury. There are also hundreds of other bills, of a less denomination, which are cleverly executed and pass readily from hand to hand, until presented at a bank or sub-treasury. American bank tellers and cashiers, as a general rule, are quick to detect counterfeit money of any kind, no matter how cleverly executed. The detection of spurious paper money has been reduced to a regular system. The counterfeiter makes his plate, invariably a single one, from which he prints. All the notes of his issue, then, will be alike, and will have certain points of difference from the genuine. These points of difference are described in publications known as "Counterfeit Detectors," and all the counterfeit notes are tabulated, the new ones being added as fast as they appear.

The machine known as the geometrical lathe, produces an intricate network of interlaced fine lines, regarded as the greatest safeguard against counterfeiting. It engraves the groundwork for the figures denoting the denomination of the note, both on face and back of bill. In United States Treasury notes its work covers the larger portion of the back in green ink. The characteristic feature of the geometrical lathe work is the perfection of the fine line which never breaks, never deviates a hair's breadth, is always the same thickness and always the same distance from the next line. The designs produced are circles, ovals, or other geometrical figures, with or without indented edges.

The patterns may vary, but the fine white line stands out clear, bold and distinct, guiding you unerringly to a correct decision as to the genuineness of the bill. The intersections of the lines in the counterfeit are always blurred and the turns imperfect. As a whole, the genuine work presents to the eye, especially when aided by the magnifying glass, a clear-cut, fine, distinct, bold and beautiful appearance. Occasionally in counterfeits there is not even an attempt at forming lines, but dots are used, somewhat like stipple work. Some contain a series of disconnected scratches that are continually breaking off, becoming too thick, stopping when they reach another line, and invariably making the crossings, if attempted, blurred and blotted.

If the genuine work be thoroughly studied, the eye can not fail to detect the deficiency in the counterfeit imitation.

The work of the ruling engine is found in the shading of the solid letters, in the ground work and body of some names of banks, and occasionally in the sky and water. Its characteristic is a perfectly formed straight line, the thickness of which depends upon the nature of the work. The genuine presents a clear-cut, distinct, symmetrical and uniform pale gray shade, which begins and ends with perfect regularity, following every curve of the shaded word with minute care; whereas the counterfeit is indistinct, unsymmetrical, differs in shade, has a scratchy look, terminates irregularly and has a dull, sunken appearance that, at first glance, distinguishes it from the genuine.

The lettering on a genuine bill, found in name "United States," in name and location of bank, in words "Will pay to bearer," in the denomination, etc., is executed by first-class artists and by hand work. Too much reliance must not, however, be placed in the perfection of this work, as it can be closely, or even perfectly, imitated by another first-class engraver. One very excellent point is to study thoroughly the name of the engraving company, found in the upper, lower or side margin, as it is very difficult even for an expert artist to imitate these small Roman capitals.

The work previously described is produced on small squares of softened steel, which, by a chemical process, are afterwards changed into hardened steel. These are then placed on the smooth bed of the transfer press and a roller of softened steel is passed backward and forward over them, under a great pressure, until it has taken up even the faintest hair line of the original. These rollers are then hardened and laid away in the vaults of the bank note company. If a plate is to be produced, they are taken out and by means of the transfer press are, one by one, impressed upon various portions of the bank note plate of softened steel, until its surface has been covered with the designs composing that bill.

There are two methods of printing—the roller and daubing methods. Roller printing may be seen in any newspaper or job office. The daubing process, used in printing engravings, consists in spreading the ink over the plate, and then rubbing it off all the upper surface, leaving in the depressed parts just enough ink for one impression. Upon this plate is laid a sheet of paper, covered with a blanket, and the plate is then drawn under a roller which forces the paper down into the depressed parts so far as to take up all the ink contained therein. The black printing on the face of the bill and the green on the back are made in this way. The seal of the United States is impressed afterward. The figures denoting the number of the bill, found in the upper right-hand or lower left-hand corner, or both, are printed by an automatic numbering machine.

The genuine black ink is of the finest quality, and possesses a body and consistency that enables it to adhere firmly to the paper. When new, it has a peculiar gloss, and retains its brilliancy to a marked extent, even after much handling.

The characteristic of the different colors is about the same; they are all bright and clear, and retain their distinctness of color to the very last. This is particularly noticeable in the red treasury numbers, which seem to become almost more glossy by age.

The counterfeit ink is wanting in the brightness of the genuine. At first it may look moderately well, but after some handling the black ink turns to a dirty, grayish tint, and the red to a dull brick-red or wood-red color. In many cases it disappears almost totally.

The genuine paper is of the very best quality, strongly woven, possessed of a solid body, finely finished and very durable. For some years past the government has used a paper termed the Wilcox fiber, the peculiar characteristic of which is a narrow, localized line of dark blue fibers, which do not form a portion of the paper, but are put on after it is finished, and can be scratched off with the tip of the nail. The majority of the bills now in circulation are printed on this fiber paper. Just now the government, in addition to the Wilcox fiber, is using on some notes a "distinctive" paper, the characteristics of which are a faint, reddish-brown line and a faint bluish line running along the whole length of the bill, a little over two inches from each other, and several twisted lines of red and blue scattered over the face of the bill with a methodical disregard of method. The red and blue lines referred to run parallel to each other, as well as to top and bottom of the bill, and are discernible on both face and back.

The counterfeit paper is of a very inferior grade, and always fails to stand the test of time, becoming fuzzy, soft and flimsy to the touch, and wearing away so rapidly as in many cases to render the printing partly obliterated. It will also be noticed that after some handling it begins to tear in straight lines, perpendicular to top and bottom. The fiber paper above described has been imitated by printing lines resembling these fibers. In the genuine the fibers can be scraped off; in the counterfeit they cannot.

On every United States treasury note is seen one of four letters, A, B, C, D, called check letters. The following useful points on the best way to detect a counterfeit note are from an authority on the subject. Experts don't judge so much by the appearance of the bill as they do by its "feel," that is, by the way it slips through the fingers; but it takes years of experience to acquire the necessary fine touch, and even then it is not always reliable. Every bill is lettered and numbered, and there is a connection between the numbers and letters, which is made in such a way that when you know about it you can tell a genuine bill almost at a glance. What are known as the character letters of a bill are placed on either side of the central figure or vignette, and are A, B, C, and D, and after the numbers, have nothing to do with the case so far as detecting a counterfeit goes, but those engraved on the bill in the places mentioned are rightly named character letters, since they serve, in connection with the numbers, to show if the bill is genuine. Now, suppose you have a bill numbered 12922826. The character letter on such a bill should be B. Why? If you take the last figures, which are 26, and divide them by 4, you will have a remainder of 2. Now, B is the second letter of the alphabet, and the remainder, after dividing the last two figures by 4, must in every case be that represented by the numerical position of the first four letters of the alphabet. That is, when one is left over the character should be A; 2 over should be B; 3 over should be C, and when there is no remainder the letter should be D. When this rule fails to work on any bill you come across, you can bet as many more as you can raise that the bill is a counterfeit. It must be remembered that this division test rule does not apply to national currency.

Coins of all kinds and every denomination have been counterfeited. The most dangerous counterfeits are those struck from a die, and are found principally among the imitations of the gold coins. Molds of various kinds are extensively used in counterfeiting gold, silver and other coins, but these counterfeits are much inferior to the class mentioned above. Coins struck from a die have a very fine appearance, the lettering and milling being sharp and clear, and the ring usually good, and are in some instances almost perfect facsimiles of the genuine. The most noticeable defects to be found in this class of coins is that they are usually a trifle short weight, and the edges or reeding are not so sharp and clear as in the genuine. Many of these coins have the full weight. In counterfeits made from a mold the lettering, milling and reeding are usually poor, weight very defective, and lacking the sharp and clear-cut appearance which is found in the genuine coin. A majority of the counterfeit silver coins in circulation are made in this manner, by molds, as it is a very expensive form of counterfeiting. Some very fair specimens have been produced from the molder's hands, but usually they are much lighter than the genuine; and if of the required weight, they differ in diameter or thickness.

Various metals are used by the counterfeiters in their operations, the principal of which are platinum, silver. copper, brass, antimony, aluminium, zinc, type-metal, lead, and their numerous compositions.

Among the most dangerous counterfeits of the gold coin are those of a composition of gold, silver, and copper. They are a low grade gold, and on being subjected to the acid test show they lack the fineness of the standard gold used by the United States mint, which is 900 fine, or 21.19 carats. These counterfeits average from 400 to 800 fine. Platinum counterfeits are very dangerous, as from the metal used in their composition the required weight is obtained, and they are very heavily gold-plated.

A large number of short weight gold coins are now in circulation, and the frequency with which they are met has led to investigations which show that there has been for some time a systematic scheme for robbing the government by stealing metal from the coins. Some years ago a series of tests were made by the government for the purpose of defining the actual loss by abrasion in the moving of gold coins. It was found that $5 was lost by abrasion every time $1,000,000 in gold coin was handled. Bags containing $5,000 each were lifted to a truck to be removed to another vault, and the mere lifting of the 200 bags caused the loss stated, and their transfer from the truck again made a second similar loss.

This shows how readily gold can be removed from the coins, but this method is much too slow for the clever rogues, who realize the value of scientific appliances. The work of abrasion is now done by electricity, after the manner of electric-plating of gold. An ordinary galvanic battery and some cheap acid is procured. The coin is placed in the fluid, and attached to it are wires from the poles of the battery, leading to another piece of metal to be removed from the coin. Sufficient gold to form a plating is quickly transferred, and, as it is removed uniformly from all parts of the coin, the liability of disfigurement is reduced to a minimum, the only effect being to blur the characters slightly.

In this way about 50 cents' worth of gold can be removed from a $10 gold piece without a marked change in the appearance of the coin. The eye of an expert, however, detects the alteration at a glance. One of the employes in the New York sub-treasury is said to have become so skilled in this branch of the work by years of experience that he can tell by mere touch, with closed eyes, whether a piece is spurious metal or has been tampered with. It is stated that the sweating of gold by electricity in this country is practiced almost entirely by foreign swindlers who have been driven from their own country for similar offenses.

When these counterfeits have been in circulation for a time the plating wears off, especially on the edges of the coin, and exposes the metal underneath, of which they are composed.

The most dangerous counterfeit of the silver coin is made of a composition of antimony and lead, the former metal predominating. These counterfeits are of recent appearance, and are of the dollar. They have a very fine appearance, are heavily silver-plated, with a very fair ring, and some are but slightly below the standard weight.

Some pieces among the smaller coins are made of brass, struck from a die, and when heavily plated are very fair specimens of the genuine. These coins lack the required weight except in a few instances.

Counterfeits of type-metal, lead and other compositions, of which the larger percentage of the imitations of the silver coin are composed, are very much lighter than the genuine, and those having the required weight are much too thick.

Genuine coins of all kinds, for the sake of gain, are tampered with in various ways. These operations are confined almost exclusively to the gold coins, which are sweated, plugged and filled.

Sweating is removing a portion of the gold from the surface of the coin. The process does not interfere with the ring, and as the portion removed is generally slight, the coin is left with a very fair appearance, the weight only being defective. It is done in numerous ways, the principal of which is the acid bath; also by filing the edges or reeding, the operator finding a profit in the small quantities of gold removed from numerous pieces

Plugging is done by boring holes in the coin, extracting the gold, and filling the cavity with a cheaper material. The larger coins—double eagles and eagles ($20 and $10 pieces)—are used for this purpose. The holes are bored into the coin from the edge or reeding, the gold extracted, and the cavity filled with a base metal. The small surface of the plugging material, where it shows on the edge of the coin, is then covered with gold and the reeding retouched.

This is done with a file or machine for that purpose. The average loss in value to coins treated in this way is from one-eighth to one-sixth. Coins of this kind are dangerous, as they are perfect in appearance, the edges only having been tampered with.

Filling is commonly done by sawing the coin through from the edge or reeding, removing the interior portion, and replacing it with a cheap metal.

Coins of all denominations, from the quarter eagle to the double eagle, are subjected to this process. When platinum is used to replace the gold extracted the coin has the same weight as the genuine. By this process coins lose four-fifths of their value, as the original surfaces are left only of paper thickness. When the edges have been covered with gold and the reeding restored, the coin has the appearance of being genuine, having the correct size and weight, and a fair ring. In some instances the covering of gold on the edges is so thin that the filling can be distinctly seen. When other and less costly filling than platinum is used, the coins are of light weight and have a bad ring. If of correct weight they are too thick.

Another method of filling is done by sawing the coin partly in two from the edge or reeding, on one side, leaving a thin and thick portion. The thin side of the coin is turned back, and the gold extracted from the center of the thicker portion. The cavity is filled with base metal, and the sides pressed back into their original position, and are soldered or brazed together. It is difficult to give the average loss to coins treated in this manner, as hardly any two seem to have the same amount of gold taken from them.

For detecting counterfeit coin, compare the impress, size, weight, ring, and general appearance with the genuine coin of the same period and coinage; and if we take the three tests of weight, diameter and thickness, it will be found almost impossible for the counterfeiter to comply with these three tests without using genuine material.

Mix the following ingredients in a bottle with glass stopper:

Twelve grains nitric of silver, crystal.

Seven drops nitric acid, pure.

One-half ounce distilled water.

Place a drop of this fluid on the suspected coin, whether gold or silver. If the coin be counterfeit, it will turn black. If it be genuine, it will remain clear. Be careful to place it on the worn corner or on a cut made with a knife, as the coin may be silver-plated, and the acid would not affect this outside silver coating.

Engravers, as might be supposed, take more naturally to counterfeiting than any other class of men. They possess the art of engraving the plates for counterfeit notes, the most difficult and profitable part of counterfeiting. The knowledge that they possess this power is naturally a temptation to use it if the idea is ever presented to them. For this reason the utmost care is exercised in the government bureau of engraving and printing, where the treasury notes and gold and silver certificates are made, to preclude all possibility of any one engraver becoming familiar with all parts of the same note. No one man is allowed to engrave an entire note-plate. Each plate passes through a great many different hands, each man to whom it is assigned engraving only a very small portion of it. But despite this precaution there have been not a few cases where government engravers have practiced secretly upon the entire plate for a particular note until they have become adepts in the engraving of every part of it, and have abandoned legitimate employment to devote themselves to counterfeiting

A simple desire for novelty and excitement and that singular longing, more or less inherent in the breast of all of us, to do anything we are prohibited from doing, especially if the charm of secrecy and mystery cling about it, lead many people into counterfeiting.

Others go into it because they really believe that there is a great deal of money to be made in the business and that a fortune may be readily accumulated. There could be no greater or more foolish error than this. Of course some counterfeiters do make a good deal of money at first, but it is only a question of time, and always a very short time, before they are detected and placed under arrest. Then every cent they have in the world, and in many cases every cent their relatives and friends have, is spent in trying to keep them from the penitentiary. The counsel fees that these people pay are simply fabulous. There is no class of criminals whom the lawyers bleed more mercilessly, for the knights of the parchment and brief seem to share the generally popular idea that counterfeiters have money galore.

Even when they do make money they live so extravagantly that they usually spend even more than they make. In counterfeiting, as in almost all other occupations, a man's value declines with age, and as these people grow older, like all who follow any vicious course, they steadily sink lower and lower, and if they do not die in state's prison they perish miserably in abject poverty, cast off and disowned by relatives and friends and even by those who were once their associates in crime. The scriptural saying that "The way of the transgressor is hard" applies with peculiar force to counterfeiters.

How are counterfeiters first detected? is a question often asked. In every city and large town in the United States Uncle Sam has secret-service agents who devote all their time to watching for counterfeit money and for those who may try to pass it. They are familiar with the history and circumstances of everybody in the place on whom the slightest shadow of suspicion can possibly rest. Their attention may be attracted to certain persons by a great variety of circumstances. If a man who has previously been poor seems to be suddenly well supplied with money without his friends and neighbors being able to account satisfactorily for his good fortune he becomes an object of suspicion, and he and all members of his family are shadowed night and day by secret-service agents. If he is making or "shoving the queer" he is very soon detected. If he is innocent the secret-service man is soon satisfied that such is the case and releases him from a surveillance for which, as it has been strictly secret, his character and circumstances are none the worse.

Every woman who dresses beyond her husband's means, every man who lives beyond his salary or other income, is an object of suspicion to Uncle Sam's secret agents. The money they are spending may be obtained by crimes wholly different from that of counterfeiting, but until he has thoroughly satisfied himself that such is the case Uncle Sam's detective keeps his weather eye constantly upon them. It is thus impossible for any one to have any guilty knowledge of counterfeit money without being speedily detected. When sufficient evidence has been secured the wrong-doer is hunted like a fox by the hounds of justice from that time till he dies, unless he gives satisfactory evidence that he has reformed.

But counterfeiting is not the only trick that may be played upon Uncle Sam's currency. A few years ago, shortly after silver coin had replaced the old fractional currency or "shin-plasters" of the war, and the dollar of our daddies had made its reappearance, every coin, from the largest to the smallest, had a hole punched in it. There were hundreds of people who made considerable money by punching small pieces of silver out of these coins. They readily passed current without question until the abuse became so great that Uncle Sam had to interfere to stop it by declaring that punched coins would not thereafter be received as legal tender.

It may have been this desire that suggested to a bright young mechanic in Philadelphia a much more clever and profitable way of doctoring coin. He hired a room with steam power, and there, with the aid of small drills, he extracted from the interior of $5 and $10 gold pieces almost their entire substance, leaving nothing but a very thin shell of the outside gold. This was affected by drilling through the milled edge of the coin. He then replaced the extracted gold with some baser metal, taking care to preserve the exact legal weight of the coin, and covered up with a small bit of the extracted gold the tiny hole his drill had made in the edge of the coin. By this most ingenious device he extracted $3 worth of gold from every $5 gold piece he handled and $7.50 from every $10 piece, and yet the coins remained, to all appearances, just as before. The "sweating" they had undergone could not be detected by any test that could be applied. Acid would not affect them, for their outside was genuine gold. For the same reason, neither would scraping, unless prolonged for a very unusual length of time. Their weight was precisely that of a genuine undoctored coin.

This device was absolutely the cleverest and safest of all the dishonest practices ever known to be resorted to in connection with money. If the genius who originated it had followed out his scheme with greater caution he might have been pursuing it in safety to-day, but he was one of those overconfident, reckless individuals whose fool-hardiness causes them to neglect due precaution for their own safety. He actually carried on his business in a room separated from an adjoining office only by a board partition which did not reach quite up to the ceiling. The sound of the busy drill at length attracted the attention of a young scapegrace of an office boy, whose curiosity prompted him during the absence of his master to play the role of peeping Tom by placing a large box upon a chair, mounting upon the former, and peck-a-booing over the board partition. He thus watched the coin-sweater in secret for nearly an hour and was still watching him when his employer returned and caught him at it. In response to the latter's query, what was he looking at? he eagerly confided to him all he had seen. The result was that his employer notified the police and the ingenious young mechanic was soon behind iron bars.

Counterfeiters do not stand anything like so good chance of making money and escaping detectives as they did thirty years ago, before the war. The national banking system was then unknown. Every little mushroom bank in the country issued its own notes. These were not secured, as our present national bank notes are, by bonds of the United States deposited with the United States treasurer. Their value rested solely upon the credit of the bank issuing them. As a result a great part of the paper money in circulation, even when not counterfeit, was quite as worthless as if it had been. Banks were breaking daily, and their notes were thus being rendered not worth the paper they were printed on, yet the facilities for carrying the news to remote parts of our land were then so limited that such money continued to pass readily long after the bank issuing it had ceased to exist.

There was no limit to the amount of notes a bank could issue, since it did not have to give any security for them, and as a result there were 100 of these worthless bills to every one good National bank note of the present day. In such a state of things it made very little difference whether a bill was counterfeit or not, since even if it was, in nine cases out of ten it was worth just as much as a genuine one. Moreover, these notes were so miserably engraved and printed that it was a very easy matter to counterfeit them with great accuracy. It has been estimated that prior to the war fully one-third of all the paper money in circulation was counterfeit and another third was the issue of worthless and irresponsible banks. This was so generlly known to be the case that every merchant kept behind his counter what was called a "counterfeit-detector." It was a pamphlet issued monthly, giving a list of all counterfeits in circulation and of all the notes rendered worthless by the breaking of the banks issuing them. Every time a customer offered a bill in payment the merchant would take down his "detector" and satisfy himself of its genuineness before accepting it.

The facilities for detecting counterfeiters, following them up, and arresting them were then practically nil, for the present thoroughly organized "secret service" was not in successful and thorough operation.

CHAPTER XX.

METHODS OF DISHONEST BOOKKEEPERS.

Moral and Physical Epidemics—Commonest Methods Used to Cover up Thefts—System no Honest Bookkeeper Will Object to—Examination at Regular Intervals—How to Detect a Dishonest Bookkeeper—What a Business Man Should Insist Upon—Things a Bookkeeper Should Never be Permitted to Do—Defalcations by Bookkeepers—What Employers Should Do—Opening the Door to Embezzlement—Suggestions for a Division of Work—Providing a Safeguard—What Constitutes a Good Bookkeeper—Words From a Boston Bank Bookkeeper—System Adopted by Banks to Guard Against Manipulation of Books—How the Work is Divided and Systemized—Requirements of a Bookkeeper—Detail of the Arrangement and Classification of Work—Bonding Employes—A New York Method of Handling Bookkeepers—Duties of the Balance Adjuster—Watching Speculative Employes—Inquiry as to Private Habits—Dishonesty Among Bookkeepers the Exception—Proverbial Honesty of Bank Employes—Preventing Peculations in Banks—Adopting Wise Methods.

There are moral epidemics as well as physical, and crime will sometimes devastate a country like disease. Particularly is this so in respect to fraud and embezzlement. In the intense race for wealth, through the desire to grow rich, that they may have money to spend for enjoyment, men seem to stop at nothing in their headlong pursuit. Forgery, fraud, actual robbery, and every ingenious form of cheating are resorted to. Men who bear the highest repute, respected citizens, supposed Christians, bank presidents, cashiers, tellers, attorneys, and trusted employes, all are found in this devil's dance. It is the result of the national characteristic—extravagance.

Dishonest bookkeepers have a better opportunity to defraud their employers than almost any other class of employes, and it is somewhat surprising, in view of the numerous defalcations constantly coming to light, that business men do not seek to place a safe check on the man who is entrusted with the conduct of the most important part of their business. It must be admitted, in this connection, however, that there is a point where checks must cease and faith begin, because unless a man thinks he has a thief in his employ and watches him constantly, he might as well keep the books himself. No honest bookkeeper will object to any system of checks that may be devised. In fact, he would rather have every verification made of his accounts that can be thought of. This does not mean that an honest man is to be subjected to a system of espionage which shall make him feel that he is watched every time he pulls out the cash drawer, but it means that he shall at regular intervals submit a balance sheet and even his trial balance sheet, as well as submit all his books for inspection. If his employer does not understand bookkeeping he is somewhat at a disadvantage, for a sharp bookkeeper can comply with these requirements and at the same time be stealing every day, and his books will apparently balance. Even an employer who understands bookkeeping can be deceived unless he goes over every account in the ledger and strikes a balance himself. That is where faith has to be brought into play or the services of a bookkeeper might as well be dispensed with. The commonest method employed by the dishonest bookkeeper is very easily explained, but cannot be detected unless a trial balance is taken. Suppose a mercantile house doing a moderate business has say 500 accounts on the ledger; John Smith owes say $500. He comes in and pays cash instead of a check. The dishonest bookkeeper gives John Smith's account credit in the ledger for that amount. No entry is made in the cash-book at all. The bookkeeper pockets the $500, which does not interfere with balancing his cash, for when the credit side is deducted from the debit the amount in the drawer will agree with the balance as shown on the cash-book.

To keep track of his customers and how their payments are being made, the merchant consults his ledger, which is the ocean into which the streams from all books of original entry flow. Suppose he looks over 400 or more accounts. How can he determine, even if a bookkeeper himself, which particular account has been credited without any original entry having been made? If he happens to be quick-witted, he may observe that where this system of thievery is carried on the bookkeeper does not enter the cash-book folio on the ledger account. Wherever this is discovered the cash-book should be examined at once, at or about the date given in the ledger credit. This method of cheating can be carried on for months without detection, even if a trial balance is presented for inspection, for cash can be debited $500 more (or whatever amount may have been stolen) than is shown in the cash account in the ledger, or even cash can be doctored by making the proper debit without the corresponding credit.

The clumsier methods employed are to enter all cash as received and then make false additions, but this is comparatively easy of detection. Every business man should insist on a semi-monthly balance sheet, if the business is not too extensive to make this an onerous duty for the bookkeeper, but under no circumstances should a statement of the condition of the business be made at longer intervals than a month. Never permit a bookkeeper to run behind-hand in posting, and for his own protection insist that he shall not keep "slips" in the cash drawer, but shall put all moneys paid out in a petty cash book for the purpose. The defalcation by bookkeepers, reported day after day, is no argument that a large portion of them are dishonest. On the contrary, the percentage of dishonesty in bookkeepers is smaller than in any other position of trust.

The main thing for an employer to do is to keep a sufficient bar between the bookkeeper and the money. If the bookkeeper is also the cashier, this is hard to effect, and the door to embezzlement is wide open Collusion with another employe is only resorted to in extreme cases.

Secrets are dangerous, and the most genteel thieves do not care to risk the confidence of another person. If the cash can be got in hand without the knowledge of anybody, the theft is so facilitated and the possibility of detection so minimized as to remove fear and scruples. This is, in brief, the history of most embezzlements. Hence no bookkeeper should be allowed to handle money or audit accounts for the cashier to pay. The system of checks or division of work is excellent, but it is new, and there are few plans now in use that have not weak points where they are least expected. The initial point of most wrong-doing is that employers lose caution. An employe of long standing is not suspected. His word is taken when it ought not to be. The habit of lumping things together is tolerated. In short, temptation is practically placed in the bookkeeper's way, when legitimate means of determination and limitation of power would prevent the evil.

Next to providing sufficient checks, one of the best means for employers to adopt as a safeguard is to give adequate pay to their help. It is next to folly to put a man in a position where he has so much responsibility at a meagre salary, wholly disproportionate to his services and his responsibilities. Yet this is commonly done. It has been shown that the largest percentage of small embezzlements among bookkeepers spring from this very cause.

The head bookkeeper in one of the largest banks in Boston says :—

"Bookkeeping as a profession is beginning, like many others, to feel the influence of popular folly. Young men, induced doubtless by a mistaken idea of the commercial opportunities offered by learning to keep books, thinking also that they can easily secure remunerative positions, learn the profession. Competition in our circles is therefore very strong. Except in the case of men who have proved their worth, and practically made themselves a necessity to particular banks, stickling for a price is out of the question. Most men, however experienced, have to begin low and work up. An inexperienced man fresh from a commercial college, where he has acquired a thorough knowledge of the theoretical part of the work, will ordinarily command but little salary.

"It must not be overlooked, however, that a good many of the so-called bookkeepers are in no wise competent. An adequate course in a commercial college is of vast benefit in the calling, but theory, after all, is a secondary consideration. Many bankers are dead set against college men. What is needed is ability to meet actual exigencies, and that is something that every bookkeeper does not possess. A fair handwriting, rapidity, the ability to debit and credit accounts and add correctly, are indispensable requisites for the calling, but after all they are compatible with a certain degree of automatism that is anything but desirable in an employe. Cashiers work themselves up to better salaries and hold their positions by personal efforts, good judgment, interest evinced in their employers' business success, and the like, and a bookkeeper's promotion and tenure of place is no less dependent upon the same factors.

" Apart from the influence of over-supply there is no reason why a good bookkeeper should be out of employment. The responsibilities of the position are great and the right qualities are not easy to find, and these facts tend to make bankers conservative in the matter of changing accountants. Employers will strain a point to keep a good man, and in case of business depression first-class bookkeepers are about the last employes of an establishment to go."

The number of robberies in banks by bookkeepers has of late years opened the eyes of bankers to the necessity of providing means to prevent collusion between customers and bookkeepers. To prevent such robberies a New York bank formulated a system of bookkeeping that is being brought into general use all over the country. The publisher of " THE FRAUDS OF AMERICA " has been furnished with a full description of the system which we incorporate herein for the benefit of the business public of the United States:

" In order to secure proper attention to the wants of depositors and to guard the bank from possible loss in consequence of dishonesty on the part of bookkeepers or of collusion between bookkeepers and dishonest customers and depositors, we have adopted the following method for handling this part of the business:

" The desks of the bookeepers of city ledgers are in an upper room of the bank. They are instructed to take off a trial balance once a month which is immediately thereafter transferred from one ledger to another, so that each one's errors are looked up and adjusted by another clerk. Bookkeepers are not permitted to make any entries upon the books of original entry of the bank, their duties being confined to posting on their ledgers and balancing pass books. All charges to the accounts of city depositors are made from the checks or charge tickets, which are entered upon the debit books by check clerks. Such charges are also entered by another set of clerks upon voucher lists, which lists are called back each day to the debit books to insure the correctness of both. The voucher lists, together with the vouchers, remain in the custody of the clerk who writes them up until the pass-book is left to be balanced, when the footing of the list is compared with the footing of the debit side of the dealer's account upon the ledger. Any discrepancy between them must be adjusted, with the knowledge and consent of both bookkeepers and voucher clerks. Balance ledgers are kept in charge of another bookkeeper for each city ledger, and separate postings are made to these balance-ledgers by another set of clerks.

"Everything pertaining to the accounts of city depositors is under the general supervision of an information clerk, and a department of the bank has been established, termed the 'Information Bureau,' for the receiving and delivery of pass-books to be balanced, or to have any entries made therein, and for attending generally to the wants of the bank's customers who ask for any information regarding their accounts. The other employes of the bank are not allowed to give such informtion, and all inquiries from dealers concerning their accounts must be referred to this bureau. The information clerk has a window opening upon the public room of the bank which is readily accessible to customers. The information clerk is required to give prompt and courteous attention to all persons applying at his window in relation to their business with the bank; to receive all pass-books left to be balanced, and to keep a record of the date of their receipt; to deliver the same to dealers or their representatives.

"Every pass-book that is balanced before delivery of the

same he is required to compare with the balance ledger and see that the balances as brought down by the bookkeepers agree with those upon the balance ledger.

"After comparing the balances he initials the same as being correct, and he must not deliver any pass-book until the balance as stated thereupon has been examined and found correct.

"The information clerk also keeps a record of dealers' accounts, and examines frequently the dates upon which their pass-books were balanced, and is required to see that every pass-book in the bank is balanced at least once in two months.

"Whenever pass-books are presented to the loan clerk, discount clerk, collection clerk, or receiving teller, to enter up credits of the current day's work that have been made in the various departments and not yet placed upon the pass-book, they are required to send the same to him for verification. He initials such entries, keeps a record of them, and verifies, by comparison with the credit books, after such books have been properly closed for the day, these different entries.

"He is also required to see that credits written upon the pass-books subsequent to the dates of the transaction are marked thereon with the dates of both such entries and the original credits upon the books of the bank. He must investigate carefully all differences in pass-books reported by dealers and cause such tickets to be made as are necessary to adjust the differences.

"In taking off the trial balance at the end of the month the balance-ledger-keepers are instructed to note the balances of each of the dealers on a separate book. The ledger-keepers do the same. They are then handed to the information clerk to strike the difference, and if there be any, to thoroughly investigate such differences and see that they are properly adjusted The city-ledger-keepers are required to balance pass-books at once when so requested by the information clerk, and to have all pass-books balanced and ready for delivery at the time specified by him. Special efforts are made to balance all pass-books within twenty-four hours from the time they are left with the bank.

"The city-ledger-keepers are also required to report to the information clerk any errors in, or omissions from, the pass-books, which they may discover in balancing, and have him verify and initial upon the pass-books, the change necessary for them to make. They are required to furnish him promptly any information he may require from their books, and to keep their ledgers footed closely, so that a balance may be struck readily when required. They are not permitted to enter upon pass-books any credits which may be of the current day's work, but must refer all requests of this character to the information clerk.

"The receiving teller is required to enter upon the pass-books all deposits of the current day, whether such pass-books are presented at the time of making such deposits or later in the day; but all deposits of a previous date must be entered upon the pass-books by the city-ledger-keepers at the direction of the information clerk, who verifies the original entry. The receiving-teller also keeps a record of dealers who habitually make deposits without their pass-books, and is required to report them. The information clerk is prohibited from making any charge tickets or credit tickets, or any entry whatsoever upon the books of the bank, except upon the record books of his own desk. His duties, so far as they relate to the entries of the accounts of the city dealers, are solely those of an investigator of errors, or verifier of entries, balances, and adjustment of errors."

Most of the cashiers and book-keepers in the great banks

are under bonds, but a hundred times more binding have been the personal and friendly relations that have existed between the presidents and vice presidents of the institutions and their employes. Defalcations pain the decent and honorable bookkeepers, and for their own protection they have prayed that different and more rigorous methods be introduced.

Bookkeepers do not handle a cent of the bank's money, and the devices for collusion with outsiders have been intricate. For that reason a number of presidents keep huge scrap books of all newspaper articles describing just how the last defaulting bookkeeper got away with the cash. The methods he used are studiously investigated, and the presidents and vice presidents have conferences for the purpose of ascertaining if such methods could be practiced in their own institutions. Many times the decision is reached that there is a possibility that these methods could be worked and then there is an immediate change in the system of bookkeeping in that bank.

There is one bank in New York whose methods of dealing with its bookkeepers preclude the possibility of cooked-up books. The bank referred to has a system by which the bookkeepers and tellers are shifted once a month or rather they are directed by the president to remain nights at the bank and look into each other's books. Each gets paid for this extra work, and there are so many employes engaged in the investigation that there is little or no possibility of collusion. The tellers and bookkeepers are thoroughly aware that once in every thirty days, and possibly oftener, their accounts and books will be examined by others, and the president of the bank does not give his orders for the investigation at any stated time. He has decided on as many as three examinations in a week, and then again he hasn't summoned his employes to go over the work of their associates for a month. Several of the presidents of leading Chicago banks, after investigating this system, have put it in operation in the institutions over which they preside.

Another precaution practiced by many banks is to employ a balance adjuster and once a month he makes an independent examination of all deposit slips and pass books and cancelled checks, to ascertain if the whole corresponds with the bookkeepers' ledgers. In order to perpetrate a swindle under this system collusion would be necessary between the bookkeeper, the balance adjuster and "the man on the outside."

There is an absurd fiction that a bank employe's time is his own outside of business hours This should be exploded at once. If the directors of a bank happen to find out that the president is taking "flyers" on the Stock Exchange they will not say it is that president's own business, but will look sharply after the cash balance and will probably find a new president. If a president, in turn, finds out that his cashier or bookkeeper is living beyond his means he will naturally infer that the bank is somehow paying for the additional luxuries. In short, every man who handles the money of others, in trust for them, is liable to have his private way of living and his personal amusements made the subject of inquiry. It is a part of the price he pays for the early comfort of being a bank employe. It will follow him through life as long as he is in a fiduciary position. And no one but the intending rogue much minds having to satisfy his superior that he is living right and doing right.

Dishonesty in banks is the exception, and not the rule. There are about fourteen thousand banks in the United States, and about seventy-five thousand bank employes, and the few black sheep that come to the front is something wonderful. There are ten defalcations and embezzlements in mercantile houses to one in banks; yet the theft of a ten-dollar note by a bank employe is heralded from one end of the country to the other, and by the time it reaches home again it is magnified into $10,000. The bankers and bank employes of America are proverbial for their honesty and integrity the world over.

One of the leading causes of embezzlement and misapplication of money by bank officials and employes, is attributed to a laxity of proper checks on the work assigned them. Once a man has a reputation of honesty, he is trusted implicitly. His accounts or work are never questioned or looked into, and if he wishes to accommodate a friend with a few thousand of dollars, he can easily do so. If the venture is unsuccessful, figures are juggled to suit his fancy.

Let a man know that on a moment's notice another man will take his place for a day or two and continue his work, and he will be very cautious about keeping his accounts straight. It may seem a species of unfair dealing, but in view of the acknowledged cause of embezzlements it is legitimate.

In regard to peculations in banks it is impossible to invent a system that would prevent small peculations with absolute certainty. A system theoretically perfect would if it worked practically render it immaterial whether a clerk were as honest as Cato or as great a thief as Fagin. But every system depends for its success upon the honesty of those who carry it out; that is its inventor assumes the majority of the honest employees will make it hot for the occasional dishonest one. The more separated the detail of the work the more new combinations will be apt to arise which will give opportunity for peculation The employees of a bank living a large part of their lives together know and appreciate each other's honesty of character and purpose. They cannot look on any one as a black sheep until he actually does something wrong. They trust each other more or less as their duties are contiguous. They form friendships or antipathies. Without a very large share of confidence in each other, from the president to the latest employee, a bank could not be run at all. Usually there is great *esprit du corps* among the employees of a large bank; they take pride in each other and in the bank. Although some bank officers encourage distrust among their employees, this oftener produces unpleasant manners and petty acerbities than it adds to the security of the cash on hand. It sometimes also damages a bank by making the tellers and others who come in contact with the public phenomenally unpleasant to every one who has occasion to address them.

The best way to secure freedom from peculation is to adopt a method of keeping accounts and papers as easily understood as the business done will allow. A method suitable for the kind of business of one bank might not do so well for another. The employes should be carefully selected, and bonded in every case, according to the supposed temptation likely to be met in their situation. The various guarantee and fidelity companies are doing a good work in making the average employe sensible of the value of a bond he has to pay for himself, and constantly making him feel the responsibility that attaches to his duties, however humble they may be. The employes should receive proper salaries, which would encourage them to feel both that they may live in moderate comfort and at the same time lay aside something for the future. If there is any business that requires men of moral stamina higher than the average it is employment in banks and institutions where large amounts of money are handled. Within a reasonable range it is well for banks to watch the outside manners and habits of their employes, and to see that they have timely warning against those that lead to extravagance and consequent impecuniosity. Very often smartness and ability, quickness and alertness, are suffered to condone other defects.

But while wise methods will reduce robberies by employes to a minimum, they cannot absolutely prevent them, although there are doubtless some large banks in which they never have occurred. Those who insist on there being some possible system which will absolutely and infallibly prevent stealing are apt to fall into the error of encouraging a distrust among their clerks, which has the tendency towards suggesting the very crime they wish to prevent. It is the human equation that has to be dealt with, made up of the good and evil, of good qualities and imperfections. The best results are obtained by encouraging right and noble traits, such as honesty and devotion, and to let the evil traits be choked out by a generous cultivation of the others. In a city where there are many banks it is well to encourage associations among bank employes. This leads to the growth of a guild and professional feeling, and raises the tone of the whole class.

CHAPTER XXI.

FRAUDULENT HANDWRITING.

INFORMATION FOR THOSE WHO HANDLE COMMERCIAL AND LEGAL DOCUMENTS—PECULIARITY OF HANDWRITING—METHODS EMPLOYED IN FORGERY—MEANS EMPLOYED FOR ERASING WRITING—CARE TO BE USED IN WRITING—SPECIMENS OF ORIGINALS AND ALTERATIONS—MEANS OF DISCOVERING AND DEMONSTRATING FORGERY—DISPUTED SIGNATURES—FREE HAND OR COMPOSITE SIGNATURES—IMPORTANT FACTS FOR THE BUSINESS PUBLIC—HOW TO USE THE MICROSCOPE AND PHOTOGRAPHY TO DETECT FORGERY—APPLYING CHEMICAL TESTS—HOW TO HANDLE DOCUMENTS AND PAPERS TO BE PRESERVED—THE VALUE OF EXPERT TESTIMONY—USING CHEMICAL, MECHANICAL AND CLERICAL PREVENTATIVES.

The following chapter on fraudulent handwriting is written by Mr. William C. Shaw, of Chicago, the well-known expert on forgery, whose services are called in all important forgery and disputed handwriting cases in the country. It is replete with facts and suggestions of the greatest importance, and will be found not only interesting reading, but an instructive article throughout :

The comparative frequency with which checks, drafts, notes, etc., are being raised or altered, as well as deeds, wills, etc., forged and substituted, has naturally created a widespread interest in the subject of "fraudulent handwriting." The importance of practical knowledge in this direction by those who are continually handling commercial papers and legal documents is at once apparent, but others engaged in any business pursuit may be saved considerable loss, trouble and annoyance by observing the principles and suggestions explained and illustrated in this article.

In approaching the subject of detecting forged or fraudulent handwriting let it be understood as a fundamental principle that there are hardly two persons whose writing is similar enough to deceive a careful observer, unless the one is imitating the other. Hands, like faces, have their peculiar features and expression, and the imitator must not alone copy the original, but at the same time disguise his own writing. Even the most skilled forger cannot entirely hide his individuality and is bound to relapse into his habitual ways of forming and connecting letters, words, etc. The employment of extreme care can be detected by signs of hesitancy, the substitution of curves for angles, etc., which appear very plainly when the writing is critically examined with a magnifying glass. When a signature has been forged by means of tracing over the original, the resemblance is often so exact as to deceive even the supposed author. In these cases the microscope is generally effective in detecting the forgery, as well as the methods employed. Perfect identity of two genuine signatures is a practical impossibility; if, therefore, two signatures superposed and held against the light completely coincide it is almost certain that one of them is a forgery.

The methods employed in executing forged handwriting are varied and depend largely in the individual skill and inclination of the party attempting it.

The most frequent class of forgeries consists of erasures, which means the removing of the genuine writing by mechanical or chemical means. Erasing with knife, rubber, etc., has practically been abandoned by expert forgers, on account of the almost certain detection which must necessarily follow the traces left in evidence. Erasing fluids, ink eradicators, etc., are more generally used for this purpose. These have entered the market for legitimate purposes and can be commercially obtained. Too much confidence should, therefore, not be placed in the careful writing of checks, etc., alone, as with the aid of chemicals the original writing can be entirely removed and forged words and figures substituted.

Second in importance and frequency, and perhaps the easiest kind of forgery, consists of simple additions to genuine handwriting. In checks or drafts the changing of "eight" to "eighty" by the addition of a single letter is a striking illustration. The change of "six" to "sixty," "twenty" to "seventy," etc., can also be accomplished by adding a few strokes and without erasure, as per specimens given:

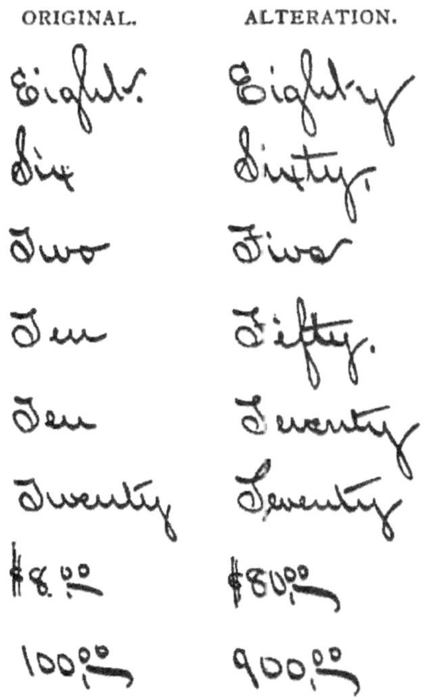

The forging of signatures and writing in general is accomplished by means of tracing as above referred to, free-hand copying, with the aid of considerable practice, and copying by mechanical or chemical processes. It is not intended here to give directions, but simply to refer to facts, with a view to preventing losses and detecting forgeries. For this reason one method of reproduction may briefly be described. The carelessness with which blotters are used in public places, bank counters, post, express and hotel offices is to be strongly condemned. The entire signature of an indorser is often clearly copied on the underside of the blotting paper, which only needs to fall into the hands of a designing party to be projected on any paper or document and in any desired position.

The means of discovering and demonstrating forged handwriting are as varied as the methods employed in its execution, and it may be some comfort to know that the cunning of the forger is more than matched by the skill and ability of the expert.

The ordinary method of identifying handwriting consists in the "comparison of hands." This, however, is only admitted in courts of justice under certain limitations. The genuineness of a disputed writing can be proved by a witness who has seen its execution, or by comparison with correspondence received in the regular course of business, or by comparison with undisputed specimens of the alleged handwriting, which must also be in evidence. Disputed signatures may be compared with other signatures acknowledged to be genuine, or with letters or documents, the genuineness of which is unquestioned. In arriving at conclusions many things are to be considered, the form of the letters, their manner of combination, evidences of habit, etc.

Another method of detecting forgery is afforded by the internal evidences of fraud of the writing itself, with or without the aid of comparison with genuine writing. These evidences may consist of alterations, erasures, additions, crowding, etc., as above referred to; tracing a genuine writing by means of ink or pencil, afterwards retraced, etc.

The copy of a genuine signature may be free-hand or composite, by which is meant that the writing is produced discontinuously or in parts. Comparison of the separate letters of a doubtful specimen of writing with the separate letters of the genuine writing of the supposed imitator or imitated always exhibits less uniformity if imitation has been attempted, the copyist being frequently led into an approach to his ordinary handwriting or into oversight of some special characteristics of the writing he is simulating. Even minor points do not escape the expert's critical attention. The dotting of the i's, or crossing of the t's, curls, loops, flourishes, intervals between words and letters, connections, characteristics of up and down strokes are all carefully noticed.

A glass of low magnifying power will, as a rule, exhibit erasures, and even bring to view the erased letters. In tracing, the forger frequently fails to cover over the first outlines, which can be plainly distinguished. The places where the pen has been put upon and removed from the paper may sometimes be noticed, which is in itself strong evidence of fraud.

With the aid of a microscope the character of the alterations, certain characteristics due to age, emotion, etc., the kind of a pen used and how it was held, the nature of ink, order of writing, with regard to time, whether produced by the right or left hand, standing or sitting, can often be determined. Indentations made by heavy strokes or a sharp pen, as well as those employed as guides for the signature subsequently written, will also be brought into prominence. Forged signatures placed under the microscope have generally a patched appearance, which results from the retracing of lines in certain portions not occurring in genuine writing.

In case of disputed handwriting photography has also been employed to great advantage. Of course the writing in question should, whenever practicable, be compared with the original, photographic copies being looked upon with disfavor and considered by most courts as secondary evidence. Still, photographic enlargements of genuine and disputed signatures are very useful in illustrating expert testimony. Certain characteristics, differences in ink, attempts to remove writing, etc., may be brought to view, which would be entirely overlooked by direct examination. The wonderful power of the camera has recently been illustrated in a very striking manner. A large ocean steamer was photographed, and on receipt of the proof the owners were surprised to see a hand bill posted on the side of the hull. Examination of the ship disclosed no hand bill there, but another photograph exhibited the same result. A searching inspection revealed the presence of the mysterious paper buried beneath four coats of paint, but defying the superficial scrutiny of the human eye.

As a last resort chemical tests may be applied, by which the identity or difference of the inks used may be established, etc. As a means of demonstrating that chemical erasures have been made a certain manipulation and treatment of the paper submitted will almost invariably bring back the original and obliterated writing.

A few words regarding papers and documents, intended for preservation, will not be amiss. Improved processes of manufacture have certainly had no beneficial influence on the durability of the products, and while inks and papers have become greatly reduced in price and apparently improved in quality, it is very doubtful if much of our book learning and many of our written instruments will go down to future generations. Even fifty years will suffice to decompose many an attractive volume at present on the shelves of our libraries, or fade the writing of finely engraved and important documents. The quality of the ink and paper selected is therefore of greatest importance. Typewritten copies particularly are subject to the ravages of time, and ought to be avoided when preservation for years to come is the principal consideration, as for instance in the case of wills, etc., which ought to be made in one's own handwriting whenever practicable.

Briefly, I may state that all the safeguards employed on commercial papers or legal documents, outside of the actual protection afforded, have the beneficial effect or tendency to make forgeries, erasures or alterations more difficult, at the same time warning prospective forgers to keep a respectful distance.

The inks used, the position of the writing, the paper on which it is written, the employment of certain chemical, mechanical and clerical preventatives are all to be thoughtfully considered by those who desire to protect themselves against losses resulting from fraudulent handwriting.

With regard to expert testimony it may be said in conclusion that it is most effective if governed solely by the evidence submitted, and not by information otherwise obtained. The microscopic and photographic examination of papers and documents, as well as their mechanical and chemical treatment, require in all cases the trained eye, the skilled hand and the extensive experience of the expert, in order to fully utilize the available material and to arrive at conclusions which are in entire accord with the facts under consideration, thereby aiding in the just and equitable settlement of weighty questions of profit or loss, affluence or poverty, liberty or imprisonment, life or death.

Another expert in handwriting says that regarding the methods made use of to determine authorship, specialists are naturally reticent. Some of them have admitted, however, the nature of the leading principles which guide them. The philosophy of the matter rests mainly on the fact that it is very rare for any two persons to write hands similar enough to deceive a careful observer, unless one is imitating the other. "Fists," like faces, have all some special idiosyncrasy, and the imitator has not merely to copy that of some one else but to disguise his own.

By careful and frequent practice he may succeed well enough to deceive the ordinary man, but is rarely successful in baffling the expert. Even the most skillful culprit cannot wholly hide his individuality, as he is sure to relapse into his ordinary method occasionally. Then again, great care has to be used, and this can be detected by the traces of hesitancy, the substitution of curves for angles and *vice versa*, which come out very plainly when the writing is examined under the microscope, as it usually is by the expert.

A plan of detection which has been adopted with great success is to cut out each letter in a doubtful piece of writing, and paste all the A's, B's, etc., on separate sheets of paper. The process is also gone through with a genuine bit of caligraphy of the imitator or the imitated, as the case may be. Comparison almost invariably shows that the letters are less uniform if imitation has been attempted, the writer being occasionally betrayed into some approach to his ordinary caligraphy, or into momentary forgetfulness of some special point in the handwriting he is simulating.

No point is too small to escape an expert's attention. The dotting of "i's," the crossing of "t's," the curls and flourishes, the intervals between the words, the thinness of the up-stroke and the thickness of the down-stroke, are all noted and carefully compared. Where only a signature has been forged, and that by means of tracings from the original the resemblance is often so exact as to deceive even the supposed author, but in these cases the microscope is generally effective in determining not merely the forgery but the method by which it was accomplished. It is some comfort to know that the cunning of the forger is overmatched by the scientific skill of the trained expert.

CHAPTER XXII.

YOUR NAME IN DANGER.

New Science of Crime—Chemistry Has Developed a High Grade of Rascals—Changed Methods of Crime—New Dangers that Alarm Business Men—Is Protection Against Forgery Impossible?—Result of Chemical Treatment—Forged Letters of Introduction—The Advice System—Paying for Forged Paper–An Expert's Easy Alteration of Safety Paper—Devices Adopted for Protection—The Business Public to Organize for Mutual Protection.

It used to occasion some comment from those who received letters from Senator David Davis, of Illinois, to see his name subscribed so near the body of the letter that it would have been impossible to have written anything between the signature and the letter itself. He left no white paper; the upper parts of the letters of his name were made to touch the last line ot the letter. Judge Davis used not to write so many letters when he was a supreme court justice as he did afterward when he became a member of the senate, and he was never a very active correspondent.

He explained why he had adopted this rather unusual custom. He said that when he was a judge in Illinois a case was brought before him of alleged forgery of a note. The signature to the note was admittedly genuine, but it was claimed by the apparent maker of the note that the body of it had been written upon a piece of paper to which the genuine signature had been attached. The trial developed that some one had secured a letter written by the apparent maker of the note. The man's signature had been written at a considerable distance below the end of the letter, leaving a sufficient space of white paper to write in the words constituting the note. The original letter had, of course, been cut off.

This experience, Judge Davis said, taught him a lesson, and he never signed his name to any document without taking care to make it impossible for any one to make a forgery over the genuine signature.

But if Judge Davis were living now, he would find that such precaution would not be a preventive to forgery. Within the past two or three years the methods of crime have very greatly changed. The cracksman is a criminal of the past. Bank burglary is almost unknown.

But it has been made apparent that crime has only changed its methods. Criminals are now expert and, to some degree, learned men. Chemistry serves the villain just as it does the true scientist, and bank officers as well as the higher grade of detectives have been aware for some time that an epoch of dangerous forgery has succeeded the day of the expert safe-breaker and masked burglar.

Recently a very remarkable case has been on trial in Connecticut, and one which would illustrate to Judge Davis, if he were alive, that his method of preventing forgery is no longer of any value. A merchant of Rhode Island, a man of very high business standing, named Peckham, was amazed when he received notification that two notes, one for $8,000 and another for $2,000, were held by banks for collection, and that he was the maker of them. Mr. Peckham repudiated the notes, although he was compelled to admit that his signature was genuine. He declared that the body of the notes were forgeries. The payee of the note was a grain merchant named Tritt, living in Connecticut, and a criminal suit for forgery was brought. The notes were submitted to experts. They were written upon sheets of business paper, at the top of which were the business cards in one case of Mr. Peckham's house and in the other of Mr. Tritt's. Mr. Peckham claimed that in each case his signature was signed by him to business letters and that the body of the letters had been bleached out by chemicals and then a note written in place of the correspondence.

A few years ago it would have been possible to have proven such bleaching and alteration. Prof. Doremus, an expert authority, testified in court that where original writing had been removed it could be reproduced by chemical reagents. But if chemicals failed to restore any writing, then it might be regarded as established that the only writing upon the paper was that which appeared to the naked eye.

These two notes were submitted to an expert, and he subjected them to chemical treatment. The paper upon which the note for $2,000 was written under this reagent revealed earlier writing, and in Mr. Peckham's handwriting. But no treatment of the paper upon which the $8,000 note had been written brought to light any earlier writing. As the first trial was upon this note, and as the only evidence of forgery was Mr. Peckham's uncorroborated testimony that he had never made the note, the case against the accused man failed. But the fact that the expert was not able to restore earlier writing is no longer proof that no such writing was ever made on that paper, and in this advance in chemical knowledge lies one of the greatest dangers to business men.

A short time ago a firm doing a large insurance business in New York signed three checks brought by the cashier to them in the course of his usual business. The checks were made payable to another insurance company. Some time after that this cashier disappeared and no trace of him has ever been discovered. It was then found by the officers of the company that he had by use of chemicals obliterated the name of the payee on these checks and inserted his own, and in that way was able to draw the money, amounting to several thousand dollars. The company brought suit against the bank, claiming that it had paid forged checks, and an expert for the bank testified that if there had been obliteration of the name of the original payee it would be established by chemical treatment. The checks were submitted to such chemical treatment, but there was no revelation of alteration.

An expert says that his investigations have taught him that the marrying of ink to paper so as to produce negotiable bills or evidences of credit cannot be done in such a way as to prevent alterations or forgeries, with the chance very greatly that the parties whose names or paper are thus forged will have to stand the loss instead of banks. These things have not made any public excitement, because forgeries of this kind have not the dramatic and sensational elements which used to attend great bank burglaries. Yet this advance in criminal knowledge is far more dangerous than the old method of crime, as many experiences indicate.

A man with letters of introduction, undoubtedly forged, went not long ago to one of the largest banks in New York City with $5,000 in one pile and $50 in another. He said to the teller that he wished to deposit this money and to take out two certificates of deposit. Having done so, he chatted with the teller awhile, who was impressed with his manner very greatly. On the following day the man returned to the bank, saying that he had a chance for business investment and would therefore draw the $5,000 deposit, handing in to the teller his certificate of deposit. The money was paid to him without question. A few days later a certificate for $5,000 was sent to the bank for collection from Canada, and then on comparison it was discovered that the first certificate which had been paid had been altered from the $50 certificate received the day before. It was done with wonderful expertness. As the $5,000 certificate paid in Canada was genuine, the bank was compelled to stand the loss.

But an even shrewder piece of criminality than this, and one which banks or business men anywhere in this country may suffer from, has recently been discovered. A man having every appearance of the habit and life of a gentleman and a business man with letters of introduction, called at a country bank in Ohio, saying that he had a considerable number of small obligations to meet and he desired to buy bank drafts on New York. He bought a number, most of them for less than $20 in amount. Some weeks later this bank began to receive these drafts, and discovered that the amounts upon them did not agree with their books. Not the slightest indication of change was apparent to the eye. Chemical treatment revealed no alteration, and yet it was certain that the criminal, being skilled in chemistry, had altered the figures. It was his method not to increase the amount very greatly. A $16 draft he made $160. Small amounts like these would not tend to cause suspicion, and such drafts could be easily negotiated. As the bank could not prove forgery or alteration, it was compelled to pay the drafts, and bank officers being extremely sensitive, they paid the losses, which did not aggregate very large amounts, and kept quiet.

A Chicago bank believed that it was amply protected against fraud, by what is called the advice system. Its habit has been at the close of each day's business to notify its New York correspondent of all the drafts it has issued that day, and the numbers and amounts of each of them. This it was supposed would prevent the payment of any altered draft when it reached the New York bank. But this advice cost the bank $12,000. A well-dressed man, well introduced apparently, with the manner of an active business man, bought two drafts of this bank, one for $12,000 and one for $120. This transaction was reported immediately to the New York correspondent. A day or two later a draft for $12,000 was received by the New York correspondent. Its number corresponded with that indicated in the letter of information sent from the Chicago bank, and it was therefore paid. But when a few days after that another draft for $12,000 of the same number was received it was evident that fraud had been practiced. The last draft was genuine. It had heen negotiated in a distant city. The first draft had been altered so that its number corresponded with that of the genuine draft for $12,000, and it had been raised from $120 to $12,000. Yet the alterations were so perfect that it was almost impossible to detect them. As the New York correspondent had paid the forged draft it was, of course, compelled to pay the genuine one, and the Chicago bank lost its money.

It has been supposed that the use of the punch was a perfect preventive of raising checks. But that depends upon what kind of punch is used. One check issued for $39 was raised to $3,900 and paid, although the figures 39 has been punched in the check. It is probable, however, that perfect punches will be invented which prevent the raising of the amount. But this will not prevent forgery.

One of the greatest banks of New York has used for some years a patent paper for its checks, for which it has been claimed that alterations are impossible without immediate revelation upon the paper itself. There are several kinds of safety paper in use and when they were first made they defied alteration, but chemistry has beaten them, and it is possible to bleach writing from them in such a manner as to make discovery impossible.

Business men who make many checks are now being made aware of these dangers, and, understanding that the tendency of the courts is to protect banks where the signature is unquestioned and the appearance of the check is such as to defy detection, are now adopting all sorts of devices for their security. Some of them have made private arrangements with their banks not to pay any checks which do not have a secret mark upon them. But this does not prevent other forgeries. The Connecticut case previously cited in this chapter, shows that it is possible for a scoundrel to take a letter written by a man of financial responsibility, obliterate absolutely the handwriting upon it and substitute for it a note. This standing over an unqestioned signature may be easily discounted, and unless the business man has some other evidence than his testimony as to the forgery the chances are that he will be compelled to pay the note.

This matter is of so much importance and the dangers seem to be so rapidly increasing that the bankers are talking of devising some new method of preventing these frauds, while business men are so seriously concerned about it that it may be made a matter of convention and agreement among them.

It is the opinion of Superintendent Byrnes that more money has been lost by forgeries and other swindles by the expert use of chemical knowledge in the last year than has been lost by burglary in the last ten years.

CHAPTER XXIII.

POSTOFFICE AND MAIL THIEVES.

A Great Business With Few Losses—Thieving From the Mails—Ingenious Methods Used to Rifle Letters—The Work of Postoffice Inspectors—Clever Ruses Adopted by Inspectors—Their Requirements—Using "Decoy" and "Test" Letters—Watching Dishonest Postal Clerks—Investigating Postoffices—Tracing Anonymous Letters—Entrapping a Thief—How the Work is Done—Reminiscences of an Inspector—Stealing Letters Containing Checks, Drafts and Other Valuables—Robbing Street Letter Boxes—Plundering Mail Sacks—Smart Work of an Inspector—Hiding Among the Mail Bags.

Considering the hundreds of thousands of dollars that are daily sent through the mails in the form of treasury notes, the few losses from embezzelment speak volumes for the general honesty of postoffice employes. In spite of the facilities offered by the government for the safe transmission of money by money orders and registered letters, the masses seem content to take chances, and it is safe to say that where one person seeks a guaranty for the safe delivery of a missive and its contents there are two who are disposed to trust in providence and to the integrity of postal clerks. Instances are on record where as large amounts as $10,000 have been mailed in unregistered packages, and misdirected letters containing sums from $1 to $100 turn up every day at the dead letter office. The average postoffice official is perfectly conversant with this fact, and if at all weak-kneed morally, the indiscretion of the forwarder subjects him to constant temptation. But there is always more or less thieving from the mails.

Probably no thief is harder to catch than the one who robs Uncle Sam's mail. His methods are so ingenious, his plunder is so easily hidden or destroyed, and his rascality is so well masked by the honesty and integrity of his associates, that he not infrequently continues his operations for years before he is finally overwhelmed with proof of his guilt, disgraced and sent to prison. Though letters, and valuable ones, too, are stolen every day, and keen-eyed inspectors are hunting high and low for the thieves, arrests for this class of crime are comparatively rare. There is a reason for this. Postoffice inspectors in running down a thief will never take him in custody until they are at least morally certain of his guilt. They will either wait to catch him in the act of rifling a letter, or keep a strict watch on his habits outside of business hours to learn whether or not he is spending more money than his salary would permit, before they will even let him know that he is under suspicion.

On this account innocent men are never submitted to the humiliation of arrest. Sometimes an inspector may not be able to prove that his man was a thief.. However, he may inadvertently have omitted some important detail from the chain of evidence he drew around the fellow, and though the prisoner is turned loose with a verdict of " not guilty " as his certificate of honesty, it is almost a certainty that he deserved to go to the penitentiary. It would indeed be strange if the thousands of clerks who constitute the great mail army of the country were all honest men. It would be stranger still if all of them could withstand the temptations that constantly arise as they handle the millions of precious parcels which are carried in pouches through all the ramifications of the railway systems. The government will not guarantee the safe delivery of a letter or parcel.

A matter of precaution, however, has provided the

money order and registered letter system, to prevent the sending of cash in letters, but even letters sent under these auspices are not sacred to the mail thief. He robs them with as little impunity as he would the humblest missive that falls into his hands. The only protection the user of the mails has against thieving is the postoffice inspector. His influence on the morals of men throughout the great department in responsible positions is simply amazing. But for him Uncle Sam's letter service would go to the bow-wows in a very short time. It is not because the inspector is such a formidable person that he is feared, but because his ways are mysterious; because he seems to be omnipresent. His clever ruses to overcome the cunning of the rascals he is after, his nearly invariable success in rounding them up, in the gangs that practice the lockstep daily, and the unlimited power he has at command to carry on his work secretly or publicly, as he may choose, makes him one of the most important factors in the service.

One of the chief duties of a most important branch of the postal service is the detection by inspectors of malefactors against the postal system. This branch is known as the department of postoffice inspectors. They number from seventy-five to 100, and are under the immediate direction of a chief inspector. They are paid from an item in the general postal department appropriation. The country is divided into ten districts, the chief offices being located in Washington, Boston, New York, Philadelphia, Chattanooga, Tenn., St. Louis, Chicago, San Francisco and Austin, Texas. Each division is under the supervision of an official known as the postoffice inspector in charge. The staff of each division varies in number according to its extent and general character. Inspectors in charge receive a salary of $2,500 and inspectors $1,600 per annum, besides a per diem of $4 when actively engaged in work for the department. Their commissions run from Jan. 1 to Jan. 1, and appointments are made under the civil service act. The chief is paid $3,000. The positions involve considerable responsibility and call for a degree of intelligence and capacity far beyond the requirements of ordinary detective work. As a rule, the clews afforded by cases presented for their investigation are of the vaguest nature. Patience is one of the rarest of moral qualifications, and yet to locate the average postoffice thief it is necessary to rival Job himself in the exercise of that virtue. The inspector in charge is the official who receives every complaint against the postoffices in his division.

When complaints are made of money being lost in the mails they are at once forwarded to the chief inspector at Washington, who classifies them under the head of A, B, C and F. It may be said in this connection that the loss of ordinary letters is classified under the head of B. All complaints are "jacketed," as it is termed, numbered, and, with directions for the prosecution of the case, returned to the inspector in charge of the division in which the complaints were made. Certain formal inquiries are sent to the writer and the person to whom the letter was addressed. It is estimated that at least 20 per cent. of the letters first reported stolen eventually turn up, perhaps having been misdirected or held for postage. The cases reported are subjected to careful examination to ascertain if a number of losses center in any particular postoffice. If they do it is accepted as an indication of crookedness, and the suspected points are at once put under the closest espionage. Sometimes complaints covering a wide expanse of country seem to center on one railroad route.

When either a railroad route or postoffice has been selected for investigation there are various methods pursued to locate the supposed thief. Decoy or "test" letters, the latter being the official designation, are frequently called into play. As soon as suspicion is fastened upon an individual half a dozen of these letters, each marked and containing money, are addressed to some obscure town and mailed the same day. If these letters come to hand all right the experiment is repeated again and again until the inspectors are satisfied that they have been misled. When any of these letters fail to come through to their destination an arrest is made so soon that criminating evidence is generally found upon the person.

The detection of dishonest postal clerks is almost certain in the long run, but there are instances where peculations have been carried on years before discovery. One dishonest clerk will temporarily cast a shadow of suspicion over many others.

This class of work, however, is but one portion of the inspector's duties. They are required to follow up cases where the parties have put the mails to improper uses. One of the most important of their functions is the supervision of postoffices of the first, second and third classes, and the investigation of any charges of inefficiency or misdemeanors preferred against the postmasters themselves. The location of offices of the above character in any town or city is selected by the inspectors who also lease the premises. In fact, an inspector in charge can temporarily suspend any postmaster for cause. In some respects their powers are autocratic.

Credentials issued by the postmaster general not only command all railroads, steamboats, and other mail contractors to afford them free passage, but require that they shall be "respected and obeyed." They are called upon to rate up the salaries of clerks and investigate the demands of postmasters for additional help, as well as to sift every case wherein there is reason to believe that the mails are being subjected to improper uses. Scores of letters are received daily by inspectors inquiring as to the reliability of certain medical and other concerns who are large advertisers. Almost invariably such letters are dated in the middle or western states. No inquiries regarding the character of individuals are even honored with an answer, but all communications coming within the legitimate sphere of the service are given careful and considerate attention. The Society for the Suppression of Vice finds this branch of postal department of inestimable value in reaching parties engaged in the dissemination of obscene literature. All questionable advertising schemes are among the many other matters that the inspectors are called upon to probe to the bottom, and their work of this nature alone is sufficient to merit the kindest consideration of the public. Save for their vigilance, it is hard to say where the depredations on society of the " skin advertisers " would cease.

The source of anonymous letters is about the most annoying problem presented to them for solution. The number of epistles of this description deposited in the mails is far greater than ordinarily supposed. To gain an idea of the depths of human meanness one can do no better than to peruse the unsigned communications submitted to the inspection of these officials by the insulted recipients. Some of them are no more than insulting, others defamatory to the last degree, while not a few fairly reek with obscenity. When a letter of the latter description comes to light, the inspectors are apt to conclude that they have a woman to deal with, for it is a rather peculiar fact that when a female stoops to this sort of thing she is likely to be decidedly immodest in expression as well as vindictive in tone. Postal cards are favorite mediums for obscene communications, writers aiming to wound their victims through the eyes of all who may chance to scan the foul screeds. It is not easy to locate an anonymous writer, but if the victim is long pursued the old adage of the pitcher and the well is likely to be verified.

An instance of this is afforded by a case in Toledo, Ohio, where a well known merchant tailor was pestered by anonymous postal cards, averaging one a day, reflecting on the character of a most estimable young lady. This was kept up for weeks after an inspector had been detailed to work up the case, and not the slightest clue was discovered. Finally a tailoress employed in the shop of the victim was detected in the act of purloining a blank postal card. Nothing was done or said about the occurrence at the time, but a few days after the inspector strolled into the shop and requested the woman to mend a rent in his overcoat. When he left the garment in her keeping there were half a dozen marked postal cards in the pocket, but when he took the coat away they were gone. The next day the tailor received one of them through the mail covered with the usual nasty inuendoes. The woman was arrested, confessed, and was punished, and the blush of shame no longer mantles the tailor's modest cheek when he reads his morning mail.

A few reminiscences and the manner of work of a famous postoffice inspector told in his own way will be found very interesting:

" You see, a letter is a very small thing, and is scarcely more to the postoffice business than a grain of sand is to a stretch of beach. It passes through many hands, and it is hard to find out just where its trip was brought to an end. When one letter disappears on a given route it is almost certain that others will go in the same way. Then we begin our work. We do not overlook a single circumstance or detail. When we have finally satisfied ourselves as to the point where the robberies were committed, we either establish a watch or use decoy letters. Either one is almost certain to bring the game down. But I remember one case in which all our ordinary devices failed. It was away out in New Mexico on one of the old star routes. Hundreds of letters, all of them containing money, drafts or something else of value, disappeared with astonishing regularity. Finally the thieves altered their methods, and instead of taking the letter entire opened it and took the contents. We sent inspector after inspector over the route.

" Every trip involved long and tedious rides, sleepless days and nights and work that was as disagreeable as anybody would want to do. We found that the rifled letters passed through many hands, and that of twenty men each one was liable to be guilty. All of them were watched and shadowed, but in vain, and we were about to give up in despair when a thought occurred to me. Calling one of my men, I carefully outlined to him the details of my plan for detecting the thief, and I was not a bit surprised when he expressed doubt about the result. Briefly, the plan was this: I went to a wholesale drug house, procured a lot of different kinds of drugs, which were carefully labeled, and then placing them all together in a satchel I handed the latter to my assistant and sent him on his mission. Just before he went he was instructed to inform every official he met that his was merely a trip of inspection, and to carry out the deception he was to make an examination of all office accounts that came under his notice. But the instruction on which I laid the most stress, however, was that which referred to the itinerant apothecary's shop he carried. I told him to be sure and examine the contents of every bottle of mucilage he saw and incidentally mix a bit of some drug with it, taking care, of course, to make a memorandum that would show just where the drug had been left. Well, the inspector made the trip and came back.

Three weeks after his return a Chicago banker brought us a registered letter which had come over the troublesome star route. A big draft was missiug from it. It had been rifled. The inspector who had 'fixed' the mucilage came in just about then, placed the back of the letter to his mouth, and tasted his mucilage. 'Ah!' he said, as his eyes lighted up; then he pulled a book from his pocket, carefully scanned the leaves, and placing his finger under a certain line he told us that the envelope had been resealed at a certain town in the New Mexican Rockies. The rest was easy and another inspector went down that way. In a week or two half a dozen decoy letters were sent over the route. The thief fell into the trap and subsequently went to the penitentiary. I won't mention his name, for he is now leading an honest life. The postoffice thief is, as a rule, a victim of his surroundings, and it rarely happens that one of them gets into trouble a second time. Once they have paid the penalty of their indiscretion they settle down to an honest existence, and it would be but little short of an outrage to publish their names.

" The case of George Wood was the most remarkable one that ever came under my observation. Wood was an educated man from Massachussetts, as smart as a steel trap and a thief by nature. For months complaints poured into the office that valuable letters were missing. Every firm in the city, I believe, lost mail of some sort. Then we began to hear rumors of a man collecting bills that had been sent out by mail, and before we could get well started on the case the thief had gathered in several thousand dollars. For months we were unable to fix suspicion on anybody with any degree of certainty, but finally we were forced to the conclusion that the work was being done on the outside of the postoffice. Either somebody had a key to the box locks or had invented some method to extract their contents through the drop hole.

One day our attention was called to a man who had paid a young German woman for some furs with a check that had been stolen from the mails. His description tallied in a general sort of way with the strange bill collector whose clever disguises had so long saved him from arrest. We put that girl on our staff, stationed her in the street near her store and kept her there for nearly a week looking for the thief. She saw him late on the afternoon of the sixth day of her tiresome vigil and followed close at his heels. The girl followed him home, made a mental note of the number of the house, and then reported to me. I had the fellow's room searched and in it we found 3,600 letters which had contained upwards of half a million dollars' worth of bills, receipts, drafts and checks. We decoyed him to the postoffice, placed him under arrest and then got a confession from him. He admitted that he had stolen over 7,000 letters, but he never would tell us the amount of money he collected. His plan was to make a tour of the mail boxes in the evening when they were loaded with business mail, extract as many letters as he could with his fingers, and then take out many more with a wire. Wood was easily convicted and sentenced to a term in prison.

" Permit me to state one more case that will show how diligently and long inspectors work to unravel thefts and detect culprits. A few months ago every inspector between Boston and New York and Chicago was hunting diligently for a thief who confined his operations to packages of sample jewelry that were sent out by some Massachusetts manufacturing firms. We traced the packages over every foot of the distance they traveled and after months of hard work and after thousand of dollars' worth of property had been stolen we arrived at the conclusion that the thief belonged in New York. That he was a discriminating fellow who knew his business was apparent from the fact that he did not touch anything but jewelry. One night when we knew that an unusually heavy consignment of samples was bound westward an inspector hid himself among the mail bags in the New York station. He stayed there for hours watching everybody in the place without being seen and managed to observe a man whose business was loading and unloading trucks extract from a Massachusetts pouch all the jewelry packages they contained. He hid them in a dark corner, and when he finished his day's labor he put them in his pockets and took them home. The inspector of carriers followed him home, placed him under arrest, and searched the house, with the results that he recovered several thousand dollars' worth of gold and silver trinkets and punished the thief."

CHAPTER XXIV.

AMERICA'S ARMY OF CRIMINALS.

WHAT SHALL BE DONE WITH THEM?—NUMBER OF CRIMINALS IN THE COUNTRY—JAILS AND PRISONS SCHOOLS OF CRIME—IMMUNITY OF PROFESSIONAL CRIMINALS — EDUCATION AND ILLITERACY—TAKING CARE OF EX-CONVICTS—PUBLIC TREATMENT OF CRIMINALS—HOW TO DEAL WITH OFFENDERS—CRIME, ITS CAUSES, ITS RESULTS AND ITS TREATMENT—THE COST OF CRIME TO THE PUBLIC—CAUSE OF INCREASE OF CRIME—SENDING CRIMINALS ADRIFT—REFORMATION OF CRIMINALS A SERIOUS QUESTION—CRIMINAL JUSTICE AND PRISON ADMINISTRATION—BORN CRIMINALS—THE HABITUAL CRIMINAL—THE SAFETY OF PROPERTY OWNERS.

The most carefully prepared statistics show that there are about 500,000 criminals in this country, and that only about 50,000 of them are incarcerated. Of this 500,000 it is estimated that one-third are under 20 years of age, one-half under 21 years of age, and a fraction more than two-thirds under 22 years of age, and the chances are that all of them will continue criminals through the remainder of their lives. It is plain, that the ranks of the criminals are recruited from young persons, and it is this fact that makes the question, What shall we do with our criminals? such an important one.

If the jails and lock-ups in our country—four or five thousand in number—are in truth, as they have been often aptly termed, in most cases compulsory schools of crime, maintained at the public expense, we shall have from this quarter alone an accession to the criminal classes in each decade of perhaps 40,000 trained experts in crime. Surely almost any change in dealing with the young, with the beginners in law-breaking, would be an improvement on the prevailing system. Jails and prisons so constructed and managed as to keep separate their inmates, such as are found in several States, and in Europe, would afford an adequate remedy for the evil. Until this can be done it would be far better to cut down largely the number of arrests and committals of the young. The case of professional criminals has been largely discussed and is well understood by prison officers and those who are specially interested in prison reform. But it does not attract the attention of the general public nor of lawmakers. The salient facts are universally known. Professional pickpockets, burglars, and thieves, thoroughly known as such by police detectives, are in all the large cities plying their vocation. They haunt all great assemblies. Recently in Boston on an occasion that drew multitudes to that city in a day over eighty professional criminals were identified, arrested, and held in custody several days and until the crowds of visitors dispersed to their homes. No specific crime could be proved against them. They were released without prosecution, but of course no suits for false imprisonment were brought against the officers who detained them.

Education is an important factor in the treatment of criminals. Investigation shows that the educated are sixteen times less liable to commit crime than the uneducated. Out of 559 criminals selected at random in a New York prison, fifty-one knew absolutely nothing, thirty-four could barely read, 214 could barely read and write a letter, 211 were reasonably educated, forty-nine had attended high schools or colleges, and but one was a college graduate. There was an inclination to doubt the representations of that one, who claimed he was graduated from Oxford, England, because he was addicted to poetry.

Such facts as these are daily spread before the public by

the press. But this blot upon our criminal jurisprudence still remains. Hence the necessity to call public attention, to arouse public interest, to bring to bear public opinion upon this monstrous abuse. The professional criminal belongs in prison, where he should be kept at work earning an honest living. How long should he be kept there? The answer is plain—until he is cured of his criminal habits, if it keeps him a convict until the end of his life. To the unreflecting all this may seem hard. But this is clearly one of the cases in which the way of the transgressor, if now safe and pleasant, should in the interest of society be made "hard." There is ample scope for the indulgence of human feeling and the practice of charity in dealing with our brothers, the criminals, in these testing days of temptation and peril, when we see our convicts passing out of the safety of the prison into the dangers of freedom. What has society, what has the law, what have individuals done to protect and encourage the ex-convict on his discharge from imprisonment?

The chief difficulty is not in the way but in the will to accomplish the desired result. Merit, ability, experience ought to be the controlling consideration in all appointments of prison officers. Mere partisan appointments corrupt the prison. Society should take up the subject and see that its representatives and agents who make and execute the laws shall understand and do their whole duty with respect to the causes of crime and the treatment of the criminal. Society and its members suffer greatly by crime, and in every community they are in some substantial degree responsible for the crimes by which they suffer.

Crime, its causes, its results, and its treatment are in a real and deep sense part of the business of every community and of all its members. Society cannot safely neglect its criminals. The cost of crime is a burden on every public treasury and finds its way to every man's pocket. Its calamities are no respecters of persons. They reach the purest domestic circles and the happiest homes.

The beneficent influence of local, state, and national societies upon prisons and prison discipline and management are plainly visible in many states, but, after all, it is safe to say that a large majority of the prisoners accused or convicted of crime in the United States are dealt with in defiance of just and wise principles in these four vital particlars:

First—The young and thoughtless, the beginners in law-breaking, and the accidental criminals suspected of guilt, are arrested and lodged in city prisons or county jails, and there detained for trial, huddled together with old and hardened offenders, to be educated and trained in the whole art and mystery of criminal life.

Second—Professional criminals are sentenced for short terms, according to the supposed enormity of their respective crimes, and at the end of their terms are sent forth to prey again upon society and to tempt and to instruct others who lead lives of infamy and of hostility to the welfare of the public.

Third—Prisoners are discharged at the end of their terms under such circumstances that the chances are that ex-convicts, with all the world against them, will be compelled to make a living by a return to their old ways, and be confirmed in their enmity to the well-being and good order of society.

Fourth—Our prisons in many, if not most, cases are under wardens and other prison officers who hold their places as political appointments, liable to be removed without regard to qualifications or experience on merely partisan considerations.

These four pregnant facts, even if no other causes were in operation, would sufficiently explain the increase of crime in the United States.

As Gordon Ryland puts in his book upon "Crime; Its Causes and Remedy": "In dealing with offenders we are to proceed entirely upon the assumption that our treatment of them is to be of a nature determined exclusively on public and not at all on personal considerations; that no result is to be aimed at which will terminate in themselves. The final object in our system of penal discipline, as in all our social arrangements, is the good of the community—its deliverance from some evil or inconvenience, or its attainment of some substantial good. This principle, says a well known writer on prison reform, is far reaching in its influence, and if adopted universally in action would, first, brush away a multitude of evil practices and obliterate mountains of vicious legislation.

"*Second*—Criminals in their characteristics are just as diverse as any other class of people, and graded prisons are just as essential as graded schools if reformation is to be made the main object of prison discipline, as it should be. Therefore, for felons, every state should have a separate prison for those under life sentence and for incorrigible, and another as a reformatory for young men convicted of their first offense. In the large states there should also be a separate prison for women.

"*Third*—In these prisons all sentences, except for life or in capital cases, should be indeterminate under a carefully grounded administration, and a criminal should be sent to prison as an insane man is sent to a hospital, to be cured, and not to be discharged until he is cured, and even then only upon parole until fully tested.

"*Fourth*—All misdemeanors, except for short sentences, should be confined in workhouses and not in county jails, and for recidivists (or repeaters, as they are usually known) sentence should be cumulative, and, if found incorrigible, should be indefinite within a maximum limit, with privilege of parole for good conduct.

"*Fifth*—County jails, almost universally, are so constructed as to compel the association of all prisoners confined within their walls—the young with the old, the innocent with the guilty, the hardened offender with the beginner—and the result is the contaminating influences morally are similar to a pesthouse physically. The cure for these conditions, and the only cure, is the absolute separation of prisoners.

"*Sixth*—Productive labor as a moral and hygienic necessity, as well as in justice to taxpayers, should dominate every prison, and, as a reformatory influence, industrial training is indispensable.

"*Seventh*—Prison officers should be as thoroughly trained for their duties as are army and navy officers, and their terms of office should be as secure and their compensation as liberal.

"*Eighth*—In all prisons moral and religious culture should be the leading reformatory influences, and a prison school, with competent instructors, should be an indispensable requirement.

"*Ninth*—Partisan politics must be absolutely eliminated from prison management if high efficiency is to be expected under any system of prison administration.

"Officers and employes of all grades should not only be men of business capacity, but also of moral character so high as to command the respect of the public and the confidence of prisoners. Character is important everywhere, but in prison management at its best it is indispensable."

Thus far prison management has been dealing mainly with effects, and as a preliminary work this is a necessity, but hereafter it would seem that causes and prevention should receive large attention if we are to make the progress we hope for in the suppression of crime. As Havelock Ellis puts it,

"The problem of criminality is not an isolated one that can be dealt with by fixing our attention on that alone. It is a problem that on closer view is found to merge itself very largely into all those problems of our social life that are now pressing for solution, and in settling them to a great extent we settle it. The rising tide of criminality is not an argument for pessimism or despair. It is an additional spur to that great task of social organization to which, during the coming century, we are called.

"The truth is the prison question is as broad as humanity and as comprehensive as human thought. The most potential influence in the prevention of crime is doubtless education. Many of our wisest phrenologists believe that if society would deal with its children as it is possible to deal with them that the present swelling river of crime could be reduced to a rivulet in a single generation. To do this great changes will have to be made in our entire educational system, and especially in our common school system, and possibly with the latter it must be revolutionized."

Havelock Ellis very truthfully says: "We now know that the more intellectual rudiments of education have very little influence indeed in preventing crime, though they may have a distinct influence in modifying its forms. Such education merely puts a weapon into the hands of the anti-social man. The only education that avails to prevent crime in any substantial degree must be education that is as much physical and moral as intellectual, and education that enables him to play a fair part in social life. The proportion of criminals with some intellectual life is now becoming very large; the proportion of criminals who are acquainted with any trade at the time of the crime is very small; the proportion of criminals engaged in their trade at the time of the crime is smaller still. We are now approaching a point at which it will become obvious that every citizen must be educated to perform some social function. In the interests of society he must be enabled to earn a living by that function. If we close the social ranks against him he will enter the anti-social ranks, and the more educated he is the more dangerous he will become."

Under the present system, in all the states, a prisoner at the expiration of his term is set adrift with a new cheap suit of ready-made clothes, a railroad ticket to the nearest city, and a few dollars in his pocket. He is to start out again in life. He must earn a livelihood. He must obtain employment for that purpose. The accident of his future may be determined by many causes. Whether it shall be good or bad depends upon numerous chances.

How many graduates of Harvard University, dropped upon the world in such a fashion, with all the benefits in character, ability and reputation which Harvard can give them, with no friends except such as beckon them to haunts of vice and criminal ways of earning a living—how many Harvard graduates, under such circumstances, would get through the next two years without being compelled to beg, borrow or steal? How, then, can you expect the discharged prison convict, with the firmest of good resolutions (as many at that moment have), but with no satisfactory references to previous employment, with no friends of whom he can borrow, intoxicated with the sudden sense of freedom, to avoid the commission of new crimes before he can earn an honest living?

The reformation of criminals is one of the most desirable objects presented to society. The methods and plans of the work, if it can be accomplished, should be subjects of the closest and most attentive study. One human being saved from a life of crime is a harvest worthy of the best exertions.

To save many is an object of the highest endeavor and the purest ambition.

But mere sentimentalism—a feeling of pity without the impulse of practical common sense—can serve no useful purpose in this work. A mere lugubrious fancy that a poor and needy criminal is more an object of condolement or charity than a poor and needy man who never committed a crime is discreditable to the mind. The convict on emerging from prison should be no more an object of pity than when he entered its doors. The taint on his life is a part of his punishment.

It is not only for himself, but for the protection of society, of mankind, that the future of the criminal should be a matter of sincere and lasting interest. It is cheaper and better for society that he should be made a good man than that he should continue as an outlaw, under police surveillance, causing further trouble and expense in the administration of justice—an expensive future inmate of prisons. To reform criminals is a great and beneficent work for the criminals, but in a larger sense for society.

The arguments and appeals of thoughtful men who have made criminology a study are worthy of consideration. The best methods of criminal justice, the best systems of prison administration and the best methods of treating discharged convicts are subjects which should attract the attention of every thoughtful and humane man.

The system of indeterminate sentences has been a theme of discussion by all who have an interest in this department of social science. The system implies a sentence on conviction that shall not be for a limited term as now provided by the criminal law, but a sentence which shall expire on the determination of some proper authority that the convict has suffered punishment enough to atone for the offense and to insure future good conduct so far as it can be insured by punishment for past misconduct. With the system is associated a plan for the release of prisoners on parole for a period of probation to be fixed according to the circumstances of the case.

The transformation of the criminal into a serviceable member of society is the only effective protection of society against crime. The mere temporary caging of the criminal as a wild beast is a protection to society for the time being, it is true. But if when he is let out of his cage he is worse than when he went in he may be more wary and cunning thereafter, but he will be more dangerous to society than before he was caged.

Many men are born criminals and very early in life come to look upon the officer of the law as a natural foe and well-to-do persons as natural prey. As the representatives of this class grow older and their ability develops they aspire to the higher walks in the profession, and finally come to look upon small thefts with contempt and common thieves with scorn. They will frequently spend a whole year in planning a big robbery, and often disguise themselves as hostlers and servants in order to gain the interior of a house they contemplated burglarizing. In cases where they become too well known they will bring a pal from a distance and give him the details they have been so long in gathering and instruct him how to proceed in carrying out the plans. Then there is the great commercial criminal, with whose methods every one is familiar. He generally winds up his career in Canada, and remains deaf to all persuasions to return to the scene of his exploits. He is generally well-bred and highly esteemed, and as a rule started low down on the ladder. He will enter a large house, work hard for a small salary, and eventually be promoted to the position which enables him to decamp with a vast sum of money. The reflection raised by his exploits is that it would perhaps be the better plan for corporations and firms to pay better salaries and secure better men.

What is the habitual criminal, and what should be done with him? He is a man whose life is devoted to warring upon society. He is an enemy to every good citizen, and imperils the peace, happiness, life and property of those among whom he lives. A man who commits a single offense may or may not be fixed in evil purposes. The second offense tends to show that he belongs to the criminal class, and has determined to live by criminal pursuits. When, having committed two offenses, and served two sentences in prison, he commits a third similar offense, it is a fair presumption that, not having been deterred by his previous imprisonments, and not having been reformed by his experiences, he has fully determined to follow a criminal life. If so, what should be done with him?

Moderate sentences having produced no good effect upon him, either to deter or reform, why should he not be taken permanently out of society and put where he cannot harm others, or wrong himself, by committing crime? No objection can be raised to this method. The property owner is certainly safer when such a man is shut up, and the man himself loses nothing except his liberty, a thing upon which he places so little value that he throws away his chance of keeping it. Why should not the state take his estimate of the value of his liberty and take it away when he misuses it?

The seeming severity of a law of this kind is mitigated by a provision for the release of the prisoner sentenced under it when he shall be thought to be reformed. It remains for him to so use his opportunities as to prove that he has reformed, and thereby earn his own release. There seems to be no sense in releasing him before that time.

The failure of prosecuting officers to avail themselves of

the habitual criminal law, which is in force in most states, so as to secure the permanent imprisonment of habitual offenders, should not be used as an argument against the law, but, rather, for additional legislation to compel its enforcement. The principle underlying it is sound, and a use of the law would be for the benefit of the community.

CHAPTER XXV.

HYPNOTISM AND CRIME.

VIEWS OF AN ABLE CRIMINAL LAWYER—WILL-POWER AND MAGNETISM—SCIENTIFIC TESTS AND THEIR RESULTS—CELEBRATED EXPERIMENTS AND STRANGE ADVENTURES—LIVERNASH THE MURDEROUS SOMNAMBULIST—MAKING HYPNOTIC EXPERIMENTS ON CRIMINALS—A PARIS INCIDENT—THE STORY OF EYRAUD—THE STRANGE CALIFORNIA CASE—OPINIONS OF EXPERTS—HOW WOMEN HYPNOTIZE THEMSELVES—REVERSING THE MENTAL AND MORAL CONDITION—DIFFERENCE IN TWO IMPORTANT CASES—HYPNOTIZING A WITNESS—CAN HYPNOTISM BE SIMULATED?—THE DUTY OF MEDICAL SCIENCE.

"What do you think of hypnotism and crime?" was asked of one of America's most famous criminal lawyers. He replied in substance as follows:

"I think there is an intimate relation between the two, in the sense that the former is a valuable adjunct to the latter. There are various 'isms'—hypnotism, mesmerism, magnetism—and I make no attempt to define the minute distinctions between them. I use the word hypnotism in its broadest sense, and mean by it that mysterious influence which some persons exercise over others, solely by the force of a superior personality. We see it in schools. I have have known a man weighing 200 pounds to fail in maintaining order among his pupils. He could not 'make them mind,' There was bedlam about him constantly. As a teacher he was competent; as an administrator he was a failure. A mere stripling afterward took the same school and became master of the situation within half a day. Every pupil, from weakling to giant, acknowledged and respected his power. How was it done? Physical fear did not enter into the problem. If this factor had been a controlling one, the big man would have had the advantage. But it was the little man, in this case, who was a ruler, and his reign was absolute. There proceeded from him something that could not be weighed, measured or seen. Every pupil felt it, and it did not seem to occur to any one of them to dispute the sway or challenge the authority which pervaded the atmosphere. It must have been something like magnetism, for want of a better term. There was certainly an imponderable agency at work that asserted itself successfully; for, if a contest of strength had occurred, there were a dozen big fellows in the room any one of whom could have picked the teacher up and thrown him out of the window. Anything of that sort, however, was a moral or psychological impossibility—the reason why I can not reduce to a cold-blooded, logical statement. We see something akin to the phenomenon in lawyers, ministers, public orators, animal tamers, auctioneers, army officers, train robbers and successful business men.

"Perhaps I branched off a little, but the connection is closer than you think. I have cited cases in which the power of one person is felt by another, or others. We all speak familiarly of executive ability, the persuasion of oratory, the art of managing men and the force of a strong will. These are but other names for a power that is constantly exercised in different forms and degrees, but the true inwardness of which is one of the mysteries of nature.

"How, for instance, do you account for fifty able-bodied men riding in a passenger car permitting themselves to be bulldozed and robbed single-handed by a stranger, who, with nothing but revolver, a steady eye and a plentiful supply of nerve, manages to convince the whole crowd that they are at his mercy?"

To the suggestion that the robber's gun might have something to do with it the lawyer replied:

"The gun, of course, plays a part in the transaction, but it is hardly sufficient to account for the paralytic stroke that projects itself into the nerves and muscles of the victims. There are many against one, and common sense teaches that a display of prompt courage and action by a carful of passengers would put the robber to flight; but common sense on such occasions seems to take wings. The whole crowd is hypnotized. A subtle influence emanates from the quiet but determined-looking man who has issued the command 'hold up your hands'—and influence that compels submission and annihilates for the time all power of resistance."

The average person has just enough awe and respect for the seeming supernatural to enable him to pursue eagerly any exposition or development of the mysterious which may be made in the progress of psychic force. It matters little as to this average person whether experiments in psychology puzzle the scientists or are accepted as entirely within the reach of human reason. In point of fact, he is willing to accept the belief in the supernatural working, and to ascribe to unseen spirits the influences that puzzle his intelligence and confound his understanding. If this average person were let alone he would very cheerfully renounce a rational exposition of hypnotism and give herself up wholly to unalloyed enjoyment of something inexplicable and superhuman. Perhaps he would institute another crusade against witchcraft and repeat the dolorous experiences of the early colonial period. But science is particularly active in this progressive age, and if science has not advanced quite as far in the development of hypnotism and hypnotic patients as might be desired, it has at least allayed popular credulity, while it has stimulated popular interest.

The purpose of this article is not to treat of hypnotism in extenso, but of its use and abuse in criminal cases. Before coming directly to the point it will be found interesting and useful to review briefly a celebrated and remarkable case, which a few years ago claimed the attention of the civilized world.

Michel Eyraud, a Parisian and criminal, after wandering over two continents, was captured in Havana, taken back to Paris, there convicted of the murder of M. Gouffe by strangling and duly guillotined. His confederate, Gabrielle Bompard, was sentenced to twenty years' penal servitude. Before the trial it was brought out that Eyraud possessed the most remarkable hypnotic power, and the girl herself, perhaps with the cunning of a criminal, declared that she had been led to assist in the crime merely through the exercise of Eyraud's baneful gift. Be that as it may, the theory impressed the department of justice to the extent that a hypnotic experiment was made on Gabrielle before a party of scientists and officers of the law, and under the influence of a celebrated hypnotist the woman was compelled to go through all the details of the tragedy. After the experiment the hypnotist called attention to the fact that this woman, whose record had been fairly good, against whom the police could bring nothing, had, by the power of a stronger will, "been made to behave like a fiend, without heart, without conscience."

The news of the experiment spread like wildfire throughout Paris and the interest of the sensation-loving Parisians was stimulated to the highest pitch when it was rumored that the experiment would be repeated in open court. In this, however, they were disappointed, and the trial proceeded and ended without the startling features hoped for. But Eyraud took his cue from the theory of the hypnotist, and just before his trial advanced a theory which, unfortunately for him, did not save his reputation or his head.

He admitted frankly that he strangled Gouffe, "yet," he added, "am I guilty? Was it I or some will stronger than mine which brought this man to his death? As I dominated Gabrielle Bompard an unseen power dominated me. I know it; I feel it; there are times when I am unaccountable for my actions. They know that I have hypnotic power, yet they will not shut me up among the madmen. They know that I am possessed of some psychic force unrevealed and unintelligible to others, yet they will not say that it can lead a man unwittingly to murder. Am I naturally cruel? Do I not love my family? In my soul I know that I have two natures. One, the good, I control myself; another, the bad, is beyond my mastery. In one character I am a good husband, good father; in the other I am an assassin."

The story of Eyraud has thus been recapitulated because it is a fitting introduction to the strange scene that was enacted in a California court-room. Unlike the president of the French chamber of justice, the California judge listened respectfully to the theory of hypnotism and permitted an experiment to be made in the court-room in behalf of the man arraigned. This man was Edward J. Livernash. Livernash had gone from San Francisco to Cloverdale, a little town ninety miles distant, and had shot and severely wounded an old man, Darius Ethridge, against whom he had no grudge. Giving evidence of an unbalanced mind, he was taken to an asylum, from which he was shortly released. His last appearance in court was the result of a suit brought by his victim, Ethridge. The supporters of the theory of Livernash's utter irresponsibility were a superintendent of an asylum, and a professor of mental and nervous diseases in a university in that state. They called his disease somnambulism or auto-hypnotism, a condition of trance similar to that of a hypnotized patient, which changed a man normally bright to one dull, querulous, secretive and irritable.

The professor explained that a man suffering from somnambulism is a changed being. His entire mental and moral condition is reversed. In most cases, the doctor testified: "The abnormal condition is brought about by an outsider, but in some cases it is imposed by extraneous objects. Women look into a mirror and hypnotize themselves. When patients have been hypnotized by the ringing of a bell the condition may unintentionally result from the bell-ringing. In about one-third of the cases hypnotism is impossible. Another third are particularly susceptible because of inherited tendencies. In this case the patient was unusually susceptible. His father was a peculiar man. His mother was on the borderland of insanity. He sat with his brother many times when the latter went into his hypnotic trances, and this fact undoubtedly was largely responsible in bringing about the defendant's condition, as the somnambulist is frequently imitative."

Perhaps this is the state that Eyraud blunderingly attempted to explain when he maintained that he was dominated by some psychic force hitherto unrevealed. At all events it prepared the audience in the court-room for the experiment, publicly made for the first time, of throwing a man into a hypnotic trance and forcing him to live over again the actual story of his crime. This part of the programme was faithfully carried out. So far was Livernash under hypnotic influence that pins were stuck through his hand, cheek and ear without the slightest indication of bodily suffering. Then, in obedience to command, he answered all questions quickly and intelligently. Of course there was every evidence of mental hallucination, but the object was to show what he did and not why he did it, the claim being that he could be put in the condition in which he was when he committed the crime, and thereby demonstrate all the wild theories and vagaries of a somnambulist. In consequence the utter absence of a motive or governing cause was immediately shown.

This, then, was the difference between the cases of Gabrielle Bompard and Livernash. The woman had no vagaries. She was merely dominated by a stronger will to commit a brutal crime in the most heartless, matter-of-fact way. Livernash, as a somnambulist, was controlled by his own diseased imagination. If the experiments proved anything they proved these facts, and the further fact of popular or judicial incredulity does not lessen the general interest or curiosity.

It is not necessary to give the details of Livernash's testimony while in the trance. He differed in no essential manner from any other hypnotic patient. He answered only the questions put to him by the man the superintendent commanded him to answer, and once when the doctor himself asked a question he refused to reply until the man had given his permission. When at last he came out of the trance he showed no effect of the experience save in the heightened color of his cheeks.

The day following the hypnotic experiment Livernash appeared on the witness stand to testify in his own behalf. As to the important events of the crime his mind was a blank and he was able to recall only flashes of reason that came to him during his somnambulistic spell. This, however, was not important, as any criminal would be smart enough to take his cue from the line of defense. But the testimony of his wife, his sister and the doctor was strong corroboration. Further than this, the superintendent of the asylum himself went on the stand and his testimony as an expert is entitled to considerable respect. The doctor argued that while the shooting, taken apart from other acts, might have been done in a sane moment, it was not probable that Livernash could stimulate the hypnotic condition, and he was quite positive that the simulation could not have been maintained.

Moreover, he had subjected Livernash to the ammonia test—that is, he had held under his nose a bottle of concentrated extract of ammonia three times the strength of the essence, and he had never winced. If he had been shamming he could not have withstood the shock. The doctor said further that the man who resists hypnotism cannot be hypnotized; if he ceases resistance and puts himself under the control of another once or twice, it is doubtful whether he can again summon sufficient power to resist hypnosis. In answer to the question whether it was not dangerous to allow a man like Livernash to roam at large, a very interesting theory was developed. The superintendent of the asylum claimed that Livernash was entirely subjugated to his, the doctor's will, and could "do nothing as long as he controls him." Then, too, his health may be built up so that this somnambulistic condition will not recur.

The two cases of Livernash and Gabrielle Bompard are the most thrilling, the most striking examples of hypnotic influence in crime. In the one case the hypnotized victim (assuming the justice of the expression) changed her entire nature at the will of a dominant companion ; in the other the dominating power came through the victim himself, but was no less irresistible, no less fatal. Yet these cases are not unparalleled in criminal records. The French have furnished at least two examples which resulted in the acquittal of the parties arrested and which were closely allied to the Livernash case. A servant girl was accused of stealing her mistress' jewels, and strenuously denied the theft. It was discovered that she was subject to "spontaneous somnambulism." Accordingly she was hypnotized in court, whereupon she immediately admitted having stolen the jewels and told where they were hidden. Coming out of the trance, she could remember nothing. Her moral irresponsibility was then established and she was promptly discharged. The other case was parallel and experiments also resulted in the acquittal of the prisoner. Readers of fiction will recall in Wilkie Collins' "Moonstone" a similar example of spontaneous somnambulism not more remarkable than the development in real life.

That such cases exist is therefore not to be denied. That they will be accepted frequently in courts of justice is, however, highly improbable. Such eminent French authorities as M. Guillot and Dr. Charcot have condemned the abstract proposition because it attacks the principle of perfect freedom in self-defense and because, as M. Leveille claims, if the hypnotist has absolute power over the hypnotized the replies may be echoes rather than confessions. Still, there are cases, like those cited, where innocence may be established, and doubtless Dr. Brouardel is right in the assumption that when the accused person shows evidence of nervous disorder it is the duty of medical science to employ every means for determining whether this person's conduct is or is not under the immediate influence of abnormal conditions.

CHAPTER XXVI.

HEADS AND PHYSICAL CHARACTERISTICS.

STUDYING A MAN'S MAKE-UP—DESCRIBING PECULIAR PHASES—THE VERMIN OF HUMAN SOCIETY—CONGENITAL TENDENCY TO CRIME—A SAVAGE CHIEFTAIN'S PASSION—RELATION OF THE FORMATION OF THE SKULL TO CRIME—THE HEADS OF CRIMINALS—MARKED PECULIARITIES OF CONSTRUCTION—COMMITTING CRIME FOR PLEASURE—STUDYING SKULLS—DECLARATIONS OF SCIENTISTS--FORMATION OF NORMAL HEAD —THE CRIMINAL AN INCOMPLETE BEING—THE AUSTRALIAN, MALAY, AND FLATHEAD INDIANS' HEADS COMPARED—THE GAIT OF CRIMINALS —MEASURING A CRIMINAL—HOW CRIMINALS ARE SPOTTED.

If there is a class of men who have a congenital tendency to crime it would indeed be strange if there were not some fundamental characteristics both physical and psychical which they display.

It seems that any intelligent observer when visiting our prisons and penal institutions and carefully noting the physiognomy of certain men there confined, would come to the conclusion that he had seen men who were as properly there as a rat in a trap or a lion in a cage. There is seen in this class an indescribable something that appeals to the intelligent mind suggesting that they are not men cast in the ordinary human mold.

It is believed, therefore, to be possible to classify by physical characteristics the thief and the burglar. The eye has been appropriately called "the window of the soul." If a man has small, twinkling, restless, furtive eyes, if while conversing he drops his eyes when you look into them, you need not fear personal injury from him, but keep your eye on him, because, ten to one, that man is a thief. The professional burglar generally has this same optical expression, but it is generally of a more sinister and vicious kind than the cunning of the thief.

We establish criminal courts, and prisons, and penal and reformatory institutions to punish criminals. They may be called the vermin of human society, capable in very many instances of considerable intellectual development, and with an intelligence oftentimes of a high order, with the avenues to honorable effort and success open to them, yet do we not find this class traveling irresistibly in the path of crime? Why? Because of their abnormal congenital tendency to crime. In other words, because they are following out natural instincts which neither education, nor intelligence, nor punishment have power to control. This class may have an intellectual conception that it is against the law to rob a bank, or snatch a pocketbook, or use the pistol or the bludgeon, and they will take all precautions against being caught in the fangs of the law if they do. Yet every day we see men sentenced in our courts who have been before punished for the same offence. Many thieves will steal with no more moral compunction than Sir Reynard has when he prowls at night for a victim among the fat pullets of the farm-yard. Men with the brutal instinct of the lion and wolf abound who yearn for the sight of human blood.

A few years ago the French physiologist Ribot called attention to some remarkable facts illustrating the moral influence of climate and diet. "The infirmities of the mind," he said, "appear to be subject to laws strikingly similar to those governing the disorders of the body. Moreover, the progress of medical science has left no doubt that the predisposition to almost every vice and every virtue can be stimulated by the action of special drugs."

And criminal aberrations seem under certain circumstances to become as contagious as physical epidemics.

Dr. Livingstone, in the chronicle of his African travels, describes a kaffir chieftain who seemed to be seized with semi-annual fits of a butcher mania, which obliged him to extend his man-hunt to tribes which had been entirely innocent of any act that could be construed into a fair casus belli, so much so, indeed, that some of them were ignorant of the very name of their invader. The commander of his swashbucklers shared his passion, and justified it on the gronnd that it was necessary to keep their men in practice.

For similar purposes Malay pirates often attack and butcher the crews of vessels carrying nothing but ballast, or such unprofitable cargoes as sea-moss and teak-weed. One of these human sea-monsters, hanged a few years ago at Singapore, confessed to have sunk or burned eighty-five Chinese junks, a circumstance which he merely mentioned because his capture had been effected by a French man-of-war, and the French were just then not on the best of terms with China. In the thousand islands skirting the coast of Sumatra the arrival of a boodle-freighted corsair will often stimulate a general revival of piracy and induce scores of fishermen to sell their tackle for firearms. An eminent English authority says that crime is contagious, and is just as susceptible of demonstration as the fact that alcoholism is a disease.

The relation of the formation of the skull to crime is a study which is being pursued at the present time with the keenest interest by eminent medical scientists. French physicians have pushed their researches further probably, than those of any other nation, and have almost conclusively demonstrated that atavism is almost certain to produce the criminal. By atavism is meant the reversion of type in the evolutionary series, or a tendency to return to the ancestral type in producing variations of structure or malformations which are normal structures in some of the lower animals. A number of the leading physicians of the United States have become interested in the subject, and have made some very interesting discoveries. The relation of the skull to crime has not been studied from a phrenological standpoint by these physicians, for the reason that phrenology lays down certain general laws which phrenologists claim will govern in every case, and, as none of these physicians are believers in the theories of phrenologists, they have been discarded as worthless, at least in making researches in the subject under discussion. Murder is classed in law as the worst form of crime, and the study of the formation of the skulls of murderers has been diligently pursued by scientists until they are now able to make some remarkable disclosures.

It is not claimed that all murderers have peculiarly shaped skulls; on the contrary many of them are possessed of as classical and fine looking heads to the casual observer as the scientist, the divine or the educator. The motive for the crime must be taken into consideration. The murderer who carefully plans his awful deed and then deliberately executes it; the murderer who kills for the love of crime; the murder who is first thief and then murderer, and the murderer who puts a fellow-being out of the way in order to cover up another and lesser crime can not all be considered in the same light. Recent developments show that in nearly all cases of willful and deliberate murder the murderer is possessed of a skull in which very marked peculiarities of construction are noticed. Such a man has the mark of a murderer upon him as clearly as did Cain. The devil has marked his purchase. Is there such a being as the born murderer? Upon this point eminent medical authorities differ. Researches and investigations made in recent years go to show that such in all probability is the case.

There are children born to become murderers; born so because the peculiar formation of the skull exerts certain influences upon the brain, which produce the murderer despite any effort the individual may make to restrain his vicious tendencies.

There are cases of record where the murderer executed his bloody deeds purely for the love of them. A case in point is that of a degraded mortal whose face struck terror into the hearts of every one who ever saw him; a man who could no more restrain his passion for murder than the starving savage could dispel the cravings of his empty stomach. He murdered, not for any purpose, but purely for the sake of committing his awful crime. He murdered, not for money, but for pleasure; it was a pleasant sensation to him to see his dying victim writhing in the throes of death and to give the final dagger plunge which laid the sufferer cold and still in death. The skull of this human monster is of a lower type than that of the monkey. It was elongated until the face became a fright; the eyes, set deep in their sockets, resembled burnt holes in a blanket; the forehead was low and receding and the top of the cranium flat as though depressed by exterior and unnatural pressure; the posterior of the skull fully developed, showing that the animal nature of the monster's brain was his ruling passion.

A study of his skull revealed the fact that the brain was so depressed in the force part of the head as to render the man devoid of all intellectual qualities. The brute forces only were allowed full sway. The effect which this had upon the brain is plainly to be seen, and scientists declare that the formation of the skull is alone responsible for his atrocious deeds.

Scientists declare that as the skull retrogresses toward the animal formation, so do the morals and intellectual qualities of the brain decrease. This assertion seems to be wholly borne out by facts. It is found that almost without exception the men who are accused of willful, deliberate murder are possessed of heads of such apparently peculiar formation that they would at once be stamped as dangerous and vicious men by any one familiar with the subject of skull formations. In the cases of those men who are thieves first and murderers afterward the head was of a higher and more intellectual order. In the cases of the men who committed their crimes in the heat of passion there is almost a universally better showing than in the cases of heads of more brutal and blood-thirsty murderers, and investigation seems to bear out the assertion that the lower and more degraded murderers have the most plainly marked skulls.

In the normal skull the sutures, or seams between the several bones of the cranium, remain open, and the bones of the head are only loosely jointed together. This enables the brain to grow, and as it grows the skull expands to sufficient size to comfortably contain it. In a murderer's skull, recently examined by an able medical gentleman, with the sutures ossified, the brain was compressed into a smaller space than it should have occupied. In the years it was thus confined it continued to grow until the bones of the skull were reduced to a sixteenth of an inch in thickness in several places, and the temporal bones were unevenly forced from their normal position, thus rendering the skull lopsided, with greater curvature on one side than on the other. The skull when held up before a light was so thin in some places that the light could be seen through as plainly as through greased paper. On either side of the ruffle, and extending parallel to it, was an elliptical indentation about a thirty-second of an inch below the surface of the bones of the skull. These indentations are about two and one-half inches in length. The confinement of the brain in this solid cavity was very like placing it in a vise. All chance for mental activity was lost, and in case of a rush of blood to his brain the man's mental balances was for the time gone and he was irresponsible for his acts.

Generally speaking, the criminal may be said to be an incomplete being. He is tainted with a morbid inheritance and shows signs of physical and psychical degeneration correlative to the imperfection of the development. The skulls of female thieves and lewd women are generally of a very marked character, and the former are generally or a higher order than the latter. The prime diameter of the skulls of thieves, as well as their horizontal circumference, exceeds that of prostitutes. The physical degeneration due to imperfect organization shows itself among prostitutes principally by the frequency of deformities of the head, of anomalies of the cranium, of the latter of which there are 41.33 per cent. Their psychical abnormality is exhibited either by feebleness of intellect or by a notable absence of the moral sense. The crania of other criminals show marked deformities in a large majority of cases.

The skull of an Australian is the nearest approach to the orang type of that of any human being. It is truly an animal head. The forehead is exceedingly flat and recedent, while the prognathism of the superior maxillary almost degenerates into a muzzle. The alveolar arch instead of being round or oval in outline is nearly square. The whole head is elongated and depressed in the coronal region, the basis of the cranium flat and the mastoid processes very large and roughly formed. The immense orbits are overhung by ponderous superciliary ridges. The Australian is crafty, cunning, brutal and bloodthirsty, placing little or no value on human life. He is at the same time cowardly and weak.

The Malay race shows another low form of skull. There is little breadth and height to the skulls of the race, and the facila angle would do no credit to the Caucasian. He has been termed the tiger and the serpent of the east. He is subtle, crafty, excitable, unprincipled, sensual and cruel. A glance at a Malay skull will suffice to show this fact.

The Flathead Indian has been another interesting study. The question naturally arises: Does the unnatural depression or flattening of the skull of the offspring of this tribe by means of a board fastened upon the head of the infants, and the consequent and necessary rearrangement of the hemispheres of the brain contrary to all natural laws, cause the tendency to murder so noticeable among this tribe? Indians, as a rule, are a murderous people, and the fact is indicated by the formation of their skulls, but does the further contortion or malformation of the skull out of the normal condition render the individual members of the Flathead tribe more subject to crime? The answer of many scientists is yes, while a few contradict it. The Flathead Indians are of a lower type than the other tribes surrounding them, and this is probably due to the practice of flattening the skulls of their offspring. They are too timid and scrawny to be warlike, but when compelled to fight are dangerous, bloodthirsty and wholly without mercy.

A curious study has been made by Dr. Peracchia of the differences between criminals and law abiding citizens, as exhibited by their walk. The doctor first made a number of observations to determine the conditions of normal progression, and found that in good people the right pace is longer than the left, the lateral separation of the right foot from the median line is less than that of the left, and the angle of deviation of the axis of the foot from a straight line is greater on the right side than on the left. But this is not all. Dr. Peracchia has not only shown us how we may distinguish criminals in general, but has laid the beginnings of the differential diagnosis between various sorts of evil-doers. The following are the distinguishing characteristics which his observations have enabled him to formulate:

1. Thieves.—In those who are predisposed to appropriate the property of others there is a pronounced widening of the base of support together with a very long step.

2. Assassins.—In those who have murder in their hearts, the base of support is not as wide as it is in thieves, since the angle formed by the axis of the foot with the median line is less obtuse, but the sinistrality betrayed by their foot prints is very marked.

These discoveries are of a very interesting character, and if the criminal could be induced to walk before the honest man, instead of following him as he usually does, they might also be put to a practical use, for then good citizens could diagnose the rogue by his tracks, and might thus be enabled to escape robbery, or assassination, as the case might be.

Measuring a criminal, a wonderful system which was invented by M. Bertillon, consists in recording the measurement of divers bony parts of the human frame—parts which do not alter with any change which age or accident or device may make in the muscular tissue and are not affected by the subsequent thinness or corpulence of an individual.

These measurments are: Full height, height when sitting, length and breadth of the skull, length of middle and little fingers of left hand, length of left fore arm and foot and full stretch of the arms; the length and width of right ear, the color of the hair and eyes and any scars, moles, etc., on hands, arms, face and bust are also accurately recorded. With these data M. Bertillon is able to establish the identity of any criminal who has been through his hands.

The way in which he accomplishes this is ingenious and merits some explanation. He divides each measurement into three classes—the large, the medium and the small. We will suppose that he has 90,000 sets of measurements before him to classify. He commences by the length of the head, selecting that measurement because the skull of the adult never grows and the measurer cannot be deceived, as he might be in taking the full height of the body. By this means he is enabled to reduce the 90,000 into three categories of about 30,000 each.

The width of the head is treated in the same manner and the classes are reduced to 10,000 each with broad, medium or narrow skulls. The length of the middle finger provides another divisor and further reduces each class to 3,300. By the length of the left foot the divisions are brought down to about 1,100 each and the length of the fore arm reduces them to less than 400 each. The original 90,000 has thus been divided into 243 groups, each containing between 300 and 400. This number is still too large for working purposes and so the 400 persons are divided into three more classes, of about 140 each, according as they are tall, short or of medium height.

The length of the little finger will further reduce this to lots of less than fifty each, and, finally, by the color of the eyes, of which M. Bertillon distinguishes seven varieties, the classes are brought to parcels which should average about seven each, but which in reality vary from three to twenty, some colors being more frequent than others. This completes the particulars used for classification, but, in order to eliminate even the remotest chance of error, there are added the length and width of the right ear—which form a valuable indication—the height when sitting and the full stretch of the arms.

CHAPTER XXVII.

BOGUS PATENT ATTORNEYS.

THE VICTIMIZING OF INVENTORS A BUSINESS—SWINDLING TRICKS OF ALLEGED PATENT ATTORNEYS, BROKERS AND AGENTS—MAKING FRAUDULENT STATEMENTS—WORK OF THE PATENT SHARK—THE INTERNATIONAL BUREAU SCHEME—HOW HONEST PATENT AGENTS ACT—A REMEDY SUGGESTED TO CHECK PATENT FRAUDS AND SWINDLERS—SOME TIMELY SUGGESTIONS.

The class of inventors has been selected by the framers of our constitution and laws as one specially worthy of protection. The patent statutes are based on a clause of the constitution especially providing for their encouragement, and the courts of the United States have devoted many sessions to adjudication of patent cases, the simple procuring of letters patent putting the humblest inventor in position to appeal to the highest class of Federal tribunals for the determination of his rights. The old time opinions of the judges in these cases are agreeable reading. They take the ground that the inventor requires special guardianship in his rights, the fact being recognized that the man of creative genius is often impracticable in business matters.

Unfortunately, there is another class of men who have adopted this opinion concerning inventors, and who try their best to exploit the community of patentees for their own benefit, and to the accompanying detriment of their clientage. When letters patent are awarded, the drawings and claims of the patent and the inventor's name are published in the Official Gazette of the United States Patent Office. This appeals at once to a large number of sharks calling themselves "patent agents," who see in the inventor a possible source of revenue. As soon as his patent is issued the inventor, therefore, begins to receive letters from various self-extolled concerns, recommending him to do various things, to apply for foreign patents, or to permit the correspondents to act as his agents for the sale of his patent on commission.

Many of these letters and circulars contain statements that are absolutely fraudulent. The inventor, for example, will be urged to apply for foreign patents in England, France and Germany, and other countries, when the agent is perfectly well aware that after the patent has issued in the United States and been published in the Patent Office Gazette valid patents cannot be procured in those countries, except under the international convention, which he is seldom able to avail himself of. The patent shark relies upon the ignorance of this fact on the part of the inventor to protect him in his nefarious traffic. He is also protected from detection by the fact that in many foreign countries there is no examination as to novelty, and in due course, and after the payment of the government fees, the patent will issue and he will be provided with the letters patent certificate to present to his "client," who sleeps in blissful ignorance of the fact that the documents are not worth the paper they are printed on.

In many cases the fees upon examination will be found to be phenomenally low, and the inventor will snap at what seems to him a bargain, simply to find that in Germany, perhaps, he has procured a Gebrauchsmuster, or model of utility patent, instead of a patent; or in Canada, he may be led to believe that he has procured a patent for one year, when he has simply filed a declaration of intention, which affords no true protection.

It is after an inventor is enticed into correspondence with

such firms that his troubles begin. He is probably told that his patent has been examined and found valuable, that otherwise the correspondence would never have been initiated. Perhaps he is told that the correspondent is the American representative of an "International bureau for procuring pateuts, with main offices in all the principal capitals of Europe," and that the foreign office has examined the patent and has found it peculiarly well adapted for the old world.

The inventor, almost of necessity of sanguine temperament, has his hopes easily raised. His probably rather exalted idea of the merits of his invention is still further increased, and he is induced to put himself in the hands of the firm. He is then exploited to the best of the practiced ability of the "firm." He is advised to engage them as patent agents for foreign patents, and perhaps he is told that they have a purchaser for the patent, provided the inventor will take out a certain number of foreign patents. He is exhorted to invest capital if he has it, if not, to get money from his friends and to organize a company. Perhaps an alleged sale of his patent or of partial rights in it will be made and a check conveniently dated a month or more in advance will be shown him—a check which, of course, is never collected. These are no fancy sketches—precisely such lines of action are followed by numerous concerns. It has even gone so far that a similarity of name has been used to dishonestly impress the inventor with the idea that he is dealing with a firm of reputation.

The conservative patent agent who will give honest advice as to the patentability of an invention, but who will long hesitate before either approving or condemning its practical utility, and the probability of its success, is the one who can be trusted to conduct the business properly. The agent who has no conscience will urge the inventor to apply for a patent, even thought he is aware that the device is not patentable.

The public is the final judge of the merit of inventions—directly or indirectly their value is settled at that tribunal—and the value of a patent can rarely be predicted with certainity. Every patent has to stand on its own merits; its exploiting must depend on the ground it covers, for a different clientele is to be reached by each invention.

The remedy for this state of things is simplicity itself: it is to be careful with whom you deal. The issuing of circulars tending to inflate the hope of patentees is in itself a bad sign, as far as the standing of the firm issuing such circulars is concerned.

Deal only with attorneys of known integrity whose long record of service makes them well known and who have been tried and have not been found wanting.

CHAPTER XXVIII.

THROUGH PRISON WALLS.

MEN OF CELEBRITY WHO HAVE ESCAPED CONFINEMENT—ORSINI'S WONDERFUL ESCAPE—ESCAPE OF PRINCE LOUIS NAPOLEON—FLIGHT OF JOHN MITCHEL, THE IRISH PATRIOT—CARL SCHURZ' PART IN A DARING ESCAPE—HOW DR. THEODORE GALLAUDET GOT AWAY—SENSATIONAL ESCAPE OF WILLIAM J. SHARKEY—OTHER MEMORABLE AND CELEBRATED ESCAPES.

There has always been a glamour of romance attending the escapes of criminals from prison, and the bypaths of history are full of stories of those who by audacity or address have triumphed over obstacles almost insurmountable and gained their freedom. The more than Oriental imagination of Dumas in the romance of Monte Cristo, portraying the escape of Edmond Dantes from the Chateau d'If, has scarcely exceeded in wonder many of the strange stories of actual fact. The escapes of Baron Trenck, of Cassanova, of Jack Sheppard, and of a hundred others rival in interest the wildest fictions of the novelists. Many instances there are where prisoners have burrowed through inside walls of enormous thickness by the aid of the most insignificant means, such as a nail or a broken case-knife, have scaled high walls by ropes made of bedding or clothing, and eluding vigilant sentries have gained their freedom. Sometimes a happy concourse of circumstances have assisted them, and at others they have displayed an almost superhuman energy in overcoming unforeseen difficulties.

Orsini, the Italian conspirator and revolutionist, who was

executed in Paris in 1858 for attempting to assassinate the Emperor Louis Napoleon, escaped from a prison at Mantua in 1856. The difficulties he surmounted were enormous. He was confined in a cell which had but one window seven feet from the floor. Twelve iron bars three inches thick crossed each other and were inserted in the stone casement, with a second frame-work of similar bars distant three feet further in the embrasure. The outside of the window was covered with an iron grating. From the window to the ground below was a distance of 104 feet, and this was at the bottom of a wet ditch. On the other side of the ditch was a wall twenty feet high and very thick.

Beyond the wall there was a bridge to cross, which was closed at night and guarded by sentries. By the assistance of outside friends he obtained some steel saws and went to work at the iron bars, and after months of the most painful labor he sawed a space out sufficient to allow him to pass through, all this while daily inspected in his cell by vigilant guards. He also prepared a rope made of his bedding to lower himself to the ground. When all was ready, after the last visit of the guards at night, he set out on his perilous journey. In descending the rope his strength gave out, and when he was yet twenty feet from the ground he fell, severely injuring an arm and leg, and lacerating himself severely. He lost consciousness for a time, and when he recovered he could hardly move. A wall twenty feet high remained to be surmounted, along which ran a roadway, over which as soon as daylight should appear people would be passing. He wandered along the ditch seeking for a place to escape, and by means of a nail he at last fixed his rope to the top of the wall, but when that was accomplished his strength was not sufficient to enable him to climb it.

He now surrendered himself to despair, knowing that he

would be retaken and executed. Then he became indifferent and lay down in the ditch and slept. He was awakened at daylight by the stirring noises of the city. Some people passed, and Orsini in desperation called to them for help, saying that he had got drunk the night before and had fallen into the ditch, but they only shook their heads at him. Finally a stout, peasant lad passed. In a voice of agony Orsini called to him for help, and asked him to take the end of the rope. The boy took it and pulled with a will, but he was not strong enough. After a tremendous effort Orsini fell back again.

"Call another man!" he shouted, being in despair. A stout man suddenly appeared and took hold of the rope. Both pulled with might and main and raised him high enough to catch him in their arms just as his strength was giving away. They lifted him to the road, and when they understood he was a political prisoner ran away with all their might, and he limped off and concealed himself in a neighboring swamp. Though a great search was made, he was not discovered. He soon made his way to a friend's and finally escaped to England. There he entered upon the conspiracy against Louis Napoleon which culminated in the throwing of the bombs before the Emperor's carriage in January, 1858, causing great loss of life, but doing no harm to the Emperor. Orsini was arrested, tried, and executed, and his stormy career brought to an end.

The escape of Prince Louis Napoleon from the Fortress of Ham was accomplished by the great address and presence of mind of the Prince. It will be remembered that after his wild and foolish attempt to gain the army to his cause at Boulogne in August, 1840, he was arrested and tried before the Chamber of Peers and condemned to imprisonment for life. He was taken to the Fortress of Ham, and for more than five years remained a closely guarded prisoner. Despairing of gaining his release through the clemency of the government, he at last determined to make his escape. He was allowed to see visitors sometimes, and Dr. Conneau, Gen. Montholon, and a valet named Thélin were with him constantly and waited upon him. The latter also was permitted by the guards to go in and out of the prison at will. Some repairs being necessary to the apartments of the Prince, workmen were brought from the village to do the work. It was noticed that the workmen were closely inspected when they came in the morning and when they went away in the evening, but that when in the course of the day a single workman had occasion to leave the prison for a tool or to carry out some old timber he went and came freely, because he passed under the governor's window and past the guard-house in the court-yard. The plan of escape formed was for the Prince to disguise himself as a workman and to leave the prison in the daytime. Some English friends who called on him two days before his escape left him the passports of their servants, which he would need in crossing the Belgian frontier. Everything being in readiness, May 25, 1846, was appointed as the time for making the attempt. Seven o'clock in the morning was the hour fixed, as at that time the governor of the prison was not up and there were fewer guards on duty.

The Prince having dressed as usual put over his waistcoat a thick linen shirt, then a clean blouse. Then a pair of blue trousers, very much worn. Over the first blouse he put on another, but a very dirty one, an old apron of blue material, and on his head he placed a black long-haired wig with a greasy cap. His mustache was shaved off, and his hands and face begrimed with paint and dirt. When all was in readiness, Thélin called on all the workmen who were repairing the stairs to come and take a glass of wine or brandy. As the last man left the stairway and went to the other end of the corridor where the drink was set out, Thélin rushed up-stairs to tell the Prince the moment had arrived to start. The latter then drank a cup of coffee, put on a pair of wooden shoes, took in his mouth a clay pipe, and with a plank on his shoulder resolutely went with a heavy step down-stairs. Thélin passed down a little ahead of him leading a favorite dog. They first met two warders, one of whom Thélin drew a little farther into the corridor, as if to say something important to him, and kept him with his back turned to the Prince. The other warder was still on the watch, but owing to the plank carried by the Prince on his shoulder could not very easily see his features. The Prince stepped through the door into the courtyard, when a workman followed him as if about to speak to him, Thélin called him and ordered him back to the dining-room to do something there. When the Prince reached the first sentinel in the court he dropped his pipe from his mouth. Stooping in such a way as to hide his face he picked up the pipe, struck a match, and lit it, the soldier continuing on his beat.

He next met the officer of the guard, but he was reading a letter and paid no attention to the supposed workman. A little farther on a few private soldiers were sitting on a wooden bench in the sun. The lodgekeeper was on the threshold of his lodge, but only looked at Thélin who was following the Prince with the dog held by a string. The sergeant, whose duty it was to open and shut the gate, turned a sharp look on the workman, but a movement the Prince made with the large plank compelled him to make a step backward. He opened the gate and the Prince was free, Thélin following him very close.

On the outside the Prince met two workmen coming upon him on the side unprotected by the plank. They looked at him very keenly as if surprised at not knowing him. The Prince shifted his plank, and just as he was in terror of being questioned he heard one of them say, " O, it is Buthon." By means of a cab which Thelin had procured to be in readiness, they now made their way to Valenciennes, where at 4 o'clock they took a train for Brussels, and that night were safe beyond the frontier. Two days later Louis Napoleon was in England. Meantime, in the prison, Dr. Conneau had prevented the absence of the Prince from becoming known until nightfall by various subterfuges, and the pretense that he was very ill. At last, when the escape was discovered it was too late, for it was before the day of telegraphs, and there was no means of cutting him off.

The escape of John Mitchel, the Irish patriot, from Van Diemen's Land made some little stir in its time, owing to certain circumstances attending it. Mitchell was engaged in the Irish Revolution of 1848, and when that was put down he was arrested and tried for treason. He was convicted and sentenced to transportation for a term of fourteen years. After being for a time at Bermuda, he was in 1850 taken to Van Diemen's Land, and then given a ticket of leave upon the condition that he would not attempt to escape from the colony. He accepted the indulgence, and for three years was allowed perfect liberty.

In June, 1853, he wrote to the governor of the island, stating that he would resign his ticket of leave and revoke his parole of honor, and would present himself before a police magistrate at Bothwell for that purpose. He did go before a police magistrate, accompanied by two friends well armed, surrendered his ticket of leave, and presented a copy of the letter he had written to the governor. The magistrate was taken by surprise and hardly knew what the purport of Mitchel's action was. Mitchel seems to have explained it to him a second time, and then turning on his heel he wished him a very good morning. As a matter of fact he did not surrender himself into custody, and before the magistrate or constables could seize him he was off into the bush. All his plans had been carefully laid beforehand, and by the aid of friends he got safely off, went on board an American vessel, and was brought to the United States. A very bitter controversy arose afterward between Mitchel and some of his opponents as to whether he had really violated his parole of honor. To say the best for him, his surrender was a very flimsy one, and as a matter of fact he allowed the magistrate no opportunity whatever to take him in custody.

One of the romantic incidents in the life of Carl Schurz is connected with a daring escape from the fortress of Spandau, a Prussian prison nine miles from Berlin. Spandau is famous as being the prison from which Baron Trenck escaped about a century ago. Schurz and Dr. John Gottfried Kinkel were prominent actors in the revolutionary movements which agitated Germany during 1848. In that year Kinkel occupied the post of Art History at the University of Bonn, and Schurz then a youth of 19, was his pupil. They both entered heartily into the political movements of the time. When the revolution was put down Schurz got away, but Kinkel was captured, tried, and sentenced to death by a court-martial. At the earnest and persistent intercession of his wife Kinkel's sentence was commuted to imprisonment for life, and after some time he was conveyed to permanent quarters at Spandau. Schurz had fled to Switzerland, but when he heard of the fate of his friend he secretly returned to Prussia, determined to secure his release. The prison is on an island in the river Havel, and Schurz succeeded in secreting a boat and suitable disguises on the river not far from the citadel. Kinkel's wife and her waiting-woman were permitted at times to visit him.

When all had been arranged on the outside so that he could escape easily from the island he went out one evening in November, 1850, passed the guards in his wife's clothes, accompanied by the waiting woman. Going to the appointed place he found Schurz ready for him. They successfully made their way to the seacoast, and thence passed over to Scotland.

There have been frequent escapes in the United States from jail and penitentiaries, though the constant supervision in the latter under the modern system now renders any attempt from the inside almost impossible. Such escapes as occur nowadays are by convicts employed at labor outside the walls. There have been quite a number where a prisoner has been allowed under charge of deputies to visit his home or other places outside the prison, and then, violating his implied parole of honor, has gotten away by some ruse.

One of the earliest cases of this kind was that of Dr. Theodore Gallaudet, of New York. The doctor lived at a New York hotel, and getting into a quarrel with Mr. Cranstown, the proprietor, knocked him down and injured him severely. For this he was arrested, tried and convicted, and sentenced to the penitentiary for one year. This was in November, 1858. After his sentence, when on his way back to the Tombs in charge of two officers, he suggested that inasmuch as he was so soon to be cut off from the world and all its enjoyments, they accompany him to a fashionable restaurant and have one good final dinner. The officers were willing, a few of the doctor's friends were invited to join, and they all had a good time generally. Wine flowed in abundance, the officers became exhilarated, and entertained the company with many stories of their adventures. They were having a splendid time, when the doctor was obliged to leave the room for a few moments. As he left his hat behind him, the officers suspected nothing wrong. He, however, did not return for his hat, but was next heard of in Havana, where he was joined by his family. He never came back to serve out his sentence. The officers were informed next day that their services were no longer required.

One of the most sensational escapes from the New York Tombs was that of William J. Sharkey, in November, 1873. Sharkey was a young man who had achieved a bad eminence as a gambler and ward politician. In September, 1872, he met another gambler who owed him $600. He demanded payment, and when refused deliberately shot the man dead. He was arrested, tried and convicted, and sentenced to be hanged. Two women planned his escape—one, Mrs. Allen, a friend, and the other Miss Maggie Jourdan, his reputed wife. Visitors were admitted to the prison to see the prisoners, and could go to the different cells and talk through the grating. Each visitor was given a ticket by the warden, which was shown to the keepers as they went in and out. On the day planned, Miss Jourdan went in the morning to Sharkey's cell, as she did every day, and talked with him through the grating. Two hours later Mrs. Allen came in to see a friend of hers, but as she passed Sharkey's cell she stopped and had some conversation with him, and gave him her visitor's ticket. She then went on and visited her other friend, and remained with him until two o'clock, when the gong sounded for all visitors to leave.

Meantime, Miss Jourdan had left at one o'clock, contrary to her usual custom, and about 1:30 a peculiar-looking female, heavily veiled, with a black cloak across a broad pair of shoulders, passed down the corridor, through the two lower gates, and out of the entrance, passing three men, who all scanned her very closely, but let her go by. A few moments later she was seen to jump on a Bleeker street car while in motion and passed from sight. The woman, in fact, was no other than Sharkey, as the officers found half an hour later when they visited his cell. There they found everything in confusion, and on a little shelf his black mustache, still wet with the lather. Notwithstanding the utmost efforts of the police Sharkey got away and reached Havana in safety.

CHATER XXIX.

SHREWD BEGGAR FRAUDS.

PRETEND TO BE DEAF, DUMB AND BLIND, PLAYING ON SYMPATHY—HOW PHILANTHROPY IS HUMBUGGED—BEGGING FOR MONEY TO REACH HOME—AN ARMY OF FRAUDS AND VAGABONDS—MASTERING THE DEAF MUTE LANGUAGE FOR SWINDLING PURPOSES—THE PUBLIC SHOULD BE CAREFUL IN DISBURSING ALMS.

Speech is so common, eyesight so precious, that he who would appeal for charity needs no better warrant than that he is dumb or blind. In an age when words are multipled and golden silence is seldom found, the very fact that lips can give no utterance is so unusual that their mute assertion of misfortune is seldom questioned. There is nothing so pitiful in all the world as an asylum for the blind. There is nothing which so draws one to share the burdens of another as the appeal of him in whom the wells of speech are all dried up. We sympathize with illness, we grieve at the misfortune which visits our friends, we mourn with them when bereavement comes, but all these things are in the course of nature. They are sad, but they may be expected. But when a figure in health rises and asks for charity in the hushed language of the mute, philanthropy halts and humanity gives alms. But if the dumb can evoke assistance, assuring of sincerity and disarming doubt, how hushed is the questioning when the blind apply! How stronger than speech or silence are the sightless eyes that stare unblinking at a darkened world! How sad is the fate of that man who was buried by demons when a God cried out, "Let there be light."

But not every man is mute who stretches his hand in silence. Laziness is such an awfully demoralizing vice that some who choose to beg a living and decline to work are even base enough to feign a misfortune they ought to fear. Fellows who find the winter pinching and the ranks of vagabonds full to repletion arm themselves with a slate and pencil and haunt the public with appeals for help on the untrue claim that they are dumb. One of the most persistent beggars of this kind makes the rounds of residence districts with a printed card on which is stated the bearer's desire to reach his home in some distant city—the destination varies from time to time—together with a long primer indorsement by a group of names which no one knows. The fraud always asks for some slight money offering—nothing can be too small—with which to assist him in the purchase of a ticket.

Usually his paper shows that he needs but a very little more, and he asks one by a series of pantomimic signs, to enroll his name, together with the sum advanced, in regular order on a blank list which he tenders with his touching appeal. He is so well drilled as never to be surprised into speech, and looks with such straight honest eyes into the faces of the women, who form much the larger number of his victims, that they can not question him and usually give up a dime or a quarter without a struggle. The beggar can readily collect a good day's wages in this manner, and it is a matter of surprise if he does not receive an invitation to partake of food three or four times a day. He never lets his list get full. However small a margin he may lack of having raised the sum needed to buy his ticket to his home he never gets quite enough, for nothing is easier than to stop in some secluded spot and erase the names of his latest donors, thus proving to those on whom he shall presently call that their help is not only needed, but will so nearly end the necessity for continued appeals. This class of beggar never looks like a dissipated man, is always polite, and bears refusal in so noble a way that nine times out of ten the flinty-hearted women who refused him at the back door hurry through to the front and give the more generously that they have harbored suspicion.

Another set of leeches have mastered the deaf mute language, and always ask with a pleading, painful face which meets you as your eyes lift from his written questions, if any one in your house can talk with him. He supplements the penciled question and the eloquent glance of eyes trained by long use in the art with a few rapid passes of his hands, a few dexterous wavings of the fingers in a language you have heard of and read about but cannot understand. If the unexpected happens and a person be present who can converse with him, your beggar is sure of some entertainment, and the unusual scene of one you know to be honest talking to one who may be equally so, and certainly seems needy, will almost infallibly wring from you the coveted assistance. It is like two minstrels at a Saxon court. You know your own has seen the holy land, though you have not, and as he tells you, this threadbare guest talks familiarly and correctly of distant realms. That is all any one can know to a certainty, but you give him the benefit of the chance that he may be honest, and help him with such loose change as comes to hand. Time and again the pretended mutes have been detected in their imposture by men who pitied a misfortune and gave money at their homes in the morning to see it spent for drink by an arguing, contentious fellow in the evening.

Some beggars even assume the appearance of blindness, and haunt the homes of comfortable people, led by a little girl, and asking alms in the name of an affliction that is always eloquent of need. He will sometimes carry a small basket full of pencils, or other little trinkets, and glazes over his evident beggary with the appearance of sales. But he does not hesitate, once the money is in his hands, to ask his patron to give back the pencils, as he cannot afford to buy any more. These people can sometimes see as well as the child that seems to lead them, and yet their eyes, when they choose to assume their professional attitude, seem covered with a film through which no light can penetrate.

The public should be chary in bestowing charity, and especially to able-bodied men who appear blind, deaf and dumb, or are still claiming to be victims of some recent disaster. Most any one who has charity to bestow can easily think of some deserving and honest unfortunate in their own neighborhood.

CHAPTER XXX.

LIFE'S CURIOUS PHASES.

Miscellaneous Frauds, Swindles and Humbugs Worked Upon the Public—Progressive Contributions—Traveling "Gentlemen"—Bogus Insurance Agents—Don't Stand Around—The Rubber Band Fiend—Trading on the Affections—The Soap Man Abroad—Bogus Bible Agents—Fraudulent Commission Houses—Peddlers Who Are Frauds—A Sufficient Warning—The Lining Thief—Boarding House Swindlers—How People Hide Money—Modern Slang Terms and Their Meaning—Traveling Doctor Frauds—Thief Sheltering Resorts—Points, Facts, and Suggestions for the Public—Old But Clever Games Worked On the Unsuspecting, Etc., Etc., Etc.

Progressive Contributions.

Awhile ago some person of a mathematical turn conceived the idea of a back-action system of contribution, which was expected to increase by a sort of geometrical progression. A letter containing an appeal for a small contribution for some alleged charitable institution (ten cents or so) was sent to two persons. Each receiver was requested to return the letter with the money; make two copies of it and send to others likely to respond. A very brief computation will show what a sum such a scheme would produce if carried even ten removes; yet its very magnitude seems to have operated to block its success. It looks fair enough, but any one who will consider can see that the returns asked for will be a great deal more than enough to accomplish the ostensible object, as the twentieth removes at six cents each would bring in $31,457.28, which is a tidy sum for a swindler to pick up in a short time.

Patronize Home Merchants.

Many farmers in various sections have been swindled by an oily-tongued gentlemen claiming to come from New York or Chicago, and who, first endeavoring to show what margins are made by country merchants, proceeds to take orders for family groceries at low rates. On a certain day his patrons meet him at the railroad station and receive the goods in packages, which upon trial, prove to be of a very questionable character. All such solicitors should be avoided. As a rule, country merchants are working for very small margins, and should be patronized in preference to any traveling agent, who has no regard for those he sells to, only to rope them into a swindling scheme.

Bogus Insurance Agents.

The lightning rod man and the tree peddler have their counterpart in the bogus insurance agent. This last-named calamity goes to the farmer's house, represents in glowing terms the importance of being insured, and the inducements offered by the company he pretends to represent. Having talked the farmer into making an application for a policy, he obtains a premium note and some cash, promising to send the policy by mail. That is the last of the money, and the farmer is peculiarly lucky if the note is not "fixed up" and sold to some innocent holder who proceeds to collect it at maturity. A very sleek, plausible man with "taking ways" in more than one sense obtained a note for two hundred dollars and some cash as premium on a policy of insurance from a Missouri farmer which, it is scarcely necessary to add, never came. It is highly important for a farmer to have his combustible property insured, but if he is wise, he will transact his business personally with a reliable local agency.

Don't Stand Around.

If when you go to some of the larger wholesale dry-goods houses to transact business or to see a friend and have with you a small package do not be surprised if, when you are ready to leave, you are requested to show what you have in the parcel. It may strike you as odd to be so queried, but it is a rule among these houses that, to put it roughly and literally, every one is suspected of being a thief until proved not to be so, and exception to this rule is not even made with the old and trusted employes of the several houses who have adopted this plan. Again, when you are examining goods and imagine yourself alone do not feel surprised or embarrassed if you suddenly come on to any of the clerks that instinct will tell you has been watching you from around the corner, or who has been following you at a respectful distance, to all appearances intent upon his work. If you are of a nervous disposition you will probably be impressed with the fact that you are suspected of something and your surmise in this respect will be correct. You are being watched as assiduously as if you were a well-known crook. Unless your appearance, standing, and reputation are known to every clerk, boy, or porter within a sightable distance you are made the especial mark of all of them in the hope that you will do something that will give them the opportunity of earning the $5 to $10 reward that is paid for the detection of a thief. It is not often that any one is caught, and when the event does take place the affair is kept a close secret, and if it be an employe of the house he is at once discharged and frequently is "requested" to leave the city on pain of being arrested.

The Rubber Band Fiend.

Men who are averse to hard work find many ways of making money easily. One of this order has for his stock in trade a piece of rubber hose, a pair of sharp scissors and a ready tongue. He drops in on business men and asks them if they are in need of rubber bands; if so, he will give them the very best sort for $1 for 500. The average man is likely to say that he has no use for so large a supply, and that starts the conversation. He of the rubber hose, scissors and tongue says that he can supply any number of rubber bands of the best quality on the spot. He can furnish one hundred in a minute if the customer wants them, and he adds that he will cut them from his hose right then and there. The customer says he can not do it, and the rubber band man smiles and says he has a dollar about him which says he can. Many a man has put up his dollar on this game, only to lose it, fairly and squarely, for the rubber band "fiend" gets out his scissors and goes through his piece of hose even as the hungry boy goes through a pumpkin pie. Those who have seen the operation say that it is easy for him to slice off one hundred neat little rubber rings in sixty seconds.

TRADING ON THE AFFECTIONS.

The ways undertaken by "men" in this world to eke out their livelihoods are more numerous than the sands on the seashore, and often more brutal than the vengeance of the savage, and their exploiters are as ruthless of the agony they cause, as they are greedy in their avarice. A new fangled notion, whereby such creatures can put money in their purses, calls itself the "Memorial Card Company," and hails from Boston, whither its whining, heartless circulars find their way into households where, as the "Company" has learned—through some scheme of correspondence with local undertakers, we imagine—the hand of death has been laid heavily. It is horrible and cowardly, this rasping anew the bleeding human hearts for the sake of a little gain—albeit the percentage of profit must be enormous—but "Companies" of character are willing to make their gains, however they trade upon the holiest affections of mourning men and women. Surely, of human nature's phases, when money is to be gained, we have new and larger knowledge every day, and are given new reason to mourn "man's inhumanity to man."

THE SOAP MAN ABROAD.

A very soapy imposition has been perpetrated recently in many parts of the country. A man goes through a section, leaving at each house a box supposed to be filled with soap; also an extra sample cake for trial. Soon after the wily agent returns, and in nearly every case the box is returned. He opens it and several cakes are found to be missing. The fellow charges the lady of the house with having taken them, and persists in the assertion with so much bluster that she finally pays for them, to get rid of him, notwithstanding the fact that there is no legal ground for the claim. Moral: If an unknown man insists upon leaving a closed package of soap at your house, set the dog on him.

BOGUS BIBLE AGENTS.

Rascals travel around the country with a big Bible, representing themselves as agents for the same, and securing signatures to an order for same, to be paid for on small instalments, the Bible to be "delivered in a few days." In a few days a note turns up. Look out for your signature.

BOGUS COMMISSION HOUSES.

In all large cities there are bogus commission houses that make a specialty of swindling farmers and country shippers and is not a new scheme. It has been going on for years and thousands of dollars are lost by country produce shippers every year by dealing with these fraudulent firms. Before shipping goods to strangers make them give you satisfactory bank references.

PEDDLERS WHO ARE FRAUDS.

A nuisance that does more than anything else to disturb the householder in all parts of the country is the house-to house peddler. He comes in an almost infinite number of forms, with a pack, a basket, a gripsack, or with the article he desires to sell concealed under his coat, and he comes every hour in the day. The visits of the man who enlarges pictures and the men who sell sewing-machines have become proverbial. They are trouble enough, but in their wake have come a set of men who have put them to the blush. It is no exaggeration to say that in many parts of the country, at the average house, a knock comes at the door or the door-bell rings every fifteen minutes, and the person who answers it is confronted by a peddler, who has something or other to sell. There is the peddler with a pack on his back, containing a variety of household goods which he is anxious to display. He has a little of everything—dry goods, cutlery, jewelry of the cheapest sort, various articles of wearing apparel, and other things too numerous to mention. He is followed by a man who has a patent egg-beater, and then comes along another with a potato-parer, which will save the buyer a small fortune in a year. The door-bell rings again, and an individual with a stove-lid lifter of wonderful efficiency, possessing points not presented by any other lifter in the market, shows himself. He is followed by a man with an oil-lamp burner of extraordinary powers, and another who wants to sell a new pillow-sham holder or a patent bed-spring. Another is selling albums, lead-pencils, or stationery in packages. Then comes a procession of seedy individuals with needles, or brooms, or coffees and teas, soap, patent medicines and cure-alls, clothes-wringers, brackets, pictures, chromos, oil paintings, iron holders, handkerchiefs, gents' furnishing goods, articles of wearing apparel for ladies and children, rugs, door-mats, perfumeries, mops, tinware, silver-plated ware, clocks, and laces. Space forbids the enumeration of the different articles these worthies have to sell. The business has been steadily growing for years, and as much of a nuisance as it is now it promises to become worse in the future. The articles offered for sale are generally worthless, as all well-informed people know, but there is still the necessity, repeated many times each day, of turning the peddlers away. Many of these alleged peddlers are sneak thieves and the public should be careful in dealing with them.

A Suffcient Warning.

The " Telegraph " instruction companies that insert their advertisements in all papers that will insert their swindling advertisements, are, to put it plainly, nothing but obtainers of money under false pretenses, because they hold out inducements which are utterly illusive, and because of such inducements, rake in their " earnings." It is easy to see, upon a moment's reflection, that there are many sound reasons for these statements. First—There is no possibility of any person becoming a qualified telegraph operator with less than the practice of a year, under most favorable circumstances. Second --The technical knowledge of an operator must be so great as to render him familiar with all the detail of his business, and hence, with " switches," " duplexes," " quadruplexes," " lightning-averters," " cut-outs," and so on, and, wanting this knowledge, which no " teacher " ever can give him, no man can be qualified. Third—Experienced operators, of first-rate skill, do not earn more than eighty dollars a month, and "plugs," as the regularly educated craftsmen name these "institute" fellows, could not earn more than thirty dollars. Forty dollars would be very high pay, indeed, because there is no room for them in any regular office. Fourth—The very names which these advertisers select to designate themselves are fraudulent in intention, because they imitate those of established companies—so nearly as they dare—with which they have no possible connection.

The Lining Thief.

The lining thief is one of the latest exploiters in the realm of crime. This is the man who trades hats with you in the barber-shop, in the sleeping-car, and outside the hotel dining-room. The mere act of exchanging is a trick old enough in itself, but with the oldest adroitness of the lining thief, it becomes a very tantalizing sort of meanness. The lining thief carries about him one or more linings which he has pulled out of old and rusty hats, and by a clever juggle slips them, as occasion offers, into the property of others, who have no means of identity so sure as the look of the inside. In this way, though you may seem to think you know your hat by its general appearance or color you are nonplussed by the changed character of the lining.

Boarding House Swindlers.

A well-dressed, slick-tongued swindler is plying his scheme among boarding houses in all parts of the country with good results. It is something new and catchy, and the apparent honesty of the scamp makes a willing victim of every landlady called upon. The scheme is to enter a house wherever a sign "furnished rooms" is seen, and after considerable parleying about price of room selected, he asks the landlady if she will be kind enough to reserve the room for him, "just for three days, please." The landlady, being of course anxious to secure a good tenant and at the same time protect herself, mentions reluctantly that her terms are cash in advance. Mr. Swindler objects to payment in advance. An idea strikes him. He will give the landlady $2 if she will keep the room three days, and in case he does not appear to forfeit the amount agreed. He gives the kind landlady a $10 bill, gets $8 in return, shakes her warmly by the hand, and bids her a friendly adieu. She learns later in the day that the $10 bill is counterfeit.

How People Hide Money.

A favorite hiding place for money, especially for bills of large denominations, has always been the large family Bible and the unabridged dictionary. This is still common in rural places. So is the practice of sticking money snugly away under the corner of a carpet, particularly under some large piece of furniture. This is a method that has much to commend it. Tea caddies or sugar bowls make excellent temporary safes. Another hiding place is the old-fashioned country clock, which is almost historic as a spot for tucking away little bundles of valuables. An old tradition was that the old clock, outside of its value as a timepiece, was particularly useful as a receptacle for three articles very much needed in the household—quinine, rat poison and money. The only trouble with the clock was that too many petty thieves knew about it. But the good housewives of the old time never thought of that. It is safe to say that the number of women who put away jewelry in pocketbooks under a mattress for safe keeping, afterward carefully smoothing the bed down, can be numbered by the thousands. This method is a favorite one among city people. The pocket of an old dress that hangs in an unconcealed way in a closet is regarded by many women as one of the safest places imaginable for spare rings, brooches and bracelets, and even for a pocketbook. Old shoes, standing in their proper place directly alongside of new ones, are likewise much esteemed, for a great deal can be shoved down into their toes, without giving the slightest evidence of the value therein.

Modern Slang Terms and Their Meaning.

The human emotions which, being struck, resound in slang, are of many kinds. There is fear and desire of secrecy that may produce an esoteric language, a kind of verbal cipher, intelligible only to the initiated. This kind of speech is very useful to thieves as long as the police are not adepts. Slang is probably much composed of Romany, "Yiddish" (that very curious pigeon Hebrew), French, Italian mispronounced, and words merely hit out in a kind of unconscious poetry, figurative and sensual. Nobody knows what ancient elements there may be in slang. By reason, however, of the never-ceasing need of new names for old things, the thief's slang is a very fugitive and evanescent speech. Travelers talk of families of savages which get separated in the bush, and when a generation has passed, the descendants of each set speak a different tongue.

Slang expressions, according to some scholars, become incorporated in a language through frequent and long continued use and ultimately become recognized as standard.

All tongues possess words which originated in the slums and finally with perhaps slight modifications find their way to the drawing room. How many of the coined words used at the present day will reach that distinction it is hard to say at the present time. Nor is it easy to determine how long the non-interpretation of old words will stick to them.

Certain it is that many expressions and words given to society in general by the select army of talent which now and then are arraigned in police courts are marvels of ingenuity. Among them are the following:

Pantata—A boss bribe taker and blackmailer who hides behind this sobriquet.

Guy—A rural gentleman who comes to pick up wealth and is assisted in his quest.

Backer—An alleged rich man who does nothing but takes all the money.

Writer—A man who edits green-goods literature and gets half of the profits.

Steerer—A man who pilots the "guy" to the place of "fleecing."

Turner—The man who turns good money into pieces of green paper.

Father—A benevolent-appearing old gentleman who adds an air of respectability to the game.

Speedy Fortune—The tempting pile of green paper which the "guy" wants in a hurry.

Tailor—A smooth-tongued individual who finishes the work done by the "turner" if the "guy" has anything left.

Throwing a Scare—Giving a man a sudden fright.

Glad Hand—The act of shaking hands with a man whose money you want.

Glassy Eye—A peculiar look given by men who have just explored pockets not their own

Marble Heart—Feeling for a man whose money you have in exchange for the paper which had been yours.

Circus folks not only have a slang of their own, but as they are past masters in the general slang of the day they talk a jargon which would be simply unintelligible to the uninitiated. They are in a line of business to catch every cant phrase going, and any new word which is only a local invention. To a circus man the manager or head of any enterprise is always "the main guy," while those in subordinate positions are simply "guys." The tents are "tops" to the circus men, and they are subdivided into the "bigtop,' the "animal top," the "kid top," the "candy top," and so on indefinitely. The side show, where the Circassian girls, fat women, and other curiosities termed "freaks" are shown, is termed the "kid show," and the man with the persuasive voice who seeks to entice people into the "kid show" is known as a "barker."

The man who sells peanuts, red lemonade, palm leaf fans, animal and song books and concert tickets are known under the general term of "butchers," while that class of circus followers whose methods are outside the pale of the law, such as pickpockets, gamblers, and short-change men, are either "crooks" or "grafters." To get a person's money without giving them any equivalent is "to turn them." A countryman is either a "Rube" (Reuben) or a "Jasper."

Thus if a countryman went into a side show and was robbed of $10 there, a circus man would say: "The Rube went against the grafter in the kid top and got turned for ten cases." From the combination of the warning cry of "Hey" and the word "Rube" comes the circus man's rallying cry of "Hey, Rube!" which is always sounded in times when a fight with outsiders is imminent.

The cry of "Hey, Rube!" has been in use among circus men for half a century or more, and in the old days it was often followed by bloodshed and even loss of life. Fights between circus men and outsiders are comparatively rare to-day, however, and serious trouble seldom occurs, except in sparsely settled regions of the South and West.

The musicians with a circus are known as "wind-jammers," the canvasmen and other laborers are "razorbacks," while a man who drinks to excess is either a "lusher" or a "boozer." These last two expressions are not confined to circus men, but have been used largely and more commonly by them than by any other class. The distance from one town to another is always known as a "jump," and traveling is "jumping." A circus that travels overland is known as a "red wagon show" in contradistinction to a show that travels by rail.

The show ground is always called the "lot," and the dining-tent, where most of the circus men get their meals, is the "camp." Horses are always "stock," and the horse tents are the "stock tops." Then there are scores of technical terms describing the work of the different performers, which, while hardly to be classed as slang in themselves, nevertheless add to the picturesqueness of the circus folks' vocabulary. Thus among acrobats there is the "understander," the "middleman," and the "topmounter." Among the riders there are rough riders, pad riders, and bareback riders, and among the funmakers there are "patter," or talking clowns, singing clowns, and knockabouts. A clown used to be called a "cackler" in the English circuses. The three-ring tents with their great size have knocked most the old-fashioned wagon circuses out of business.

Traveling Doctor Frauds.

Beware of the traveling doctor who goes about the country announcing in showy advertisements or gaudy-colored handbills that he is to be in your place on such a date, and in the adjoining town on the next day. Ninety-nine times out of a hundred he will charge you an excessive bill, and kill instead of cure. Persons suffering from chronic diseases are especially inclined to consult this kind of quacks, and to their sorrow they generally find, sooner or later, that the traveling doctor, in order to produce a sudden impression upon the system or a special organ, has given them poisonous medicines which will leave the patient in a worse condition than he was before. Beware of traveling doctors.

Thief Sheltering Resorts.

One of the typical forms of robbery practiced in all large cities speaks for itself of the necessity of doing away with thief-sheltering saloons. Cases of the kind are revealed almost daily in the regular proceedings of the police courts. An unsophisticated stranger in any city is accosted by a confidence man, with or without a "pal." The stranger, who is generally traveling and provided with money, has time on his hands, and the confidence man suggests that they go to see some of the city's sights. On the way the stranger is induced to enter a saloon where the confidence man is sure of securing the connivance both of the bartenders and of fellows of his own vocation. With drink or dice-shaking or a mere bet the bunco men contrive to make the stranger show his money, and after that he is helpless. Either by ruse or by open violence they rob him before he leaves the place. This is only one very common illustration of the uses to which a certain kind of saloon is put by the criminal element. Places of this sort shelter criminals and assist them; they are the headquarters of the gangs which infest certain parts of all cities. They make it easy to commit crimes which without them would be difficult and rare. Strangers should be careful about making up with every one they meet.

Hunting for Pedigrees.

A young man in New York has gone into the business of searching out pedigrees and hunting up coats-of-arms and crests for all who apply. He styles himself a "pursuivant of arms" and is doing a rushing business. This is not exactly a new vocation, for there are many genealogists in this country who earn considerable money by tracing out the ancestry of families. But this young "pursuivant of arms" is not, properly speaking, a genealogist. The preparation of family trees is no part of his business. He relies solely upon patrons who have but one thought, and that to secure a coat-of-arms, which they may have emblazoned on their note paper and cut upon their seal rings. For all such there is always a chance of securing the coveted prize. Coats-of-arms are nearly as plentiful as lamp posts. Books of heraldry give the names of thousands of families entitled to arms and a description of the device accorded to each. If a man has an English, German, French or Italian name he is almost sure of finding that name in one of the heraldic books. It does not follow that he is entitled to the arms of the family of his name, but a small matter like this never worries the crest hunters.

Wanted his Horses "Boarded."

A farmer from Iowa, who was not up to the dark ways of Chicago sharpers, was victimized in a manner which left him no chance for legal redress. He was in a hotel with several other farmers, when a rather engaging man entered, and stated in a general way that he was looking for a place in the country where he could have a span of horses boarded. He was willing to pay twenty dollars a month for each horse. The man from Iowa seized promptly upon the chance, and accompanied his prospective customer to his stable. There he was shown the team in question. A rather good looking black horse was also standing in one of the stalls, to which his attention was directed. At this point another well dressed stranger entered the stable and remarked to the ostensible proprietor, "I have made up my mind to take that black horse at your offer of three hundred dollars." "Did I offer it to you for that?" asked the other. "No; but you did to a friend of mine." "Well, I'm sorry, but I can't sell it to you at any price. The horse belongs to my wife, and she insists that it shall not be sold to a livery stable keeper." With a crestfallen look the would-be purchaser took the man from Iowa aside and told him, in a confidential tone, "See here; you buy that horse and bring it around to my stable and I'll give you twenty-five dollars for your bargain. I'll advance the money if you don't happen to have it with you." At this he handed the farmer a business card of a "livery and sale stable" which he said was his own, and slipped out. The man from Iowa at once opened negotiations for the black horse and was told that he could have it for three hundred dollars cash, to be paid that day. Paying ten dollars—all he had with him—as earnest, he started out to the address given on the business card. The place was not a livery stable, nor could he obtain any trace of his expected customer. Then it began to dawn upon his mind that he had been victimized, and he returned to the stable where the sharper took him. His original customer was still there, and the farmer demanded the return of the ten dollars he had paid. The answer was, "You bought that horse for three hundred dollars; you can pay the balance to-day as you agreed to, or I shall sue you for it and the keep of the horse until it is paid for and taken away." With the prospect which this opened before him, the man from Iowa was glad to compromise by leaving the ten dollars in the hands of the swindler, who with his confederate is now looking for the next victim.

TRICKS OF FORTUNE-TELLERS.

The nonsense of fortune-telling is one in which not only our servant girls indulge ; the daughters of wealth and education are addicted to it. Surreptitious visits to a fortune-teller are among the common escapades of society matrons and maids, and anything new in that line is bound to recompense its operator. An astrologer has set up a curious variation of his business of humbug, and his specialty is the telling of fortunes by the means of moles. He pretends to be able to read character and make prophecies by means of these blemishes. It would bother other than an ingenious man to put this method into practical use, but the difficulties are surmounted by the "professor" in question. He has printed on cards four outlines of a female figure, showing the form from each point of the compass, so to speak. His clients on their first visit are provided with a set of these cards, which they take home and mark in just the right spots with the moles which they happen to bear. Then they return to the fortune teller, and he reads their attributes and destiny from the diagrams as filled out. A mole on the shoulder means one thing, and on the side has a totally different interpretation, and so on through a vast number of locations and combinations. The fellow has adapted himself to his particular humbug by growing a tremendous beard, which makes him look like a wise man of the East, and increases his impressiveness. His gravity is perfect, he talks like an educated man, and he is doing a lucrative business, his price being $2, and his customers are so many that usually one has to wait an hour or so for an audience.

THE WORK OF FLIM-FLAMMERS.

" Fim-flam," as the trick is known in the vocabulary of the confidence fraternity, is so old a scheme and has been worked in so many different ways that it is nearly played out. The trick is worked by two confederates, one of whom attracts the attention of their victim while the other, who has already got his mind confused in some ingenious manner, either defrauds or robs him. One confederate enters a store and, making a small purchase, cheats the proprietor on the change while the other distracts his attention. The trick has almost passed into disuse among the crooked fraternity, as overworked, but occasionally it bobs up in small cities and towns and the public should be put on their guard. A grocer in Rochester, N. Y., was recently flim-flammed and we reproduce his experience as recited by himself:

" A nicely dressed, gentlemanly fellow came in and said: 'Could you accommodate me with a five dollar bill for these five one's?' and threw a roll on the counter. Change was scarce and I gladly passed out a five. I picked up the roll and found four one's and a five. 'Oh,' he said, 'that's a mistake,' and took the five, replacing it with a one, which he took out of his vest pocket. Just then another fellow, about twenty-one years old, came in and said, in a nervous, hurried sort of way: 'What is the name of this street, please?' At the same time the first fellow shoved back my five among the five one-dollar bills and said: 'You might as well give me a ten while you're about it.' I passed out a ten and he went out with it, leaving the five ones and the $5 bill on the counter. All this time the second fellow was annoying me so about the name of the street that I got all mixed up. Finally I showed him the name of the street printed on my business card, and he said, 'I guess I'll just take it with me,' and went out. It was all done so slick that I didn't discover the fraud till about two hours afterwards. I almost believe if he had passed out the $5 bill which he took from his vest pocket, thus making $15 on the counter before me, I should have pushed it back to him, telling him he had given me too much."

Fools and Their Money.

One of the latest games of swindlers is advertising campaign badges at $5 each. "They send circulars," says an old detective, "to officeholders, saying that as money was needed for current expenses by the party, it was thought well to give a chance to all to subscribe in small sums, so the badges, which of course are expensive, were to be sold. Of course he reckoned on a good many people sending the money, under the impression that they would be really contributing to the party's expenses. He was picked up very quickly, but within three days he had received several hundred letters, and nearly all of them had money enclosed."

It is hard to realize that there are so many fools in the world as there are, until you come to know of the various ways in which they are swindled. Of course there are millions of varieties of the game of the swindler, from the elaborate bogus corporation on Wall street to the humbug of the snide evangelist who passes his hat around for pennies, but the records for the postoffice show up the average idiocy of the human race rather better than anything else. It seems to be only necessary for some rascal to appeal to the cupidity, the curiosity, or the generosity of mankind in order to reap a harvest. Obviously if he can do this by advertising, and get the money back through the mail, the speculation will be profitable.

The green goods swindle is the most notorious of all the

schemes that are worked in this way, but there are dozens of them that are being worked all the time in spite of the law and all the vigilance of the department. The only safe rule for a man who is gullible enough to be deceived is for him never to send any money to a stranger until after he has received his money's worth. It is a grave offense to use, or to try to use, the United States mail for the improper receipt of money, but there isn't a crook in the country who won't run big risks when the amount to be won is commensurate with the danger. That's a part of their business, and then, they always rely on their dexterity and cunning to enable them to escape.

A notorious trick was the old one that was played in England. Some clever rascal in London advertised that he would, on receipt of sixpence in stamps, return to the sender one shilling. The advertisement was published prominently enough to attract considerable attention, and it naturally excited remark. To most persons it seemed a very transparent humbug, too silly to be called a fraud, but there were a few curious individuals who determined to see whether the advertiser was a crank, or whether he had some game, so they sent on their sixpences. By return mail each one received the shilling. A few days after the same advertisement appeared again in several of the newspapers, and everybody who had tried it before told all his friends about it. The result was that several hundred sixpences were received, and next day as many shillings went back. The third time the advertisement appeared the mail received by the clever sharper was simply enormous. Letters came from all parts of the kingdom and from all sorts of people, high and low, rich and poor. The rogue pocketed several thousands of pounds, and curiously enough neglected to made any returns.

Less ingenious are the various tricks of fellows who advertise offering information for a certain sum, generally for a dollar. One advertised that he would tell people how to get rich, and told those who remitted the money to him to do as he was doing. Another offered a method for fat people to get thin, and wrote to them to stop eating. How to make money at the races, according to another of these clumsy fellows, was always to bet on the winning horse. This class of tricksters seem to be trying to be facetious as well as dishonest, but their games are trivial and their gains small.

A much neater swindle, which was really almost witty as well as wicked, was perpetrated by a man who advertised some time ago that he would send a very fine steel engraving of Washington for fifty cents. He received a considerable number of half dollars, and to each sender he returned a postage stamp. That was no more than dozens of so-called manufacturers are doing all over the country now. You can hardly pick up a country newspaper which does not contain advertisements of cheap watches, guns, sewing machines, tools and what not. Articles are offered for preposterously low prices, and enormous numbers of people are swindled by sending on the money asked. Of course, many such advertisers may be doing a legitimate and an honest business, but there are many who are really swindlers, and swindlers of the meanest type, for they are afraid to face the risks of the law, and cover themselves up with pretenses that are morally, though not legally, false.

It is to be said to the credit of the newspaper press generally that the worst of these "ads" are now refused by all respectable publishers, and there are few papers with any pretensions to respectability that will publish any which seem to be crooked. The business, however, goes on merrily all the time, and it will go on as long as the rogues want the fools' money.

" Agents' Directories."

The public is familiar with advertisements appearing in many journals for persons to send their names to fill up an " Agents' Directory," and bring as perquisites sundry " samples, circulars, books, newspapers, magazines," etc. Beware of such schemes as this, however low or slightly to be considered the actual cost may be, because names are sought to be used in a multitude of ways, whereof many are very tortuous, and lead to much inconvenience and often loss. Again, there is a curious business in this world, which is none other than the gathering names for sale to newspapers with imaginary subscription lists, to magazines with tentative life, to vile dealers in unmentionable quackeries, and to the makers of worthless and worse than worthless books. All sorts of endeavors are put forth for inducing people to forward their names and addresses to some central point, and thus prepare the stock in trade of these peculiar merchants. Naturally, there will then be a torrent of circulars and " books," " newspapers " and " periodicals " and trashy literature.

The Man and the Hat.

It is true that a man's disposition and traits can be readily deciphered by intelligent confidence men and crooks by his hat and the way be wears it. There is a close intimacy between the styles of men's headgear and the science of phrenology. The hat is the bump which infallibly denotes the most prominent trait of character. When a man buys a hat he is governed in the selection by the peculiar organism of the brain. It doesn't make any difference whether the particular hat he selects is becoming to him or not, he prefers it because he is built that way. If he wears an unbecoming hat he is not responsible for it. A man never looks in a mirror when he tries a hat on. A woman always does.

The tall silk hat denotes financial ability. Bankers, hotel clerks and police reporters always wear silk hats. Rich men do not always wear silk hats, nor are men who wear silk hats always rich. Still, the silk hat is an unerring sign of capacity for handling finances successfully.

The derby hat denotes energy. A man who wears a derby always has the appearance of being on the go. It is a ready-for-all-occasions hat. It is at home whether at church or on the base-ball grounds. The derby is a nobby little cross between the silk and the slouch. It is an accommodating hat. The clergyman looks well in it, and it fits the bartender to a "T." And all the time it has a pushing goaheaditiveness in its appearance that makes everything sideswitch when the derby passes by.

And then there is the slouch hat. Ah, there is the hat of liberty for you. The slouch hat is the original old commoner. It is the hat for the masses—democratic in its style and republican in its simplicity. There is nothing that symbolizes pure unadulterated Americanism so well as the slouch hat. The slouch hat denotes sociability. It is the unfailing index of genial temperament. It means that the wearer is a good fellow that will do to tie to. He may be a bank president or he may be a cowboy, still you can rely on his being a hale companion wherever you meet him, possessing sturdy independence of character, and always ready to extend a helping hand wherever it is needed.

The man who wears his hat perpendicularly, whether it is a tile, a derby or a slouch, has the bump of self-esteem well developed. He thinks that he is the upper crust of the pie and is entitled to recognition. The man who wears his hat down over the forehead is a thoughtful man. He is studious, and communes with himself a great deal, and sometimes inclined to moroseness.

But the man who wears his hat on the back of his head is the one who doesn't care whether school keeps or not, and is of a class that a swindler who studies human nature steers clear of. He is independent and self-reliant, and one day is with him as another. He takes note of neither time nor individuals. He is usually popular because he is always generous. Sailors and soldiers, and jockeys and base-ball players, are not included in this classification, because they always wear caps.

Material for Detectives.

Fearlessness, coolness and self-control, are the chief requisites of a detective. Without these a man can never be an artist in the business, for, though he may be useful in some of its branches, he can never attain to the highest eminence in all of them. In addition to the qualities named he must also have strong perceptive faculties and that power of generalization which will enable him to jump at once to correct conclusions. Memory is one of his most important essentials. One sight of a face must imprint it so idelibly upon his recollection that he can never forget it, and he must remember not only the face itself, but the time, place and circumstances with which it is associated. A memory of faces alone is not sufficient. The detective must have a strong memory for names, numbers and dates as well. He must be intelligent and there is no knowledge of any kind that may not sometimes be of value to him in his profession. His eyesight and hearing should be of the best and he should cultivate a power of observation which will enable him to carefully note, without seeming to do so, everything by which he is surrounded. Detectives in real life are very different from those in novels and plays. The latter are represented as wearing various disguises, such as wigs, false whiskers, etc., which they suddenly pull off at the most unexpected moments, thereby revealing their identity. Dion Boucicault, in one of his plays, represents a detective, who is quite a young man, as making himself up for an elderly gentleman of 60 and going about in broad daylight and talking to people who knew him well being entirely unrecognized by reason of his disguise. Charles Reade and Wilkie Collins represent some of the detectives in their novels as doing the same thing. This is simply nonsense. It is utterly impossible for the most skilful hair-worker to make up a wig or a set of false whiskers that cannot be detected as false when worn, and every theater-goer knows that the most skillful artists in "makeup" cannot put upon their face the lines and wrinkles which indicate age in such a way as to decieve, even when aided by the glamor of the footlights. No detective in real life ever attempted to wear any such disguise. To be a good detective a man must have a natural gift in that way. Detectives, like poets, are born, not made. Many of them begin as amateurs. For instance, something occurs in their own lives which causes them to turn detective for their own purposes. They work up their own case successfully; they find they like the work and they embark in it as a business.

Smart Tricks of Thieves.

At Philadelphia not long ago, a thief was detected in the act of stealing a gentleman's watch, and in his haste he ran into the arms of a detective, who had been watching him for some time. Naturally, the thief must have felt somewhat excited at such a moment; but if he did he showed no symptoms of being so. Although instantly secured by the unenviable handcuffs, he had the presence of mind to pass the watch unobserved into the pocket of a passer-by. This person was puzzled to know how he became the possessor of the watch, and being afraid of keeping the gift, was sufficiently honest to hand it to the police.

Another instance of the remarkable coolness and audacity of a thief, though perhaps not an uncommon one, is worth relating. One day a Boston "stalk"—a man capable of doing mischief of any kind for a trifle—having watched his opportunity, took up a coat that hung outside a pawnbroker's shop. Flinging it over his arm and carrying it into the shop as if intending to make a purchase, he offered it for sale. Not recognizing his own property, the pawnbroker bought the coat. But even this did not satisfy the thief. He handled some silk handkerchiefs, and in choosing one remarked carelessly: "Take pay for this out of the money for the coat." "But I have given you the money," indignantly answered the pawnbroker. "Oh, no; you haven't," said the thief.

A warm altercation ensued. In vain the shop man protested that he had paid the money; and at last the thief went out in search of an officer to settle the dispute, taking with him some silver spoons, several silk handkerchiefs, as well as the silk handkerchief in question, which in his excitement the broker had forgotten. But the thief is not always so cool and collected as we are wont to believe him. He is especially unnerved by hunger and the police.

Jewelry and Your Money Back.

A sharper is going about the country playing a game so old that it is revived with impunity. It is as follows: Securing the best turnout to be had at a livery stable, the fellow drives to the public square or a conspicuous street corner and halts. Then standing up in the carriage he displays an assortment of "Australian gold jewelry," which he offers at low prices, the purchaser to keep the jewelry and also have his money back. After an active trade in gaudy sleeve buttons and similar articles at twenty-five cents each, the purchase money is all returned to the buyer. Then higher prices prevail and chains at two dollars are eagerly taken, the purchasers, as before, receiving back their money and keeping the "goods." Then the sharper drives to another corner and reopens trade, saying nothing about refunding the money. But the eager crowd, which has followed him, fail to notice the omission and rush to buy watches at twenty to fifty dollars. Suddenly the fellow announces the sale closed and drives rapidly to the railway station and departs on the first train. There is no law that can reach him, for he has made no actual misrepresentations. Those who are left with worthless watches in exchange for good money have only their own greed to thank.

Wants a Loan.

A cheeky fraud goes into a town and calls on a monument dealer or painter and says he is a member of a committee to contract for the construction of a large monument or painting of a church, as the case may be, in a neighboring town. He tells his victim that his presence is desired in said town to bid on the contrct and then departs. Presently he returns and says he lost his pocket-book and obtains a loan of several dollars. This is a cheap swindle, easily worked, and is liable to be worked on any class of trade.

Ingenious Device of a Woman.

A woman named Robinson used to walk about the streets of New York in the day time, and when she noticed a crowd around a pharmacy—an inevitable sign that an accident had occurred—she went into the establishment to see the victim. If the injured person were unconscious the good Samaritan, Mrs. Robinson, immediately claimed him or her as her own, unless, of course, the object of the druggist's care had an appearance of abject poverty. In this way she succeeded in getting the victim put into a cab. He was her cousin, her brother-in-law, or the husband of a dear friend, and everybody believed her and praised her for her tender solicitude or deep disinterestedness. She would get into the vehicle with her charge, and during the drive to a fictitious address she contrived to ease the insensible or half-dazed victim of watch, chain and money. She then got out, told the cabman to drive on to the address given, adding that she would rejoin him after she had called for a friend who was also interested in knowing about the accident. This able female was found out while she was taking a person in an epileptic fit to a false address. The patient became suddenly conscious while the charming Samaritan was fumbling in his pockets, and the situation feebly dawned upon him. By exercising a little duplicity he was able to signal to the cabman to stop, and the deeds and doings of Mrs. Robinson were later on revealed to the public.

HOW SMART THIEVES ACT.

The thieves who ransack dwellings during the absence of families have nothing to learn in the way of disarming suspicion. A gentleman when about to go into the country with his family said that he felt quite safe regarding his house, as a widow who lived opposite was worth a dozen policemen. She saw everything and knew everybody, and no thief could carry off a coal scuttle under her eye without having a hue and cry at his heels. When the gentleman returned from his vacation he found that his house had been raided, and that his neighbor had watched the proceedings in serene contentment. The thieves had provided themselves with a key tagged with his name. They had put on overalls and jumpers to look like honest workmen, and had driven up to the house in a cart with an imposing display of tools. But their finest touch—the device that blinded the widow—was the calling a police officer to point out the house for them. They ascertained when the officer on the beat would put in an appearance. Then they waited till he had passed the premises, drove after him to ask where Mr. Blank lived, and brought him back to show them the place and see that all was right. That settled their standing for the widow. The absentee had overrated her acuteness. Instead of being as good as a dozen policemen, one officer was quite too much for her.

Foiling Dishonest Waiters.

The public will be interested in a scheme adopted now by many hotels to prevent swindling either on the part of waiters or guests. It is a novel check system. Printed checks are used containing the name of everything enumerated on the hotel bill of fare. Whatever is served by the waiter will be punched by a man stationed at the entrance to the kitchen. When the waiter gets a plate of soup for the table d'hote the owner of the check, who purchases his ticket on entering the room, hands it to the waiter. The printed word soup is punched. The same when the waiter gets the guest meat and dessert; so that neither the waiter or the guest can fool the cashier. Each check is finally dropped into a lock box. In the drinking bar the amount of the drink is written by the bartender with an indelible pencil. The same system is practiced at the oyster and eating bar.

INSULTS ON ENVELOPES.

Debt-collecting agencies which confine their work to legitimate means of collecting honest dues from dishonest men and deadbeats may be encouraged, but some debt-collecting schemes are out-and-out-frauds. They are run by unprincipled men, who send (in envelopes with "BAD DEBTS COLLECTED" printed on them in big type) threatening demands to people for small bills which the agency claims are put in its hands for collection. Occasionally there is some foundation for the bill, but often the charge is wholly fictitious and fraudulent. People who are easily scared, or who are sensitive about such matters, are not infrequently pestered into paying these sharpers the amount called for. The sum is never large, and many prefer to pay it rather than have any bother. This contemptible and criminal proceeding can be suppressed under the new postal law which is now in effect. The law prohibits "any indecent, lewd, lascivious, obscene, libelous, scurrilous or threatening delineations, epithets, terms or language reflecting injuriously upon the character or credit of another, on the envelope or outside wrapper." The fine for each violation of this law is not less than $100 and imprisonment for one year. Postmasters may determine whether anything appearing on the outside of an envelope, wrapper or card, is contrary to the law, and are authorized to restrain any such apparently unlawful mail matter from going through the mails.

CRIMINALITY IN WOMEN.

It is a fact, according to science, that in all countries there are fewer convictions for crimes of women than men. European statistics vary from from the highest, 37 per cent., in Scotland, to the lowest, rather less than 6 per cent., in Italy.

It is also noted that there is a very wide difference between city and country. The proportion of female criminals is always higher in rural districts, sometimes reaching nearly to that of the males. Various explanations of these facts have been suggested. Some are complimentary to the sex, as that women are not given to intoxicants nor to gambling, nor to roving; they are more timid, more religious, more tender-hearted, and their sexuality is more passive.

Governing Ugly Men.

The superintendent of one of the leading prisons in America, in speaking of managing refractory prisoners, gives facts and makes suggestions that will prove of interest to the public:

"Of course, in an institution that has about twelve hundred inmates in confinement, there is bound to be considerable variety of character. It is not always the worst criminal that is the worst convict, although the inmates confined for crimes that show a preponderance of the animal nature in a man can be relied upon to furnish the most troublesome customers in a penitentiary. Most men, after they get to understand the rules of the prison, settle down to their observance. I do not allow any punishment by guards, and if a convict breaks a rule in such a way as to need their interference, all they are allowed to do is to cage the convict—that is, to lock him in an empty cell—and then report the case to me for action. I always allow the prisoner to tell his own story, and, after full investigation, if I find he is in the wrong, I try to adapt his punishment to the offense in such a way as to keep him from further repetition of it. Ordinary simple punishments answer. If a convict says he will not work, I generally say to him, 'If you won't work you can't eat,' and lock him up by himself. Four ounces of bread a day, and nothing but cold water to drink, will soon bring the most refractory convicts to their senses.

"Stubborn prisoners do not hold out long under this treatment. Some of them stick it out for a day and a half, but most of them wilt within twenty-four hours, and send me word that they are ready to take hold. Where something worse is needed, I have a walking track, and a bag of sand weighing forty pounds, and when a man is put on the track and made to carry the bag around the required number of laps to make fifteen miles, with a rest of only ten minutes at the end of each three hours' walking, he is generally sore and tired enough to keep him from repeating an offense which merits such punishment.

"Cases that require heroic treatment grow to some extent out of the fact that there is a classification of criminals in prison as well as out of it, and you cannot keep convicts who have been in the same lines of crime from finding each other out and sticking together to some extent; the burglars have their pals in the penitentiary as well as out of it, and so on through the whole catalogue. When one of these men gets into trouble his friends rally round him, and there is sometimes danger of a riot when the guard comes to take out the original offender. Still, even in these cases, we usually get along without having to resort to extreme measures. I do not remember but one case where it looked as though we would have to go to the limit, which in this case means the killing of the offender, and I will tell you about that so you may see what means are necessary to preserve authority, without which we could do nothing. It was a case of a man convicted of brutal murder, and when he came to us it was apparent that we were going to have trouble with him. Most convicts have some goodness left in them, of which we can take hold in our management of them. The man seemed to be simply an ungovernable animal. We put him to work in the foundry, and the first week he was there he quarreled with the convict who worked next to him and nearly killed him with a poker. I put him in a dungeon that was absolutely without a ray of light, and kept him there as long as the physician thought he could stay and live. When he came out he blinked like an owl from his long confinement in darkness, but was still unsubdued, and when he went back to work he struck a second convict with a ladle full of hot iron, injuring the man so badly that his life was for some time despaired of. Then the offender ran out of the shop, defied the guards, and when the case was reported to me he had got into the supper room where the most of the convicts had gone, and was seated in the midst of a hard crowd of his own kidney. It looked squally, but it was evident that the time had come to see who was master. I took a tough hickory cane in one hand, went to where he was sitting, touched him on the shoulder and told him to come with me. He raised up and drew off to strike me, but I used the cane vigorously on his head and face, backed him down the aisle into the ante-room and locked him up. As I backed him out a second convict threw a teacup at me, and others stood up and seemed inclined to interfere, but I told them to sit down, and there was no further disturbance. When I had my first man caged I went back to the man who had thrown the cup, knocked him down twice with the cane, and gave him a liberal dose of it after he was down. There was no further demonstration or violence, although it had been the boast of many convicts that no warden could take a man out of that room. Now they say, 'When the old man wants you, you've got to go.' As to the first offender, I had him stripped, took a whalebone buggy whip and gave him forty or fifty as sound lashes as could be laid on without breaking the skin. Every blow raised a welt, and I was prepared to give him as many more as he had got when he gave up and said he had enough.

" Corporal punishment, in some cases, is the best means of enforcing discipline. There are some offenders whose devilish impulse cannot be checked in any other way. I think there is something in the humiliation as well as in the pain inflicted that does the work needed. I don't think I am a man with any inhuman tendencies, but when one is placed where he has to maintain the mastery or go to the wall, he has to use the best means within his reach."

A Trusty Watchman.

An enterprising burglar entered a house, and after purloining everything he could find he prepared to remove a large photographic camera that was standing on a table. In some way he touched off a magnesium flash light attachment that was part of the machine, and fled precipitately when the thing flared up. The next day it was found that the camera had taken the photograph of the burglar. The negative was placed in the hands of the police, and by its aid they quickly nabbed their man. It showed the burglar with a jimmy in one hand and a box containing jewelry under his arm, while he carried a sack over his shoulder with valuable pieces of plate, books, etc., and was gazing at the flash light in open-mouthed amazement. This was the unimpeachable evidence of a mechanical eye-witness, and the fellow was sent up for six months.

Inferior Rubber.

The fraudulent tricks practiced by dishonest shoe dealers are many. Rubbers supply a favorite field for fraudulent propensities. Consumers know little or nothing of quality from appearance. The cheapest goods made, if highly finished, may readily be sold for the best. The best boot made is known as pure gum. Ranking next to this, but still graded as first quality, is the best dull finish. But of the dull boot there are, of course, as many grades and qualities as there are companies making them. When wearers come to buy them it is surprising how many pure gum shoes some dealers have, and how cheaply they sell them. A few years ago a manufacturer, remarking upon this rather curious feature of the business, undertook to remedy the evil. He ordered the "dull finish" boots stamped "*not* pure gum." The audacious dealers erased the first of the words, and the remaining two aided sales materially. Certain label manufacturers have done considerable business printing and preparing paper labels stamped "pure gum," for the use of retail shoe dealers, to be pasted on their boots. The trick of substitution is practiced by some dealers. The shoes are selected, fitted, paid for, it may be, and left to be delivered at the home of the buyer, or taken to another part of the store to be put up in a parcel. During the latter progress a cheaper and altogether inferior pair, same size and width, are put in their place for those purchased. One would hope for the credit of human nature that swindling of this nature was rare.

Blackmailing Physicians.

The reputable physician shrinks from the light of publicity. The story of his practice is and should be a sealed book. Sometimes, however, the physician, weighted with responsibility as he is, feels that he would like the confidence of someone to whom he can go. Other people, in every vocation, do it. A man who has no confidential friend ought to be avoided. Utter selfishness and exclusion make a man narrow and he looks at the world through the little end of a field glass. He is opinionated and hidebound, and if such a man lives to a good age that man becomes a crank who is an enemy to himself and to society. If a reputable doctor has a confidant—and he is entitled to one, at least, outside of his family circle if he has a home—he can tell some interesting facts which the public ought to have, so long as the doctor does not impale the subjects, and in some instances it would really benefit the public if names were given. One of the most frequent occurrences in the life of a physician is that in which an attempt is made to blackmail him. The reputation of a physician is as delicate as that of a woman. It is easier besmirched than that of the minister. There is more of this sort of thing in a large city than in smaller towns, for the very excellent reason that there are more designing people in a city and because city physicians do a large share of their business in private. The designing person in the attempts to blackmail is not always the patient. In many instances the patient is merely the tool. It will be nothing new to reputable lawyers to read that their profession is used as a mantle by some of the most unscrupulous and contemptible creatures that live. There is nothing which the average good citizen dreads as much as a lawsuit, and particularly where that lawsuit threatens to throw a light upon the life of the person which cannot, possibly, be avoided, or even if the light be an absolutely false one. These men, standing behind the honorable profession of the law, know the timidity of such people as the ones referred to, and, watching like rattlesnakes for an opportunity, they hiss and strike. No reputable attorney will be a party to a blackmailing suit, and no sane man will allow himself to be blackmailed, whatever the cost.

Horses for the Innocent.

Everybody admits that prevarication, to put it mildly, is a never absent factor in a horse trade. But there is a limit to sharp play there. A certain combination of individuals, that might very appropriately be called "a gang," are operating just now very successfully on the other side of the limit, and gentlemen who have no intimate acquaintance with politicians and think that mankind is naturally prone to be honest are being seriously affected by it every day. Horses are advertised for sale in the daily papers, the price being low and the horses are kind and fast, and will be sold at a ruinously low price to close a gentleman's estate.

The "gang" have stables in two streets. At one it is always announced that seven horses are for sale, while at the other the number is nine. Perhaps these numbers are chosen because they are considered lucky—not because they represent the number of horses, as each stable can boast of but one animal, and that of such a kind that in a good fair count it would be set down as only half a horse.

When the unsuspecting purchaser appears at the stable he is promptly "spotted," and half a dozen gentlemen, who have previously been lounging around the corner with their hands in their pockets, suddenly become very deeply interested in the prospective purchase of the one horse. Nobody pays the least attention to the real purchaser at first. He thinks business must be very brisk indeed and his chances of getting a horse at what he begins to believe must be a bargain quite as slim. Finally he edges into the conversation and becomes the central figure.

"Where are the other horses?" he asks.

"Just sold four this morning, and the rest are out on trial. A gentleman is coming around to try this one in an hour, if he is not sold before," replies the dealer.

"All right; let me take him out on trial?"

"I am sorry, but I can't. I promised to hold him for that other fellow unless some one bought him outright."

At this point the decoys evince further signs of purchasing, and the result is that the victim makes an offer. After a little haggling the price usually settled on is in the vicinity of $100. The money is paid and the purchaser drives off, happy in the consciousness of having a good bargain. When about two blocks distant his joy wilts down to several degrees below freezing point. The horse begins to wheeze and cough, and finally chokes and falls down. Then the sad-faced farmer leads the horse back to the stable and demands his money. At first he gets no satisfaction whatever. The dealer insists that the horse was all right when he left and he can't understand it. At last a compromise is made and the victim thinks himself lucky in getting $50 of his money back.

" I tell you what," said one of the decoys to a bystander, " that old horse is a dandy. He's got that choking racket right down to a fine point, and plays it elegant."

" Has he been sold many times ? " asked the reporter.

" Many times ? Well, I should cough up a cat. Every day, sure, and sometimes twice. Oh, you can gamble on his knowing his business now. Funny, now, ain't it ? That horse, as a horse, ain't worth two cents; but as a piece of property, I'm a gilly if he don't bring the old man in $50 a day, easy. Yes, sir; he don't look it, but he's one of the most valuable animals in the country."

At both places the same *modus operandi* is pursued and with the same profitable results to the dealers. The average man does not like to admit that he has been " played," and prefers to pocket his loss and keep quiet rather than air the affair in court. A few victims, more brave than the rest, have caused the heavy hand of the law to drop on the dealers. The heavy hand clutched savagely enough for awhile, and then, after the usual manner, let go and the dealers serenely went back to their business and their faithful old trick horse.

Salting Mines to Swindle.

About once every decade schemers and bunco operators in mining claims come to the front. Sometimes it is the discovery of a mine, bursting with gold nuggets, other times a silver mine, and sometimes it is a diamond mine. Around the newly found gold mine is heard the old story of the dying miner, who attempted to reveal the site, but died in the attempt. This gives the "local coloring"; the schemers send out prospectors, who dig a hole and secretly bring valuable ore from a genuine mine and bury it. When the good ore is dug up the richness of the mine is proved—to the satisfaction of the investor—and he buys the hole in the ground. After this scheme has been worked for awhile there is a lull and when the robbers have been forgotten by the public a new mine is discovered. The same old game is always being played for the benefit of wise men, many of whom seem to believe that gold grows as the flowers that bloom in the spring. The false reports of these scheming bunco men bring out a number of prospectors, restless mining men, who are ever hunting for the rich fields, which, like the mirage they often see in their wanderings, are ever beyond. They trudge along over the sandy, trackless desert, and when their provisions are exhausted they sink from exhaustion, thirst and hunger and die on its burning sands.

These false reports have whitened the desert with the bones of thousands of prospectors, besides causing the financial ruin of many too-confiding investors. One of the most gigantic swindles ever perpetrated in the far west was the "great diamond swindle" of a quarter of a century ago. It was hatched in San Francisco, with a portion of the plot in Kentucky. Some of the schemers purchased in London a few bushels of crystals from the South Africa diamond fields, and, under the guise of prospectors, visited a remote portion of the desert. The expedition was conducted secretly, and at night these diamonds were "planted" in a district of several acres.

The schemers returned, located the land as mining and mineral lands, and then kept quiet for several months. Finally they sent out a "prospecting" expedition to "uncover the stuff," as detectives would say. Reports of the discovery of diamonds in the sands of the desert soon reached all over the country, The conspirators shrewdly circulated the reports, yet pretended that they knew knothing of the facts. Specimen finds were examined by experts and reported to be of the "purest rays." The country was thrown into a fever of excitement and speculation ran high. Many sold their mining properties at a sacrifice, thus bearing the market and ruining others, and many mortgaged real estate and houses in order to buy stock in the "diamond fields."

Millionaire speculators accompanied some of the conspirators to the fields, and with spades they burrowed in the sand and turned up diamonds. So plentiful were they that by digging with a pocket knife, diamonds were found. Some of these were worth from $100 to $500 each. They had been carefully planted and located by the comspirators, and these occasional rich finds led to the belief that there must be many others. One man unearthed about a quart of crystals, greatly resembling diamonds, and among them were several genuine stones. There could be no doubt about that—the millionaire's own expert was on the ground and saw the diamonds taken from the earth, and pronounced them to be without a flaw. These millionaires influenced their friends to make investments, and the conspirators gobbled in money galore. The public ought to learn by this time that investing in any kind of mines or mining stock is a hazardous experiment at best.

THE SHORT CHANGE MAN.

An old Boston detective who was asked by the publishers of this work to give some of the swindlers that had come under his observation, writes as follows:

The public, especially the rural public, should be on guard against the short change rascal. Nearly everybody knows more or less about all the attendant feature of a circus—the side show, the horse tent, the cooking tent, the dressing room, the red-lemonade man and the peanut fiend. But not many people, even among the foxy old-timers who have patronized circuses for forty years, know anything about the "short-change man." His victims are many, but they prefer not to trumpet their fish-like quality from the housetops. They swallow their chagrin and keep silent, while they economize in a number of ways to get even on the money that the short-change man has taken.

A number of years ago I ran across one of the most accomplished short-change workers in this country and got well acquainted with him. He didn't suspect me of being a detective, and in the three months that I knew him I didn't enlighten him. He grew very confidential and chatty, and gave away to me the innermost secrets of his craft. He was a little, slim fellow, of Irish extraction, and as bright and sharp as a new needle. He had a way of tilting his head back and looking at folks with half-closed eyes, while he smiled slightly, that was clever enough to make a great hit in a dramatic creation. It was perfectly fetching, but the fine contempt he had for the "suckers" whom his kind bled, and the way he had of speaking of them was much more so. It was winter time when I knew him, and he was resting until the season opened up. I approached him a dozen times to get him to tell me all about the short-change act before he became pliable. He would take a coin and palm it as cleverly as Mr. Herrmann and laugh and turn away. But one evening he opened his heart to me.

I had been talking about the "telegraph" method of making short change, and he spoke up and said quite scornfully: "That's no good. There's no money in that. You can only get 50 cents or $1 out of that. There's lots of ways stronger than that!"

I asked him what they were.

"Well," he said, taking a roll of small bills, mostly ones and twos, out of his pocket, "they're worked this way: Do it with the 'long green.'"

He smoothed the bills out straight and caressed them affectionately.

"Ah! When these new ones were first issued," he said, "the boys worked all the banks in the country for them. They were the best graft the boys ever struck. You see they look just like a five or ten if you don't show the figure. Well, this is the way the boys take the money away from the 'suckers.' You've noticed a lot of hustlers in the crowd selling tickets and saving people the trouble of getting in the jam at the ticket wagon, haven't you? Well, you naturally think they are hired by the proprietor of the show because they sell tickets at the regular price. But they are not. They pay 100 cents on the dollar for every ticket they sell, and they depend on their ability to swindle the buyers out of a few dollars now and then for their profit.

"A young man with his best girl comes along—or an old man alone, or a solid business man with two or three of his family; it doesn't matter who it is, they're all victims—and he sees a great crush around the ticket wagon. There isn't much chance of getting a ticket there in less than ten minutes, and here at his elbow is a young man with 'Choice reserved seats at regular price! How many? We're here to relieve the rush at the wagon. No extra charge, sir! How many? and he says: 'Two please,' which, assuming that the man buys reserved seats, would be $2. He gives the young man a $10 bill or maybe $20—if there's any place on earth where a man will flash a big bill and where he hadn't ought to it's at a circus. We'll say he offers him a $20 bill this time for the sake of a better illustration of the story. The young man takes it, puts it into his pocket, draws out a handful of bills, takes a ten, a two and five ones, and hands the lump to the buyer of seats. It is $1 short, but the man has handled it so quickly and counted $18 out of it so easily that oftentimes the man takes it and goes, but the fakir is sore if he does. If he is a cautious and knowing party who is 'dead onto' the tricks of 'these circus sharps' it suits the 'short-change man' exactly, for then he will carefully count his change and say: 'Here, young man! You're $1 short here. Only $17 here.'

"That's beautiful and just as the fakir wants it. So he says: 'Sure of that? Just count it again, please.'

"So he counts it again, while the fakir watches, and when he has turned over the last bill he says, with the air of a man who knows too much to be cheated by those flip circus folks: 'That's all—seventeen.'

"But the fakir is a little doubtful, so he says, as though wishing to make sure: 'Just let me count it, please?'

"Serene in the belief that he has cornered his man, the buyer hands it over, and the fakir takes the bills in his left hand, with the $10 bill underneath, straightens them out, and then bends the whole bunch back over his left thumb. Then he turns them over, one by one, and they lie straight out—full length. When he reaches the last one he says cheerfully: 'You're right—my mistake and your treat,' or some such amiable chestnut, hands the bills back to the man, still at full length, goes down in his trousers pocket with his right hand and gets a silver dollar, at the same time tucking away the five dollar bill that he had palmed while counting the money the second time. If the young man spends any more money it will be the silver dollar without taking the paper money out of his pocket. If he makes complaint he is told his pocket has been picked, or that he hauled the money out while taking the silver dollar out."

Defense to Notes.

As many people are swindled by securing their signature in various ways to papers and documents which afterwards turn up as notes, the following points will be found of interest. When the maker or indorser of a note is sued, there are various defenses or excuses he may urge as reasons why he should not be compelled to pay it.

1. Infancy.—If the maker was under twenty-one years of age the note is void both as against him and against his father, unless given for necessaries.

2. Usury.—In states having a usury law, the note is absolutely void if given for a usurious consideration. No holder can enforce it, even though he was a purchaser in good faith without knowledge of the usury, and had paid value for it.

3. Alteration and Forgery.—An altered or forged note is absolutely void. It is not necessary to constitute the crime of forgery that the maker's name should be forged. An altered or forged note is void in the hands of everybody, even of a purchaser in good faith. A bank or individual who pays such a note loses the money. The maker is not liable.

4. Want of Consideration.—When a note is given without consideration, it is only void between the maker and the payee. A *bona fide* purchaser from the payee can collect it

of the maker. One who buys a note from the payee or any holder for less than the face value, can nevertheless recover the full amount from the maker.

5. Fraud or Compulsion.—A note obtained by fraud or threats cannot be enforced by the payee, but it is good in the hands of a purchaser before maturity

---

THE FARMER AT CARDS.

A new swindling scheme has been sprung upon the unwary travelers along the line of railroads, by which the swindlers have succeeded in obtaining quite a large sum of money. The following is the way the scheme was worked upon a Minnesota farmer who was on his way home from market with the proceeds of the sale of his potatoes and onions stowed away in a shot-bag in the depths of his trousers pocket : Just across the passage-way from him in the car sat two well-dressed men of middle-age who looked like prosperous merchants of sporting proclivities. They were engaged in playing a game of euchre. Finally one of the men apparently became tired of the sport and threw down the cards. His companion urged him to play on, but he refused. Then, as if actuated by a sudden impulse, the man turned around and, addressing the Minnesota farmer, said: "You play him a game; I'm tired."

The farmer said he did not mind "playin' a little old-fashioned euchre to while away the time," and so he took a seat opposite the stranger. The man who had suddenly become tired of the game sat beside the agriculturist, and now and then suggested a brilliant play for the farmer, which pleased the latter very much. In a few minutes the farmer obtained what he thought was a good hand of diamonds, having the right and left bowers, seven and eight spots, and ace of clubs. The stranger remarked that he was glad diamonds were trumps, because he had a hand he would not mind wagering a lot of money on

At this his confederate gave the farmer a familiar nudge in the ribs and said: "Go in and clean him up. That hand that you got is worth a farm. Bet him $50."

The farmer at once adopted the suggestion and counted out $50 in bills which he gave to the confederate. This attracted the attention of the passengers in the car, and they gathered around to see the fun. The farmer led the right bower. All it captured was the nine of trumps. Then he led the left bower, which captured the ten-spot. The farmer then became a trifle nervous and led the ace of clubs, which quickly fell a victim to the ace of diamonds. Then the stranger took the remaining trumps from the farmer with the king and queen, and the agriculturist was euchred. The farmer gasped.

"Let's see how that was done," he said.

Some one sorted out the cards and showed him how easy it was. By this time the strangers had pocketed the money, and the first time the train stopped they got off and walked away rapidly.

The farmer was completely nonplussed by his ill-luck, but awoke to the fact that it is never too late to learn.

Can Crimanls Be Reformed?

Thomas Byrnes has the following to say regarding criminals which will be read with interest:

"In considering the character or moral nature of criminals we should remember how most of them become malefactors. Most thieves sent to prison for the first time have stolen simply because they wanted money at the time for some particular purpose. In an unfortunate moment they happened to steal; they are found out, convicted and sent to jail, though probably they know nothing about criminal life, as such. But through that one unfortunate occurrence they are sent to prison, and when they come out they are thoroughly experienced in crime, because all the time they have been in prison they have been associating with criminals.

"The methods of solitary confinement, however, as pursued under the British penal system is, in my judgment, inhuman. There are prisons in the United States where solitary confinement is resorted to, and when the men who have been punished in that way come out of prison they are generally idiotic for six months or a year afterward. I do not believe in the British system under any circumstances; I do not believe the solitary system ever has the effect of reforming the criminal, and I will say that, according to my judgment and experience, no confinement ever reforms a criminal.

"Of course my business has always been to catch criminals, not to reform them. When it is asked what are the best methods of reforming criminals, we touch a problem that some of the ablest men in the world have been considering for very many years. As I say, my business all the time is to send thieves to jail. There are other people who devote their time to reforming the criminals; they had better settle the question of reform among themselves. My personal opinion is that it is utterly impossible to reform criminals. There are certain fancy measures pursued in this world for the reformation of criminals, but they are all bosh; they do not reform the outlaws. To some extent such efforts are made for the purpose of public notoriety. I know people in this world who claim that they want to reform thieves. They get hold of notorious scoundrels when they come out of state's prison, and so long as the thief is a good 'star actor,' and goes from place to place and tells all sorts of things that are villainous and bad about himself (no matter whether they be lies or truth) he is lauded around by these people as a great attraction. The moment he discontinues this kind of performance they throw him out in the street becuuse he is of no use to them; he doesn't 'draw.' I know of criminals who have gone through that kind of experience, and have come to me and asked for a few dollars to help them out of trouble.

" My experience has taught me the truth of the old saying, ' Once a thief always a thief.' There are certain intelligent criminals who have served terms in state's prison and who may in the latter part of their lives become more careful in their conduct. A man of that sort may have accumulated a little money. He will take a new thief and use him, send him to the front where there is a chance for him to go to jail, while the planner of the scheme will sit in the background where there is a fair share of protection and two-thirds profit. That is the only kind of criminal reformation I know of.

" So far as the efforts of religious people are concerned in this matter of criminal reformation, I say that their efforts are laudable. They certainly mean well. They devote time and money to the work, but they have no practical experience with criminals, and their efforts count for very little. It is sometimes claimed that under the influence of prayers and preaching the criminal's heart is touched, he sees the error of his ways, he is converted. I do not believe it. As the word ' reformation ' is ordinarily used, I know there is no such experience among thieves."

CHAPTER XXXI.

STATE OR GENERAL AGENCY FRAUD.

FARM PURCHASING SWINDLE—THE EGG FRAUD—BOARDING HOUSE FRAUD, ETC.

One of the most extensive schemes by which many of the best people are inveigled into loss of money is the general or state agency fraud. This scheme is made secure to the promoters by a contract which is so adroitly drawn and so ingeniously written that it stands the test of the courts of law. Clergymen, lawyers, doctors, teachers and business men of every kind are among the victims. As a large cash payment is required, all the victims are those whose industry and prudence have enabled them to save something for a rainy day.

The promoters of this fraud use newspaper "Want columns" to draw attention to their schemes. They also use the mercantile reports to learn names of bankers and other business men, and address personal letters to them, requesting name of some substantial and reliable man in the neighborhood, as the firm wishes to secure a local manager for its business. This letter is extremely well prepared, and is capable of easily leading the hasty reader to the conclusion that it is written by a prominent and reliable manufacturing firm, which has a good position open for some worthy man.

After due correspondence with different persons the firm writes a letter, similar to the following, to the would-be general manager:

DEAR SIR: We are in receipt of your favor of the 18th inst., and contents noted. In reply, we shall go further into details, giving you a clearer insight into our business and methods of conducting it. We own the largest subscription manufacturing plant in the country, averaging 5,000 books a day. The majority of these publications are of a religious and historical nature, and are sold by subscription; that is, to canvassing agents.

Our books are especially selected to meet the wants of the masses; also the people who live in the small towns and rural districts, who have not the advantages of public libraries, large book stores, etc. The line of goods that will be handled through this department will be what we call the "popular price" sellers, and range in price from $1 to $6, according to the size of the book and different styles of binding. Of course, we have much higher priced goods also. The agents for these publications are secured by newspaper advertising, circularizing and correspondence, and are employed on a commission basis.

Should we make an arrangement with you, your work will be the general management of the business. You will have no canvassing to do yourself, but will secure others to do this work; encourage these agents in their work, answer their reports, fill their orders, and give your best efforts to furthering the interests of the work intrusted to you. We would send one of our subscription department managers from the main office to open up the department and instruct you thoroughly in all the details of handling the business. We pay all running expenses, such as rent, advertising, postage, etc., and in addition to your salary, pay you a liberal commission on all goods sold through your department.

As a business man, you can readily see that in order for us to make money out of the enterprise, you will handle a considerable business, and on all sales you will receive a commission referred to above, to-wit: 10 per cent. Your commissions for the first year ought to amount to as much as your salary. At the beginning, you would not need additional office help. This, however, would probably be for only a few weeks, as you would soon need others to assist you; and as a matter of course, this additional help goes in as an expense of the business. The amount of cash capital required on your part, to-wit: $800 to $1,000, is to carry a part of the stock which is necessary to have on hand at all times in order to supply the trade of your department. We would require you to carry the stock, not merely as a matter of security, but in order that you may be financially interested in the work. Experience has demonstrated to us that when a man has a few dollars in a business he is sure to look after it more carefully, and push it much harder than he otherwise would.

Your capital is perfectly secure, from the fact that at the expiration of the term of agreement you return to us the original amount of stock placed with you, and we return your original capital. Meanwhile, we are replacing all stocks sold from your department, so that at all times you have the original amount of stock on hand, or the money for the same. It seems to us, therefore, that the only thing for you to consider, so far as this part of the matter is concerned, is our general business character and our financial ability to carry out any agreement that we might make with you, and that you are entering into an arrangement with the largest and most successful subscription book house in the country.

As a business man, you can readily understand the importance to us in the establishment of an office, and the interest that we naturally have in a man with whom we arrange to take charge of the office; hence, before making or entering into a permanent arrangement with you, we shall require a personal interview—in fact, a personal interview is the only satisfactory way for both parties.

Our object in having you come to see us is, that you may look over our manufacturing plant, and we may talk over the matter thoroughly, and then draw up an agreement that will be satisfactory to both parties. We would suggest, therefore, that you get your financial matters in shape, and come and see us, with funds, prepared to close an arrangement, provided everything is satisfactory.

Kindly wire us in advance just when you will be here.

Yours very truly,

——— Publishing Co.

———, President.

In accordance with the above invitation the victim visits the establishment and has the "personal interview." He is shown a large book manufacturing plant of an entirely different concern from that with which he had been corresponding. The publishing company who has been corresponding with the victim has no real capital nor effects; it occupies an office in the same building with the large manufacturing plant above referred to. This is permitted, inasmuch as this fraud company is very successful in the selling of left-over stock and books known as "slow sellers." The victim is much impressed by the big works, the daily out-put, the wonderful results, and the very expensive books published.

The visit is one of the important factors in the development of this scheme of fraud. A little later, the would-be general manager will find in the contract to be signed, a clause that "must give him pause." The visit is intended to quiet the fears of "the party of the second part" when he reads in the contract, "The sales of each month must amount to at least $250." His thought is, "Suppose I fail to meet this condition; the contract is then void." But I can without fail make sales of books sufficient to meet that condition. But if I should fail, this company is too great and too honorable to take advantage of that clause." So he signs, pays his money, and is caught. It is a case of angling. The fisherman is after the $800; the bait is the $125 salary per month with the added commission of 10 per cent. on all sales; the hook is the clause in the contract which requires the sale of a certain amount of goods. Perhaps in most cases the victim sees the hook, but thinks he can avoid it by meeting all the conditions, or believes the angler is too honorable to pull the line when the fish bite. But the hook is largely concealed under the belief that the goods are salable. The actual fraud appears when the kind of goods is revealed.

The contract is drawn up in due form, and it is necessary here to quote only three paragraphs, which give the key to the whole matter:

"*First:* * * * Parties of the first part agree to pay to said party of the second part a salary of one hundred twenty-five dollars ($125) monthly, and ten (10) per cent. commission on all sales of said office."

The party of the second part

"*Agrees:* * * * to carry a stock of books amounting to sixteen hundred dollars ($1,600) at list prices, consisting of an assortment of various books in the different bindings, published by the parties of the first part, *such stock and assortment as may be selected by the parties of the first part*, said stock to be billed to said second party at fifty (50) per cent. discount from retail prices, amounting to eight hundred dollars ($800)."

"*Fifth:* The success of this business depends upon a reasonable amount of books sold, and it is understood and agreed that the *sale of each month shall amount to two hundred fifty dollars ($250), which shall be considered the minimum amount of business necessary to a proper fulfillment of this contract.*"

After the victim has signed this contract and handed over his mǒney, the promoters at once become too busy to bother with him further and he is told that the books will be shipped very soon, and a representative will come with them to instruct the victim in the details of the business and to purchase office furniture, etc.

When the books arrive, a very smart and plausible representative appears to open the office and instruct the "manager." He usually spends a day purchasing an office outfit and making a few perfunctory suggestions and departs. The books received are the leavings and accumulations of a regular subscription publication house. Some of the books sold when first issued. All of them are books hastily and carelessly written, of small literary value, merely compiled to sell by agents long accustomed to talking their wares. These books are usually found in the homes of the uneducated, who were caught by the smooth tongue of the agent, the pictures and binding, and who wanted something to put on the parlor table. To the inexperienced man, unaccustomed to the book business, they are as unsalable as so much waste paper.

The "manager," hitherto called the victim, having received his books and his "instructions," at once gets busy arranging his office, having his sign painted on the door, advertises in the daily papers for agents, and begins to write letters.

He receives many replies to his advertisements and letters, and a few inexperienced people attempt to sell the books, but fail.

At the end of the first month the "manager" writes to his firm, sending a long list of expense items, and a report showing no sales, and requests that a check for his expenses and his salary be sent him. But the next mail brings him a letter saying that the victim has failed to keep his contract, and refers him to it. No salary; no expense money enclosed; but a point blank refusal! He now awakens to the fact that he is out $800, a large sum for expenses, and he has in return several hundred unsalable books—and a bitter experience.

Out of the thousands caught by this scheme, only a few ever complied with the contract, though many worked energetically to do so. From the nature of the books and the terms of the contract it is practically impossible to succeed.

There are other forms of the same scheme, but the fundamental fraud is practically the same; that is, to get the agent's money for worthless goods on a contract which is impossible to fulfill.

This form of swindling is sometimes practiced by men who stand high in society.

A company with a high-sounding name was organized to make and sell school supplies. The president of the company was a lawyer of eminence and a writer of some note. The other officers were business men well known to the community. The company was listed by Dun and Bradstreet as safe and honorable. The business of the company, with the general public, was without a flaw. And yet the company was a fraud, known to be such by all of its officers.

The general plan of business was the same as that given above, except that the goods were school supplies. These supplies were of a special character and unsalable at prices demanded by the company.

In this case, the company, without showing its identity, advertised for general agents to sell school supplies. School teachers were, as a rule, the victims in this fraud. The agents were required to put up from $1,000 to $2,000. The salary and commission were the same as in the book fraud. The goods supplied, while of some value to those who could use them, were absolutely unsalable at prices demanded by the company. This company had its victims in all parts of the United States.

The fact that the victims did not wish to let it be known that they had been caught in a sharper's trap, shielded for a time the company's fraudulent methods. The company also covered its tracks by doing all its advertising under cover—its name never appearing in print when advertising for agents.

We are glad to say, however, that one of the victims began proceedings against the company. This brought to light its fraudulent practices, and it was unable to weather the storm that arose as the result of this prosecution.

Most of these dishonest schemes for getting hold of "other people's money" may be successfully prosecuted before the law, provided fraudulent motives can be proved.

Real Estate.

But one of the most profitable schemes, and one in which no element of actionable fraud exists, is that of the real estate agent who advertises that he can "sell real estate, no matter where located, *for cash*;" that he has an improved method and system enabling him to reach buyers anywhere and easily and quickly turn real estate into cash. The advertisement and the printed matter was to the highest degree efficient and excellently well prepared. The popular weeklies, daily newspapers and magazines were the mediums through which he reached the people. To those answering his advertisements he would send attractive advertising circulars and a letter, upon which it would be impossible to improve for its purpose. The inquirer was told to forward an accurate description of the property to be sold. On receipt of this the real estate man wrote for a preliminary fee, at least $15 cash and often more, which he said was to pay for the advertising of his property in accordance with his plan. The commission and expenses in case of sale were remarkably low. Many thousands sent this preliminary fee, and their property was advertised, not as the owner expected, however, and in some instances sales were effected, though not often. The scheme netted a large fortune to its originator.

The Farm Purchasing Swindle.

A stranger, dressed as a well-to-do business man, drives up to the house of a wealthy farmer, and says that he has heard that the farmer is a good judge of land. The stranger wishes his judgment, and asks the farmer to accompany him to look over the land. Mr. Farmer jumps into the buggy, and the two drive off. On their way they meet a man who stops them to ask a question, and a conversation begins. Stranger No. 2 after a short time mentions the fact that the land under consideration can be bought cheap, and that he has heard that some rich man is about to buy it, and that there is a good chance to make money. He, himself, had thought of buying it, but had only about $2,500 to put into it. Finally an arrangement is made whereby all three are to go into partnership to buy the land. They look it over very carefully, and then drive to the bank. Mr. Farmer draws out the amount he will invest, say $5,000. The strangers put in the remainder. Stranger No. 1 remarks that it is pretty late in the day to attend to the rest of the business, and that they would better wait till to-morrow. To this all parties agree. All the money is then inclosed in a package or box in the presence of all the parties, and the package or box is intrusted to Mr. Farmer to keep till morning, as the bank is now closed. In the morning no strangers appear, and Mr. Farmer opens the box to find only worthless paper, or perhaps nothing at all.

On the previous day, by a trick of the hand, or perhaps

while the farmer's attention was drawn for a second by one of the strangers, the other had substituted the empty box for the one containing the money.

Egg Fraud.

A swindler, whom we will call M., claimed to have an extremely valuable egg-preserver, and proposed to Mr. A., a commission merchant, that he make tests as to its virtues. These experiments were to be made under the watchful eye of Mr. A. Permission was promptly granted. Day after day M. was seen bathing eggs in a liquid, supposed to be the egg-preserver, and carefully storing them away. At the end of four months the eggs were examined by Mr. A. and found to be in perfect condition—fresh, as if but recently laid, which in fact was the case. A. willingly paid M. $10,000 for so valuable a recipe. But more than that, he placed $15,000 in the hands of M. to be used in the egg-preserving business. Presto! M. disappears, and A. is $25,000 short. The swindler had exchanged the old eggs for fresh laid ones. It may be well to state that Mr. A. is a wide-awake, pushing business man in one of our large cities. But in this case he had failed to watch all the links in the chain of testing.

Boarding House Swindle.

A scheme sometimes practiced on boarding-house keepers is managed as follows: A respectable looking man, who is somewhat particular, comes to look for a room and board. After engaging a room, he informs the landlady that he will go down to the depot to have his trunk sent up. When he returns he asks to go to his room to take a bath and brush up a little as he is warm and dusty from travel. While he has possession of the room and is supposedly refreshing himself with a bath, he takes occasion to visit such rooms as are unlocked, where he appropriates whatever he can lay hands on that can easily be carried away. He then saunters out carelessly, looking up the street to see if he can see any signs of his luggage. He may even stop on his way out to tell his hostess that he will be back in time for tea, and unless she is naturally suspicious, or has had previous experience in these lines, she may not notice that his pockets are full, or that he has an extra suit of clothes on under his own. An instance occurred in an Illinois town, where a man thus admitted to a house took a bath, arrayed himself in a clean shirt taken from one room, a dress coat and vest from another, and disappeared before the eyes of the landlady without exciting the remotest suspicion till tea-time, when he failed to put in an appearance.

www.ingramcontent.com/pod-product-compliance
Lightning Source LLC
Chambersburg PA
CBHW020706190526
45164CB00005B/472

9781519213556